The Cocaine Eaters

The Cocaine Eaters

Brian Moser & Donald Tayler

1724

Longmans

LONGMANS, GREEN AND CO LTD
48 Grosvenor Street, London W.1

*Associated companies, branches and representatives
throughout the world*

© *Brian Moser & Donald Tayler 1965*

First published 1965

*Text printed in Great Britain
by Butler & Tanner Ltd, Frome and London*

*Colour and black and white plates printed in Denmark
by Kurt Victor Hansen, Bredgade 25, Copenhagen K*

To Our Parents

Contents

Plates

Plates

ix

Drawings in the Text

Maps

Barranquilla
Cartagena

PANAMA

VENEZUELA

Bogotá
Villavicencio

LLANOS

Buenaventura
Cali

COLOMBIA

R.Orinoco

4

3

2   Mitú

ECUADOR

BRAZIL

R.Amazon

PERU

R.Solimões

R.Marañon

Leticia

N

0   50   100 150 200 250 miles

Acknowledgements

Without the support of many people our expedition could never have taken place. Firstly, we are greatly indebted to the Government of Colombia and to the following institutions: the Royal Geographical Society, the Department of Ethnography of the British Museum, the Isaac Wolfson Foundation, the Frederick Soddy Trust, Instituto Colombiano de Antropología, the British Embassy and the British Council in Bogotá, the British Institute of Recorded Sound, the BBC Recorded Programmes Library, Radiotelevisora Nacional de Colombia, the Catholic Missions at Buenaventura, Mitú and San Sebastian de Rabago, Fuerza Aérea Colombiana, Força Aérea Brasileira, Servicio Nacional de Erradicacion de la Malaria (SEM), and *The Times*.

We should also like to thank the companies who gave us equipment, helped us financially and offered assistance in many other ways: Avianca, Banco de Londres y Montreal Ltda, Brooke Bond Tea Ltd, Casa Inglesa Ltda, Fi-Cord International, Glanvill, Enthoven and Co., Ltd, Grace Brothers, Ilford Ltd, International Petroleum (Colombia) Ltd, Kodak Ltd, Stefan Kudelski, the Metal Box Co., Ltd, the Pacific Steam Navigation Company and SS *Reina del Mar*, Rollei-Werke, Shell Colombia S.A., Tracey and Compañia S.A., and UNDRA Ltda (Schering Corporation).

On our travels we were joined on the various journeys by Nestor Uscátegui, Horacio López, Alec Clark, Ben Curry, Niels Halbertsma and his wife Hanna, whilst Dr Donald Wood looked after our interests at home – to all of them we are greatly indebted.

Also, we relied to a great extent on help and kindness shown by many individuals, and to mention but a few we thank: Padre Atanasio, Don Vicente Arango, Antony Barrington Brown, Don Carlos Balcazar, Peter Bohanna, Dr G. H. S. Bushnell, Dr Audrey Butt, Sta Constanza Camargo, Eduardo Chacon, Mrs Clark, Dr José Antonio Concha y Venegas, Dan Conley, Adrian Digby, Dr Gerardo Reichel Dolmatoff, Dr Luis Duque Gómez, Don Rafael Escalona, Hugh Franks, Ronald Graham Kerr, Dr Jaime Gómez Salazar, Peter Harrison, Joan Haworth, Roland and David Hughes, José our Amazonian guide, L. P. Kirwan, CMG, Erwin Kraus, Robert Krummenacher, John Levy, Dr Federico Medem, Charles Moser, David and Mona Parry, Roger Perry, John and Hanka de Rhodes, Capitán Antonio Brun de la Rosa, Patrick Saul, George de Sauzmarez, Dr Richard Evans Schultes, the late Dr Marian Smith, Professor J. A. Steers, Dr David Stoddart, Michael Tayler, Mike Tsalikis, Sta Cecilia Vargas, Richard Williams and Hans Zenke.

Acknowledgements

Finally we thank our agents, Peter Janson-Smith, Simon King and Deborah Rogers for all the help and encouragement they have given us. We are also very grateful to W. Edward Roscher who selected and arranged the colour illustrations; to Pat Holtby and everyone at Harkstead for their kindness; to Leonora and our parents at Woolhanger and Chelsea; and last of all to the Indians whose hospitality was unlimited.

Prologue: Beads for Barter

Would anyone be interested in sponsoring or patronizing a small ethno-
graphical expedition setting out to make recordings of folk music in
Latin America?

THE TIMES

It was July 1960. One of us had just returned to London after two years on a
dam survey in Papua, the other was still working on an oilfield in Patagonia.
Five years before, we had first met at Cambridge, and then we had both gone
our own ways – by chance, almost to opposite ends of the earth. Occasionally
we wrote to each other, and from the rare letters which crossed the Pacific
one thing was certain: we both were eager for the day when we could throw
off the shackles of employment and disappear for a year into the forests of
South America.

The fascination of visiting primitive people, living with them and above
all recording their music, had long ago fired our imagination. Though neither
of us were musicians we had always been interested in music. Donald played
the guitar and had learnt many folk tunes on journeys he had made in
Norway and Spain, while Brian had been on an expedition to North Borneo
where he had recorded the music of a tribe living in the interior.

But why did we choose Colombia, why not for instance Brazil? Perhaps
it was more through coincidence than by plan. Two Cambridge expeditions
had gone to Colombia in the last three years, both had visited the same
mountain range and on each occasion one member had stayed behind.

Grand flights of the imagination, to ride from Panama to Tierra del Fuego
or to search for a lost city in the headwaters of the Orinoco, could well cover
sheets of paper or consume hours of conversation, but to reach the decision
that an expedition should go into the field with a series of definite objectives
was another matter. Some may well have wondered 'Who are these fools?'
when they saw our hopeful advertisement. At first there was only one reply
and it came from two girls – they were used to 'roughing it' and would be
delighted to come as cooks, secretaries or whatever we willed. They seemed
to have much the same spirit as ourselves.

For nearly two months our plans simmered; feelers were put out to
various foundations but met with little success. During this time Brian left
Patagonia and returned to Bogotá, while in England Donald, in spite of the
routine of a consultant engineer's office, managed to talk over his ideas with
a friend in the BBC. Which tribes were to be visited? For how long? Most

important of all, where was the money coming from? The whole expedition was to cost between four and five thousand pounds, and at this stage we hardly believed we would eventually have to put up three-quarters of this ourselves. But our work abroad had given us ample funds. To wait spelt failure, we were free agents and we might never be so again.

It was two o'clock in the morning of 27 August when the telephone rang in a flat in Drayton Gardens.

'Is that Mr Donald Tayler?' the New York operator asked.

Sleepily: 'Yes.'

'Then just hold the line a moment. I have a personal call for you from Bogotá, Colombia.'

'... Are you still coming, Donald?'

'Yes, certainly, Brian.'

'Then if you buy all the equipment at your end, I'll make the arrangements and plans here in Bogotá.'

'All right. I'll try and get everything done in a month and fly out at the end of September, but it won't be easy – I can't leave my job for a fortnight.'

'Anyway, let's definitely go ahead ...' – our two voices seemed to re-echo this last phrase down the line. For seven minutes the exchanges took place across the Atlantic, and the expedition jumped to reality.

Preparations now had to go forward in earnest. We were, to many people, aiming to achieve the impossible, to organize an expedition in the space of only a few weeks, when normally such organization would take at least six months and often as long as a year. Still, we had two decided advantages: at this stage there were only two of us, and with one in London and the other in Bogotá we could make our plans at maximum speed. It was still a difficult task. To say we were going to record the music of various tribes in Colombia was one thing, but to decide on which tribes, and when was the best time of year to visit them, was quite another. The relief and climate of the country varies enormously. At one moment you can be flying over peaks of ice and snow, at the next over dense jungle, equally formidable and equally unknown. There are mountain people, those who live on the plains and others who lurk deep in the forests. We needed advice, and there was one man especially who could help: Dr Gerardo Reichel Dolmatoff of the Colombian Institute of Anthropology, a recognized authority on the tribes of the country, many of which he had visited himself. Through talking to him a plan evolved.

'How long do you want to work with the Indians?' he asked Brian, in his office in a wing of the old National Museum. Tall and immaculately dressed, like a cavalry officer of the Austro-Hungarian Empire, he was an imposing figure. His questions, though searching, were kind and above all he was enthusiastic.

'So you want to spend about a year on this, or should I say as long as your money holds out,' he said laughing. 'I think it's a splendid project, especially as Indian music is a field which is virtually untouched. There is no limit to what you can do. All the tribes play different instruments and there are of course their songs and dances. Some sing in large male choruses, others chant extraordinary harmonies. Just listen to this ...' – and Dr Reichel emitted a series of strange grunts and guttural sounds. 'That's a Motilon war song I heard when I was there ten years ago.'

Page after page was covered with notes on different areas, on introductions to guides, interpreters and tribal chieftains, on goods for trading and the medical supplies we should have to take. Barely a day went by when Brian did not plague Dr Reichel for more information, and as the plans formed it became increasingly obvious that our main journey would be to the forests in the south, to one of the headwaters of the Amazon.

'I don't really know very much about the Amazonas,' Dr Reichel continued, 'You should go and see Dr Medem in the Institute of Natural Sciences, he's an expert on snakes and crocodiles. Also, Dr Schultes has just arrived from Harvard with a group of botanical students. Try and find him. He knows as much about that part of the country as anyone can. He was there for long periods doing a survey on wild rubber for the Government.'

Dr Schultes, a sturdy bespectacled man with close-cropped grey hair and a lively wit, was staying in a small pension kept by an old Englishwoman.

'Yes, there are many remote tribes in the rain forests of the Amazonas. You want to know which to visit. It just depends what your interests are. I have always collected plants and the Indians have only been a sort of hobby. They are so varied. There are the Kofan on the borders of Ecuador with their magnificent feather head-dresses. Then on the Vaupés and Apaporis are people who pound coca leaves into a powder.[1]

'The missionaries have often tried to obliterate their customs, but there are some rivers they have never penetrated. The Piraparaná is one of these and the Tukano living there have managed to keep off the white man for the past fifty years. I have never travelled its full length but you might enter it near the source, though don't go too far down – the rapids are very dangerous. Remember, you must reach the northern Amazonas by October, or November at the latest. By December the dry season will be upon you and travel by river extremely difficult.'

It was September, so time was short and we would have to start as soon as possible. But first we would be well advised to find a Colombian anthropologist, who would be willing to spend much of the coming year at work in the jungle with two Englishmen. By a stroke of good luck, the English

---

[1] Cocaine itself is a white crystalline alkaloid isolated from the leaves of the coca plant. As a narcotic, it is injected and is highly addictive. The Indians who chew coca leaves or take coca in the form of powder receive only a very small proportion of the active principle in their blood, and the effect is correspondingly less harmful.

pension was a meeting-place for some of the more eccentric people in Bogotá and living in one of the minute attics at the top of the house was a young ethnobotanist, Nestor Uscátegui. To look at he seemed almost an Englishman, in a sports jacket and puffing away at a pipe. Two years before he had been a research fellow under Dr Schultes at Harvard. Now his main interest lay in the use of narcotics and stimulants among the tribes of Colombia.

Dr Schultes thought he might be just the man.

'Mind you, he's a bit vague and will smoke his pipe and philosophize as you go through the rapids.'

It took Nestor himself little time to decide. Yes, he would come, though first he would have to obtain permission from the Director of the Institute of Anthropology. We could even use his old Morris Minor to visit a tribe which lived in the mountains near his home.

One introduction led to another. The days and nights became a hectic rush of engagements talking to scientists, photographers, explorers, merchants, musicians, tropical-fish experts, indeed anyone who might be able to give Brian information on the various areas we thought we would cover, and the equipment we should take. Was the compactness of a US Army jungle hammock of greater value than the comfort of an ordinary one? Would an aluminium canoe survive the forest crossings between rivers? Which was the strongest, lightest and most economical outboard motor? So the questions went on. Perhaps Horacio López had the most convincing answers. An explorer and photographer, he had only just returned from the Llanos, where for months he had paddled his canoe filled with provisions and a pile of books. Now he was rather inappropriately working in a bookshop. He loved to talk about the forests of the Amazon and the Orinoco, to describe his adventures, and as he talked he became a new man, no longer lonely and harassed by city life, his thin and slightly stooping figure straightening as he studied maps and pinpointed the rivers he knew so well.

'How I wish I could come with you to the Piraparaná, but I must work here to keep body and soul together.'

Within a fortnight the plans and maps were in London with Donald who put forward our proposals to the Director of the Royal Geographical Society. They understandably met with a cool reception.

'To organize a year's expedition in under two months and to expect to gain our recognition and support at three weeks' notice is out of the question. However, I shall do all I can to have your request considered at the next Committee Meeting.'

If we waited till then, not only would our funds run out but our journeys would conflict with the rains. The plans were ambitious and it was not always easy to convince directors and professors that we would be able to achieve what we set out to do. Donald wrote, 'I have noted your programme – three months in Amazonia to contact five tribes. Hey man go easy – whose advice is this? I leave it to you, Brian, but fear there will be some anthropological eyebrows raised on this side when they see this!'

Yet many looked on the project with enthusiasm. The late Dr Marian Smith, then Secretary of the Royal Anthropological Institute, was delighted with our ideas which she compared to the spirit of nineteenth-century adventurers. The Keeper of the Department of Ethnography in the British Museum was intrigued. There was no collection from Colombia, would we please make one and 'be sure to bring back as many canoes as you can, even an Amazonian house if it's possible. I shall try and get you a grant when the Trustees meet next year.' Still, there was little hope of material support. We received everyone's blessing but nothing more.

The worst headache of all was Donald's, who had to assemble all the equipment in time. He had barely a month and until the last fortnight was still working full-time. The most important items were the tape recorders which would have to survive many months in the jungle, being transported in canoes or on the backs of mules. So we were very lucky that the only other reply to our advertisement in *The Times* came from the musician and recordist John Levy who had recorded music in many parts of the world. He at first wondered whether he might come with us.

'On second thoughts I don't think I can risk my recorders,' he told Donald, 'but if you really want to use a Nagra, I'll ring Stefan Kudelski in Lausanne. He is an old friend of mine, actually a research physicist, who invented the Nagra as a sideline. You will never get one in this country, there's a waiting list of at least two years.'

Once more a long-distance telephone call worked a miracle. Within a week the latest Nagra with all its accessory microphones and extensions was lying in the customs shed of Bogotá airport. But it was the more unusual things, a sudden request for milk churns or minute glass beads – 'if you see small cheap Italian beads in London, white, yellow, red and black, then bring a sack' – which caused most consternation. For a whole morning Donald might be tethered to the telephone, desperately searching. A year later an aluminium milk churn was to save our film. The glass beads were found in a store in Tottenham Court Road, and the girl behind the counter looked aghast as her stock disappeared.

When she heard they were for Indians in the forests of the Amazon she looked even more bewildered. Small half-pound packages of these tiny beads were later sent out to us as non-commercial samples. They were contraband, and if found would certainly have been confiscated. Nonetheless, they remained our most treasured trade goods with the Indians. Only a request for sola topis proved beyond Donald's capabilities. In Harrods, Moss Bros and the Army and Navy Stores the reply was the same: 'We are terribly sorry, sir, but our supply ran out years ago.'

Many items were easier to obtain and sympathetic manufacturers gave us great encouragement. Huge reels of plastic were donated to be made into plastic bags. One day a crate of tea with hundreds of quarter-pound cans appeared at the foot of the staircase to Donald's flat and during the coming year we were to bless the makers time and time again.

In Colombia the time schedule had now been checked and rechecked by many people who had travelled in or near the various areas which we were to visit. Some gave us much encouragement, others said we would never complete half of what we set out to do.

'Do you really think you can visit five distinct groups of Indians scattered over some of the remotest parts of the country, and climb a mountain of over 18,000 feet, all in the space of one year? Besides, what value can your work have when you plan to stay with each tribe for such a short time?'

In this there was much justification. Our major aim, however, was to record music.

The first journey during late October and November would be to the Pacific Coast, to visit the Noanamá, a tribe who lived in the rain-soaked delta of the Río San Juan. Then we would return to our base in Bogotá, reorganize, and fly south into Amazonia, to visit the remote Tukano on the Río Piraparaná, close to the frontier with Brazil. This would be the longest and hardest journey of all. We would travel by canoe and would take at least three months to cover the route. So we would not return to Bogotá before March 1961. After two journeys through tropical rain-forest, the third was to provide a complete change. By April we would be on the northern slopes of the Sierra Nevada de Santa Marta, the highest mountain range in the country, rising straight out of the Caribbean. Here we would live with a strange mountain people, the Kogi. We also planned to climb one of the highest peaks, and then cross the range to the Bintukua, the more amenable cousins of the Kogi living on the southern flank. Many people told us that while in the area of the Sierra Nevada we should visit the Guajiro Indians, a nomadic desert people living in the arid Guajira Peninsula. The last main journey would start in June. We were to move eastwards to the hills bordering Venezuela to visit a pacified branch of the Motilon. The war-like branch of the Motilon, the Kunuguasaya, are among the most dangerous Indians in the whole of South America – we were not planning to visit them. The whole expedition was to last from October 1960 until August 1961.

'Yes, I think your plans can stand,' Dr Reichel told Brian, when he was shown the last of many final drafts. 'But there's one thing you don't mention. You were at one stage talking of making films.'

'It seems a shame. I wonder whether a young Dutchman is still in Bogotá. He made three good films of Indians and I think he is now making commercial films for one of the oil companies. Why don't you get in touch with him? He is an excellent cameraman and a very pleasant person.'

Some nights later Brian met Niels Halbertsma at a party. Very tall, with fair hair and an eagle-like nose, Niels listened to the plans and then commented, 'The journey to the Amazonas is out of the question for me, it will take far too long, but if I have some free time in between my commitments, then I'd be delighted to come with you for one journey. You say you are going to the Sierra Nevada, that's my favourite part of Colombia, the scenery is marvellous and there will be a festival in Atanquez during May. I should love to film it if I can.'

Two weeks before, the expedition had consisted only of ourselves. Now we were to be joined – at least for some of the time – by a Colombian anthropologist and a Dutch cameraman.

Now, more than ever, speed was essential. A fortnight of September had slipped by and Donald had just left his job. There was no longer time to test fibre-glass canoes on an Exmoor lake. The experiments had to be scrapped, for all the equipment had to be assembled and reduced to the absolute minimum. Much would come out by air, but the rest had to go by sea and this had to be crated. Donald's rooms became a mass of boxes, cartons, ropes, tape recorders and medicines. His landlady threw up her hands in despair – and so did Donald when the evening papers suddenly announced a threatened dock strike. There was only one answer, to pack everything and take it down to the docks immediately. In the haste the car skidded and nearly knocked down a docker, a fight was just avoided. The equipment was heaved on to a cargo boat due to leave for Colombia that day. Any later and it could have been delayed indefinitely.

By the third week in September some official bodies had given their recognition, for they now realized from our persistence that the plans were in earnest. On 29 September Donald left London Airport, bound for Paris and Bogotá. At Orly a change of aircraft was necessary. With the two hundred pounds of excess baggage, chaos ensued. For an hour all the equipment disappeared, it was put in the wrong stream and instead of remaining in transit was about to enter France! The customs officers delved into packages; discovering shotguns and cartridges, they eagerly searched for more – the mistake was found out just in time.

Leaving the Caribbean the plane flew northwards past the dazzling peaks of the Sierra Nevada, brilliant white in the clear blue atmosphere, then over the broad plains and forests of the Río Magdalena. Suddenly the land rose to a high plateau, the savannah of Bogotá. We circled and came down to the modern Eldorado airport – and the customs again.

'We are sorry, *señor*. Scientist or not, you can't proceed any further with this luggage. All these items are prohibited imports.'

So everything was impounded. For a week there was dismay, and also amusement: one moment we were arguing with warehousemen in the airport, the next endeavouring to persuade the Chief of Imports that the goods were not contraband. The cargo boat arrived in Barranquilla, the import agents exclaimed in horror that a thousand rounds of ammunition and a crate of tea would never get past the Aduana, but an official telegram was despatched to the port. By the end of the week all our stores lay strewn over a bare attic floor. A kind Lancashire woman was starting a private hotel, and at the top of her house was this enormous room which was to form our base whenever we returned to Bogotá.

The final preparations for the first journey were now complete. As we repacked the equipment to leave for the Pacific Coast, we were frequently interrupted by people who wanted to join us: Pancho, a young Austrian photographer, who had been with Camus during the filming of *Black Orpheus* in Brazil; Delia Zapata, a folk dancer from the Caribbean coast who with her troupe had travelled as far afield as Washington, Paris and Peking, and was excited by the idea of being able to adapt new tribal dances. But we had to say no.

Part 1

Noanamá

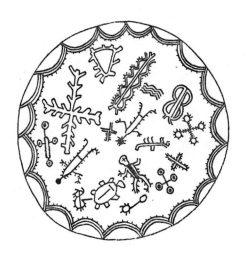

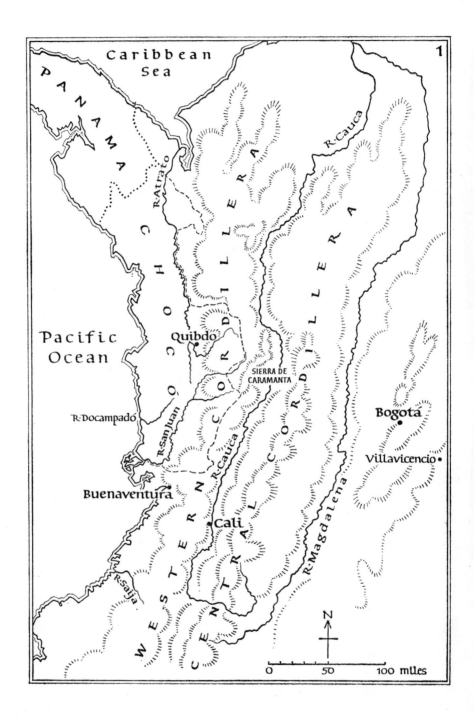

1

Caribbean
Sea

P A N A M A

Pacific
Ocean

C H O C O

R-Atrato

R-Cauca

Quibdo

SIERRA DE
CARAMANTA

R-Docampadó

R-Sanjuan

R-Cauca

Bogota

Villavicencio

Buenaventura

Cali

R-Magdalena

R-Saija

W E S T E R N   C O R D I L L E R A

C E N T R A L   C O R D I L L E R A

N

0   50   100 miles

I

A Home by the San Juan

Early on the morning of 23 October, only two months after our preparations began, we flew westwards over the flanks of the Central Cordillera and down to the fertile plains of the Río Cauca. Nestor, whose family farmed there, joined us in Cali, the capital of this rich agricultural province, and the next day the three of us were on our way into the laterized hills of the Western Cordillera. From the divide hairpin bends twisted away to the west, streams cascaded down over the rocks and often across the road. It was humid and soon began to rain. In no time we were in a downpour, but Umberto, the driver of the one-ton truck which we had been loaned, seemed unperturbed as the vehicle continued to splash its way over the pot-holed road towards Buenaventura.

'This is the wettest part of Colombia,' he said as he swung the wheel from side to side. 'It never stops raining here in the Chocó and we'll be lucky if we get through without meeting a landslide or a collision.'

For a moment the rain abated. In front a heavy grey cloud-mass hung low over the deep green carpet bordering the coast. There seemed no end to the forest stretching in every direction like a vast peat bog.

It was night when we reached the town. Long strings of lorries, their cabs decorated like Christmas trees with small lanterns, lined the shanty roadway leading to the waterfront. Every hour of the day and night freight was being shipped to and from the docks, between the port and the interior. Among the tin-roofed huts were groups of brightly clad negro men and women, their children playing by the side of the road. Originally from Africa, these people had migrated from the Caribbean down the Pacific coast, settling at the river mouths and then moving inland. Today they form the greater part of the population of the Chocó.

In the centre of the town were modern concrete shipping offices which seemed strangely out of place in this sleepy, humid atmosphere. In the bay illuminated ships rode at anchor. We discovered a small boat moored at the fishermen's wharf. She belonged to a timber merchant who owned a sawmill on the lower Río San Juan. No larger than a fishing smack, the *Fluvia Marina* carried provisions to the outlying settlements and returned laden with timber for the mills in Buenaventura. Two days later we were chugging northwards.

In the fast-gathering dusk a dark shape loomed out from the river bank, moving swiftly over the water. At the moment when our boat would have swept by, the Indian, standing upright in his canoe, deftly balanced it over the high bow wave and with a stroke of his paddle drew alongside. Grabbing the boat's rail with one hand and his mooring rope with the other, he vaulted the rail to stand beside us on the deck. . . .

It all happened so gracefully, so quickly and with such little effort, that it seemed for a moment as if he had really been with us all the time and our imaginations were playing tricks.

Nestor, puffing thoughtfully at his pipe, was the first to break the silence and asked the Indian tentatively where he came from. By way of reply, he pointed to the river bank – so they understood Spanish. In the failing light he seemed to be watching us with curious half-amused interest, his paddle in one hand, his liana canoe rope clutched in the other. He was wearing a white shirt, and very large silver ear-plugs with shining pendants.

We were about to ask him another question when, as quickly as he had arrived, he was gone. Balancing his light canoe in our seething wake, he was soon swallowed up by the darkness, and the old boat continued to shudder and grind her way upstream between the dark forest on either side.

All day long we had travelled northwards from Buenaventura along the coast. It had been fine and the water like glass, so we had stood out to sea passing a reef-wrecked Norwegian tanker about noon. In bad weather it was safer to stay inside the reef, but now there was no need, and the flying fish scudded over the translucent water in front of our bow.

To the east the coastline remained a green ribbon on the horizon, but behind it, over the distant Sierra de Caramanta, great piles of cumulus were massing. It looked as if there would be rain again tomorrow.

Late in the afternoon we changed course and within the hour we were moving up the delta of the Río San Juan. From then on we kept careful watch for the Indians. But as the mangrove swamps gave way to dense tropical forest, as the banks and the darkness began to close in, we wondered whether we had come to the wrong river. There was no sign of life or habitation. And then, from nowhere, we came face to face with our first Noanamá.

That same night we arrived at a negro-owned sawmill and mission settlement. In the darkness we transferred all our food supplies and equipment from the *Fluvia Marina* to a small wooden hut. This was to be our base and our stores kept dry in the hut where the rafters acted as a chicken roost, while we slung our hammocks above a sheltered pile of timber.

We felt at the time that our staying in a negro settlement might cause some resentment, as there is always antipathy between the two peoples. Only once, however, was any open discrimination shown in our presence, and that by an old Noanamá who confided to us one day that we were all one people – meaning ourselves and the Indians – but the negroes were different.

Mainly as a result of contact with the negroes and the growing influence of the Mission, a few Indians could speak a little Spanish, as could many of the children. So we had no need for an interpreter, and if we did get into difficulties, Nestor would always unravel them. With his slow thoughtful manner, he seemed to find an affinity with the Noanamá – perhaps more than ourselves.

The Noanamá are a handsome people; tallish and well built with the heavy chest and shoulders of men accustomed to the paddle; their dark hair in a bowl-like fringe around the head; light-skinned, narrow-nosed and high-cheekboned, mongoloid in appearance with shrewd, penetrating dark eyes. The women are often beautiful, with long flowing black hair and wearing no more than a cloth about their waist. Sometimes they put *bija*, a red dye, on their faces, and flowers in their hair. For ceremonies they cover their bodies with blue *jagua* dye in a series of designs. But it is left to the men, especially the unmarried boys, to dress up for all special occasions: with magnificent silver ear-plugs and hanging silver pendants, carefully worked bead skullcaps, strings of blue, orange, red and white porcelain beads – which come from Panama, and are an indication of wealth – so many that they can scarcely move their heads from side to side, and finally the glistening white shirt, a symbol of status and the only European garment we ever saw them wearing.

These people, expert cultivators, hunters and fishermen, have lived in the river deltas and the coastal lowlands of western Colombia – the Chocó – for hundreds of years. They are a small tribe numbering probably no more than two thousand, speaking a language similar to that of all the Indians living in the coastal lowlands from Ecuador to the borders of Panama. Where they came from, and when they arrived, remains a mystery. Legend connects them with the pre-Conquest civilization of San Augustin. Their characteristic stirrup pottery might suggest a link with pre-Inca Peru. Other considerations suggest that their earlier home lay in the Amazon basin and that at some time in the past they moved westwards across the Andes and finally halted by the Pacific (this is generally thought to be the case). And yet their appearance, their almost wholly water-borne existence, even the habit of wearing flowers in their hair reminds one of far-away Polynesia.

Wherever they came from, they have lived in this region of the Chocó, between the lower reaches of the Río San Juan and the Pacific Ocean, for a very considerable time. Unlike the Indians of the highlands they were un-affected by the advance of the *conquistadores*, which led to the break-up of the Andean tribes. The forest, the heavy rains, the humid heat and the unhealthy swamps all discouraged the early explorers. It was not until the relatively recent rise of Buenaventura as Colombia's major Pacific port, that the life of the Noanamá was disturbed by foreign influence.

To the Noanamá the river is the centre of activity. During the weeks that we spent with them, the traffic never stopped. Men, women and children, at times whole families, would move up and down the river in large and small canoes – some to their plantations, others fishing, or hunting up the numerous side-creeks, or transporting the great jars of ceremonial *chicha* made from fermented maize. The younger children seemed to spend all their days on the river; the small boys learning to swim and overturn their canoes, sink and refloat them almost before they could walk.

Often as we went up and down with our outboard engine attached to a large canoe, the children would paddle alongside and hold on. As we progressed, more and more would join in the game, until there was a trail of canoes behind us.

Usually every member of a family had his own canoe; the children sometimes had small ones, no more than eight feet long. Then there were bigger canoes, perhaps twenty feet long or more, used for fishing or when the whole family embarked. Some Indians seem to be particularly skilled in canoe-making. A tree is selected, often many miles away in the forest – a cedar or similar resinous wood is preferable; the roughly-hewn trunk is floated down creeks to the river, and then with axe and adze the canoe is shaped under a small shelter beside the riverside house. It may take more than a month for a man to make one, but once completed with its sweeping lines and platformed ends, it lasts for years.

Noanamá houses stand singly along either side of the wide muddy river, often a mile or more apart. Perched on stilts, seven or eight feet off the ground, on the high silt bar where a small creek issues into the main stream, they seem almost to stand in the water.

In front of each house are canoe moorings – long tree-trunks, floating on the surface or lying on the river mud. Attached to stakes driven into the river bed, they act as pontoons for the Indians as they get in and out of their canoes tied alongside. For the lower reaches of the San Juan, even when the river is in flood, are still tidal. Early in the morning the water may be lapping around the house posts, yet in a few hours it will have sunk eight to ten feet down the steep muddy banks.

Only a few of the houses on the San Juan still have the steep conical roofs traditional among the Noanamá. These would be crowned by the *diponghú* (see drawing on p. 20): a large inverted clay bowl with a woman's breasts and the figure of a man with outstretched arms shaped at its apex. The *diponghú* served both to keep the rain from leaking through the point of the thatch, and as a symbol of fertility, a guardian spirit to the house and to all those who lived under its roof. Now the Indians have adopted the simpler, long ridge-pole roof used by the negroes, which gives the house a more rectangular appearance and obviates the practical need for a *diponghú*.

The approach from the mooring is along a path of dried sugar-cane stalks laid over the mud. The house is entered up a sloping pole with notched steps. At night this pole is revolved so that hunting dogs cannot stray off and wild animals cannot enter. The palm-thatch eaves reach to within a foot of the split palm-wood floor. Yet inside it is both light and airy, the sunlight chases rippled reflections off the water on to the smoke-darkened ceiling, and even on the hottest days the cool river breeze moves freely under the raised floor.

In the centre of the main floor is the *trapiche*, a press for crushing the juice out of sugar cane. Around it are raised platforms on which the family sit and work during the daytime, the women making baskets and etching designs on drinking gourds, the men making new flutes, carving figurines or binding shafts for new arrows. At night they place their barkcloth sleeping mats on the same platforms.

At the back is a slightly lower platform where the women cook over a big open fire. A rack stands above on which pottery is hardened after being placed in the sun and dried. Near by is a stone for grinding maize.

Everything is spotlessly clean and the floor is swept many times a day. Even outside there is no sign of refuse. The children are taught at an early age to defecate in the river, sitting on the edge of a canoe. Even the dogs are house-trained and are punished if they misbehave.

Hanging from the roof in the centre of the house is a rack with hunting weapons: bows, arrows and blowpipes and, for fishing, *ataraya* nets, lines and basket traps. Baskets of all shapes, patterns and sizes hang from the rafters, some for catching fish, or for carrying maize cobs back from the plantation, others – a type of square basket with a lid – for keeping personal possessions.

Stored in the cross-beams overhead are musical instruments, wooden *batea* drums, vertical and horizontal pipes and flutes and – usually well hidden – prayer-sticks, figurines and other objects associated with the spirit world.

The Indians rise as soon as it is light, the children run down to the river to swim, the women to the creek to bring fresh water. Soon maize soup is being prepared for breakfast. Before noon they eat again, usually fish, meat and bananas, the fruit of the *chontaduro* palm and a drink of *chicha*. When the sun has risen over the river, some of the younger women with their children go by canoe to their distant forest plantation to collect maize, bananas and wild fruits. Others may move off singly to fish for shrimps and prawns in the reeds with baskets and bark-fibre nets. The older women stay in the house making pots: stirrup-spout and duck-shaped ones, which they use for drinking water, and great urn-like pots for *chicha*. They roll grey-brown river clay between their hands and carefully mould each strip as they apply it coil by coil to a shaped clay base. This work may only be undertaken during the phase of the new moon, for they believe a pot will crack if fired at any other time. The women also make baskets from cane fibre or collect sugar cane from the nearby riverside plantation. Later they have to prepare the evening meal and tend the children. Each new day brings the women much the same routine. To them falls the greatest burden of the daily work.

The men, who may have been hunting during the night, pass the day repairing nets, replacing an arrow lost in their hunting, fishing with hook and line or *ataraya* net, or making a new fish trap at the mouth of the creek. In January, after the rains, both men and women go to the forest plantation to sow maize and cut the undergrowth, working side by side. Later, in August and September, they return to sow a second crop. Four months after each sowing, the maize is ready for gathering – by the women alone.

At nightfall the family congregates once again, and after the babies are asleep in their bark hammocks they discuss the day's events. A man picks up a flute and starts playing. Soon sleeping mats are spread out on the platforms and the house falls silent. . .

Each day we would move up or down stream slowly adding pottery, baskets, weapons and even canoes to our collection. We soon had many recordings of flutes, drums, dances and songs. Inevitably we got to know many families and individuals – some better than others: Severiano, the shaman who lived across the river from the sawmill; and Marialeeto, an elderly Noanamá who often came to see us, to talk and to listen to the tape recorder or to admire our recent acquisitions, on whose workmanship he would give his professional opinion. We would often visit him in his own house, for his days were not so active now and he spent much of his time there. He had broad shoulders, skin like old tanned leather and – unusually for an Indian – a bald patch on the crown of his head. Reserved, with a rather mournfully distinguished manner and a puckish sense of humour, he was unfailingly friendly and polite and answered our numerous questions without any sign of resentment in his slow, halting Spanish.

We learnt very little about Marialeeto – about his early days on the Río San Juan – though it was possible from his recollections to understand how his life may well have been. Perhaps like all old people he recalled the better days of his youth. He remembered the time when only the Noanamá inhabited the riverside and all the land was theirs. No one spoke Spanish then, nor had shirts come into vogue. In the forest animals were plentiful and the river was never short of fish.

His earliest memories of childhood were of lying on his barkcloth mat and listening to the men talking far into the night, sitting on their stools. The firelight flickered on their faces as they recalled the day's adventures and old hunting stories, and the older men recited some of the tribal legends. To Marialeeto they seemed to drone on and on, while outside the cicadas whirred endlessly and a bullfrog started to croak in the reed pool close by the river. Suddenly the men, among them his father, reached for their bows and arrows from the rack overhead and called to their hunting dogs. They went down the ladder and off into the night with the light of a beeswax torch. Somewhere in the forest close by they had heard the grunt of a wild boar.

Often the hunters did not return before dawn. By then the women were preparing the maize gruel. Later everyone left the house for the plantation. But Marialeeto was too young to work. Together with the other children, he would go off in the new canoe which his father had just made him, and spend the day paddling it up the creek behind the house. Sometimes he would sink the canoe on purpose in the strong current, swim in the water, refloat it and then resume his journey. Often he felt far happier in the canoe than he did on dry land with his two feet.

He was given a small wooden carving, a figure of a man, by an old Indian. This old Indian, he learnt later, was a *haibaná*, one of the most powerful shamans on the Río San Juan. To him it was just another toy to play with, but his father and mother made sure he never lost it. When he grew older, he was told that the figurine represented his spiritual guide, his *haí*, and that he should treat it with great care. Only this figurine, kept by his side, could protect him from evil and the revengeful spirits of wild animals.

The day came when his father took him out to fish. First he was shown how to bait hooks and string them across the width of the stream with liana or tie them to balsa-wood floats; then how to build the big fish traps used at the mouths of the small tributary streams. But much more difficult was learning to throw the weighted bell-shaped *ataraya* net. This was heavy and required all the strength he could muster. Sometimes the men pounded the leaves of *barbasco*, a jungle creeper. They filled baskets with the pulp and placed them in the streams to poison the smaller fish.

Some nights a party of men, armed with fish arrows and *ataraya* nets, went through the forest to a nearby stream, where, burning beeswax to attract the fish, they encircled them with the net and speared them.

As he grew up he began to take part in all the men's activities, the making of paddles and canoes, fish traps, bows and arrows. Some of the arrows had a hard wooden point, some a blunt point to stun birds without damaging the feathers; others used for catching fish had barbed metal ends. The Indians used blowpipes, and the darts had a poison made from frogs' glands and other ingredients, which only people living to the north knew how to make. He learnt to make an oval wooden *batea* and beat time with it at a dance, to play the flute and alter its pitch. He went to the plantation, he cut the undergrowth with his machete and threw maize seed like the other men. One day he was bitten by a bushmaster which had been frightened by the noise. With great excitement and shouting, the snake was killed. Its fangs were almost an inch long. The Indians thought its pointed tail was poisonous as well. All he could remember later was lying on his barkcloth mat with the *haibaná* waving a stick over his body, sucking at the fang marks and chanting in a monotone, asking the ancestors to help to take the evil spirit out of his body.

Marialeeto was nearly fifteen years old when he started to look for a wife. He covered his face with red *bija*, hung a many-coiled bead necklace around his neck, silver ear-plugs in his ears and flowers in his hair. With a party of his friends he set off by canoe to a neighbour's *chicha* ceremony. It was August, the time of year for celebrations, and everybody joined in. Later that summer he found a wife. She was slightly younger than him, but she had been through the puberty ceremonies and her father was willing to let her go with Marialeeto who proudly took her home. From then on she lost contact with her family and worked hard with the other women in her new home. She made baskets, cut designs and figures on new calabashes which would be used to drink out of at the next *chicha* ceremony, and watched the older women making pottery – something she would have to do later.

The following year she gave birth to a son. The men of the household had built a framework in the centre of the house and covered it with barkcloth. Inside this small house the baby was born with the assistance of the other women. They at once painted the child with blue *jagua* dye, to protect him from evil spirits. Like Marialeeto himself, the baby when barely a year old was given a small figurine, his *haí*, to guard him against evil.

After some years, when he had had two more children, Marialeeto began to think of building his own home. His father's house was getting over-crowded. He was not the only son of the family, and now there were many children besides his own. He chose a site about a mile further up the river. It was not too far from the riverside plantation, at the mouth of a creek where the high ground afforded some protection from floods and where fresh water could be easily obtained, the river water being muddy and un-drinkable. Here with the help of his wife he cut the heavy posts on which the floor of the house would be built, and the beams which would support the roof. *Chontaduro* palms were cut in lengths; the soft core was left and strips cut from the outside were placed on cross-beams and bound with liana to make the floor. A framework for the roof was made from saplings, and palm fronds cut for the thatch. These were often difficult to find in suffi-cient quantity, and it took a long time to obtain enough to cover the whole roof. When complete, the conical roof was crowned by a clay *diponghú*.

Marialeeto's father remained head of the household till his death. He was

Sunset on the San Juan: young Noanamá canoeists.

the supreme authority to whom everything was referred, but he had no power outside his own family. This is customary among the Noanamá. There are no chieftains, no central power, only the heads of families. Occasionally an outstanding man may have some influence over his neighbours – but no more. Many years had passed, perhaps hundreds, since it was necessary for the Noanamá to band together under a leader and fight a common enemy.

Not long after Marialeeto set up his own home, his father died. They carefully wrapped his body in barkcloth and took it by canoe to high ground beside the river. There the men started to prepare the grave: they dug a narrow trench, then a side vault. Into this the body was lowered in a horizontal position. Before the trench was refilled they placed sticks over the mouth of the vault so that earth would not touch the body.

Probably the old man had died a natural death, for he had lived to a very great age. Yet some said the spell of a shaman had cursed him.

The shaman, like the head of the family, holds no formal authority except through his medicinal and magical powers. He is in a sense both a herbalist and a magician in that he can cure people, yet also bring evil on them if he so wishes. But it is for his power in invoking the help of the ancestors and the spirit world that he is respected. The greater his reputed power, the more people will go to him, and as there are several shamans, even on the San Juan itself – the office being often a hereditary one, passing from father to son – there is constant competition and often ill-feeling. Marialeeto's father was not a shaman, but he may at some time or other have incurred the enmity of one.

As the years passed Marialeeto gained a certain dignity. As a fisherman he became very skilled. As a hunter few could equal his cunning. His dogs were the most willing and the quickest on the scent. He grew good crops and his family prospered.

Some years he travelled up the coast to visit his Noanamá relatives living on the Docampadó, the Dotenedó and the Usarragá, rivers smaller than the San Juan, which rise in the foothills to the east of the Pacific coast. One year he went as far north as Panama and brought back many beautiful beads of blue, red, white and yellow porcelain, a new machete, an adze for shaping his next canoe and an aluminium pot for his wife.

One day Rotilio, his eldest son, now a man himself, returned from Panama and suggested that the family should move north. He said that there was much good land and few people, many fish in the rivers and good hunting. Marialeeto knew that several Noanamá families had already moved north

---

ABOVE: *Noanamá house on the San Juan.* BELOW LEFT: *A Noanamá woman cuts a design on a gourd.* BELOW RIGHT: *Girls painted with purple-blue jagua dye.*

to Panama. Since his youth the river had changed. Now there was a mission station only a mile from his house and several of his grandchildren were even going there to learn Spanish. The negroes had moved up from the delta and lived beside the river alongside the Noanamá houses, and they had taken much of the land. Nevertheless, he felt too old now to move. Like his father he wished to be buried by the side of the San Juan.

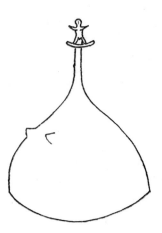

2

The Chant of Canta Hai

It was a dark, still night and only the croak of bullfrogs troubled the heavy air. Suddenly a cry rose and fell over the wide river, a high-pitched wail like the cry of a maimed animal in its last spasm of pain. Across the river a light flickered on the bank; it seemed to shine from the house of Severiano, the shaman. Quietly we went down to our canoe and set off upstream. To reach the shaman's port in silence we would first have to travel up river, then make our way through the fast midstream current and drift slowly down towards the bank. We noiselessly brought the canoe through the reeds and up to the tree-trunk which formed the family mooring place. The water lapped softly against the canoe as we tied it to the trunk.

The house stood high on stilts above us. Ahead we could see the crouching figure of Severiano, lit only by the flickering of a lamp. His naked body barely moved as the cries shrilled out into the night. We made our way over a mat of discarded sugar-cane stems, infested with pincer-jawed ants, to the notched entrance pole. The chant ceased. A young boy came over and beckoned us to climb on to the split-palm floor. Without a word the three of us walked to a corner of the house, sat down and waited.

In the centre of the floor, between the four central posts, Severiano crouched low on his sacred wooden stool. In his left hand he clutched a prayer-stick carved in human shape, the head capped with silver, the face dominated by a long aquiline nose and the body merging into the black hardwood which tapered to a point. In his right hand were three interwoven palm leaves. Placed side by side on the floor in front of him were seven more prayer-sticks, all minutely carved of black polished wood. Not all were human effigies; two represented spearheads and one a hand with eight projecting fingers.

Facing the shaman in a corner was a younger man: Rotilio, Marialeeto's eldest son, recently returned from Panama. He too sat on a low wooden stool holding a carved figurine in his left hand; other prayer-sticks lay in front of him, but he had no palm frond. He was apparently lost in meditation as he gazed towards the shaman. A carved balsa-wood boat hung from a beam above his head. In it stood small roughly-shaped figures, some with guns in their hands.

For a long while the two figures remained motionless. Then Severiano began to wave the fronds rapidly over the prayer-sticks. He took a prayer-stick in his left hand, then, exchanging it for others, with his mouth barely opening he started to hum almost inaudible words. The uncanny song grew louder, but the high-pitched nasal notes remained restrained and controlled.

Severiano, the *haibaná*, was chanting the magic words of Canta Haí. He gazed trance-like into the darkness as he sang to the ancestral spirits, using an idiom passed down from generation to generation, no longer intelligible to the Indians or to himself. Occasionally he stopped, laid down the sticks, uttered a series of words and then, picking one up again, continued his chanting. Rotilio never moved, not even when the *haibaná* rose from his stool and, clutching his silver-capped figurine, paced round and round the remaining effigies. The continuous rustling beat of the palm fronds and the steady thud of the prayer-stick on the floor of the house accompanied his strange cry.

Severiano was the most respected *haibaná* in this part of the Río San Juan, and old Marialeeto, who knew him well, had asked him to initiate his eldest son Rotilio. This the shaman had agreed to do, though he said it would take a long time, perhaps many months. Rotilio would have to leave his young wife and children to come and live with him. It was agreed that once the instruction was over Marialeeto's whole household would go and help the shaman's family collect maize at harvest time. This would be a form of payment for his teaching.

So Rotilio had left home. Each evening, once the sun had gone down, he listened to Severiano. He had carved a balsa-wood boat and inside it had placed fifteen wooden figures, the images of his ancestors. When at night he sat underneath them, he thought he heard them moving above his head. He knew that Severiano was talking to them and one day he hoped he would be able to do the same. The *haibaná* also showed him how to carve the sacred figurines and he spent hours sitting on the palm floor, often alone, shaping effigies of his ancestors, then the image of a human hand to ensure good harvests and two spearheads which would protect him against his enemies. Perhaps in years to come a rival shaman might want to break his magic power, or even to kill him, but with the help of the two spears he would be able to ward off his rival's evil influence.

Rotilio did not as yet have the power to summon spirits. Severiano had given each of his effigies a *haí*, and he himself could chant Canta Haí, but until the shaman gave him two of his own magic prayer-sticks, he could not enter the world of the ancestors. Even then his power would be limited, for until Severiano died he could not take his place, and if he should ever lose one of the sticks, his power as a shaman would vanish.

All the tribes we were to visit believe, like the Noanamá, in some form of supreme being, and to a lesser or greater extent in their ancestors. These are considered good spirits. The bad spirits are mostly associated with the forest, and with the Noanamá this world of evil is that of the hunted forest animals; wild boar, monkey, armadillo, crocodile, water rodents and certain birds. Often they appear as monsters in their dreams. They believe in a giant mermaid who emerges from the water to drown canoeists. Whenever an Indian sees cranes flying together downstream, he knows this is a bad omen, for in crane formation people's spirits fly to the underworld. The evil spirits of the animals manifest themselves in illness and to cure these the shaman will invoke the help of the ancestors and use medicinal herbs.

These herbs were of particular interest to Nestor. He spent hours talking to Severiano, who told him that one leaf was for curing fever, another for stomach-aches, the juice from a third root for clearing sores. Severiano grew many of the plants in an old canoe which he had raised above the ground between posts and filled with earth, but some came from the forest. Nestor would return laden with creepers to soak the leaves in formalin before pressing them between newspapers in readiness for the return journey.

One place remained a mystery: Severiano's retreat, his secret plot deep in the forest, where he grew the most important of all his magic plants, the narcotics which gave him hallucinations. On occasions he would retire to the forest for days, to prepare the juices. He was under their influence when we had watched him chant Canta Haí and look into the world of his ancestors.

To Nestor these were the most interesting plants of all. It was already known that the Noanamá used two main narcotics, one of which remained very much of a mystery. The first, *borrachero*, a small bush with large white flowers, is quite common throughout Colombia. The second, *pildé*, is a liana which often grows wild, climbing over large trees near river mouths. Only shamans could distinguish this liana, by the smell of its sap. Nestor slowly gained Severiano's confidence. They both smoked pipes. Sometimes Nestor would exchange his briar for Severiano's clay pipe or give the shaman cigars which we had diligently sealed in plastic bags with desiccators against the damp of the Chocó.

With this increased attention Severiano became more and more friendly and even started to paddle his canoe across the river to come to see us. One day he brought a branch of *borrachero*, but it was not in flower and so we could not prepare the narcotic. The next day, to our surprise, he arrived with a length of liana – *pildé*. He told Nestor what to do. We crushed the liana between stones and boiled it. The liquid turned a dark brown. Nestor started to drink the bitter juice; the more he drank the more vivid the hallucinations were meant to become, but nothing happened. After an hour, he felt slightly drunk, and the next day he had violent stomach pains. Probably Severiano had no intention of telling us the real secret of *pildé*, for some of the negroes, it is said, have been driven to madness by this narcotic, and a Noanamá shaman can inflict total blindness on an enemy.

It was mainly through Nestor's great interest in narcotics that we came to know Severiano, that he allowed us to watch him, even record him singing Canta Haí. The *haiband* had none of the assurance of old Marialeeto, he seemed at times almost anxious to please us, as if he knew in the back of his mind that his authority was being slowly undermined. Perhaps the interest we took in him, and Nestor in his plants, to some extent re-established his disappearing prestige. The negroes ignored him. The Mission was hostile towards him. Even some of his own people no longer came to see him about their illnesses. It may have been for this reason that he allowed us to watch him calling the spirits of his ancestors.

With the arrival of the short dry season at the end of August, the second crop of maize ripened. The time for celebration had arrived. Many families were preparing for one of the largest festivals of the year, the agricultural ceremony when they would pray to their god Evandama to give them a good harvest and look after their future crops. To the Indian, Evandama was a benign old person, the first man to have inhabited the earth. Though he controlled the universe, he did not interfere with their lives – that was the ancestors' role. Therefore, before any ceremony could begin, Severiano retired to the forest to take *pildé* and to talk with the ancestors through his visions. He was away a night and a day. When he returned he said that the spirits were in favour of the ceremony taking place and that maize should be collected for the *chicha*.

Early next morning, with the mist still lying low like white wool over the river, Severiano's old wife, her two daughters and three of their children paddled downstream to Marialeeto's, where they were joined by Rotilio's wife. The two canoes left the main river and disappeared up a small creek towards the plantation. Only the raindrops from last night's downpour broke the silence, shaken into the still water as one of the canoes touched a treetrunk or was levered round a tricky bend. A bird screeched, a kingfisher swooped from its fishing perch, bright orange star-pointed creepers hung down over the deep opaque water. Here was an enclosed world, different from the open sky of the main river. Suddenly the darkness changed to bright greens where maize plants grew to the water's edge. The women left the canoes moored to a floating trunk and climbed the bank, half running, their baskets slung over their shoulders. While their children splashed in the water, they quickly plucked the young maize cobs. The sun came up and it was time to return, for the tide was ebbing and the creek would soon be dry. They glided back over the dark water as the sun's rays filtered through the tree tops, glinting over the bodies of the girls as they sat at either end of the canoe and sang, their short paddles guiding them around each bend.

They brought the maize to Marialeeto's house, for his was the oldest and its conical roof was crowned with the clay *diponghú*. Here the ceremonies would be held. For the rest of the morning the women ground down the maize, their long hair beating their bodies as they rubbed the corn between two stones; they poured water over the grounds and squeezed them through colanders made from gourds. That afternoon, as the liquid simmered over a fire in two great earthenware urns, Marialeeto's youngest daughter, a girl of fourteen, collected the husks which had been wrapped in banana leaves. She undid the packets and sitting by the fire started to revolve the husks round and round in her mouth, mixing them with saliva and then spitting them into a gourd. Slowly she filled the gourd with this sickly paste as her mother stirred the two urns with a snake-shaped wooden spoon. Once the gourd was full she tipped it into the boiling liquid. Together they lifted the two urns from the fire, covered them with banana leaves and left the *chicha* to ferment.

Late that night Severiano arrived. In the darkness, as the rest of the household slept, he and Marialeeto lowered the long thin ritual canoe from the roof. Blackened with age, its eight-foot length was inscribed with twisted lines; at each end was a notch from which it could be suspended diagonally from two of the four central poles. They hung the canoe with the end nearest the river just above the floor and then retired to their sleeping mats. Only an occasional growl from one of the hunting dogs curled up near the dying fire, or a baby wanting to be fed, broke the calm. Outside, as usual, it rained hard.

For some weeks word had been passed round that this year they would pray to Evandama in Marialeeto's house, and next day canoes laden with people started arriving. Many families came with large urns of *chicha* balanced precariously in their low-lying canoes. For us there were many new faces; some, we were told, had come from the delta, others from the headwaters of a distant river, the Taparral, the home of Marialeeto's mother. All the men had their faces painted red with *bija*, their necks coiled blue, yellow and red with beads, their ears pierced by shining silver plugs with crescent-shaped pendants. Some wore their treasured white shirts, others only loincloths. The women had their bodies streaked with creeper-like designs of purple-blue *jagua*. Gradually the house filled and the urns of *chicha* were piled near the fire. Each family sat in a group round the edge of the springy palm floor; with them they had their most prized possessions, wrapped in barkcloth in beautifully patterned baskets of woven cane. All the men brought long wooden flutes, the boys smaller ones; one family had two small conical drums, each with a wild boar's skin stretched over one end of the light balsa-wood frame and held with thongs of hide and little wedges. For a long time the families continued to arrive. The *chicha* was not touched but left to ferment. The centre of the floor remained empty. Four elders stood by the four posts: Severiano the shaman was one, Marialeeto another, the other two we did not know. Each carried a long wooden flute, the *ursiri*, without holes, and blocked at one end with a balsa plug. They stood rigid and silent, their eyes fixed on the ritual canoe. The continuous chatter which had prevailed all morning died away. Rotilio's young wife left the side of the house and walked to the lower end of the canoe. With one hand she led her baby son, in the other she held a small wooden stave. She uttered a few words and started to beat the inside of the canoe; all the time her eyes stared out in front of her. The hollow notes resounded around the house, every sixth beat louder than the rest. No one moved, even the four elders appeared lost in a trance as they watched her. Then very slowly the shaman, followed by Marialeeto and the two men, started to circle the canoe. They hardly seemed to move, their feet barely left the floor as they solemnly went forwards. They held their long vertical flutes in front of them. By altering the angle to the mouth and the amount of air they blew, they were able to produce three strange notes which wavered beneath the steady, monotonous, strokes on the canoe.

Three times they circled the canoe and then stopped. This must have been a signal to the waiting people. The elders continued their circling almost immediately, then the men, carrying their flutes and followed by the women and children, joined the procession. From time to time the elders stopped and slowly raised their flutes towards the roof, to the *diponghú* and Evandama. Then just as slowly they lowered the flutes to the ground, seemingly to transfer the power of Evandama earthwards to assist their crops. The flute-playing grew louder and louder, until quite suddenly the women broke into a piercing cry. It was a plea to Evandama, asking him to give them good harvests and to stock the rivers and forests with game for their husbands to hunt. Gradually the cries died away and the shaman left the procession.

It was now time to drink the *chicha*. Marialeeto's wife unwrapped the urns and stirred the fermented liquid with a long twisted spoon. The shaman's wife helped her to pour the bitter drink into gourds which each family had brought. Some of the gourds bore intricate designs of birds and beasts or human figures – perhaps their ancestors – all incised into the thin dried shells and rubbed red with *bija*. The close-knit family groups laughed and talked together, the slow voices of the women almost cooing, and the strong staccato tones of the men demanding more *chicha*. Sometimes a man broke into a jolting song, striking the *batea* in time to his words, but the women all remained quiet and, somehow, resigned. Their songs were usually gentle plaintive refrains about the river on which they lived, how one might want to live by a creek with fresh clear water to drink, or how another wished to catch prawns with her barkcloth net. Now they complained of their husbands' drunkenness and how they had been left alone and sometimes deserted. They often accompanied each other in beautiful harmonies; at times a girl might break into descant. It was their singing as much as their playing of instruments which made the Noanamá such a musical people. As the sun set,

Rotilio's son sat on the bank gazing across the river. In his hand he held a *pipania* flute. Again and again he repeated one lovely tune and the notes rang gently across the water.

In the failing light Severiano once more summoned the people to invoke Evandama, and the procession continued to move round Rotilio's wife, beating the canoe until nightfall. Then they returned to *chicha*. The flicker of oil lamps caught the ear-plugs and great coils of beads which adorned the men. Some wore fine *sirri* skullcaps, triangular designs of beads which crowned their Roman fringes. The women were bare to their waists, their straight black hair flowed down their backs, with sometimes a white water-lily behind the ear; their grace of movement, beautiful form, and gentle dignity made them quite the most feminine of all the Indian women we were to meet. A sweet sensuous smell filled the dank night air and these Gauguinesque forms began to dance. They moved round in a circle, hands linked, at first humming, then singing the words '*Kar-ichi-pari*' louder and louder. The boys formed another circle: one beat a drum; the rest whistled in shrill bursts as they danced boldly outside the girls whose delicate steps were in such contrast to the heavy stamp of the men. Finally the two circles joined; the girls continued to sing as they were swept away by the men, surging back and forth across the floor. The singing, dancing and drinking continued into the night, until eventually the families settled down to sleep. A young girl lay stretched out on her barkcloth mat, her eyes closed, and as she dozed she sang to herself: it was a song of how she wanted to marry a man living far away beyond the mountains she could see, a man who had a gold tooth.

For many days and nights the festivities and prayers to Evandama continued. We were told they would go on for weeks; other houses had ritual canoes hanging up in their roofs, while downstream, living apart in the delta, were more Indians under the influence of another shaman. They too would celebrate. Throughout, the people seemed almost oblivious to the world around them; they no longer worked in their plantations, hunted or fished; instead they paddled aimlessly up and down the river, to and from Maria-leeto's house, dressed in their beads, the women dyed with the almost indelible *jagua*, and all steeped in *chicha*.

They did not wish to talk to us, nor did they like us to see the procession around the ritual canoe. They tried to ignore us. We were strangers, intruders upon ceremonies which played such an important part in their lives. Times had changed since Marialeeto was a young boy; in those days there were no strangers living on the Río San Juan and no one interfered. Now modern civilization rapidly encroaches upon the Indians. Buenaventura lies only a few hours away by motor-boat. Sawmills are springing up along the river and boats like ours make frequent journeys to collect planks from this, the country's most prolific source of timber. With the steady exploitation, negroes have filtered into the San Juan in ever-increasing numbers from Buenaventura and Quibdo in the north; for years they have settled along the river's banks, leading a life which is basically far removed from that of the Indian, though the conditions of life are the same. They are the traders and their little planked stores are dotted along the riverside; they cultivate sugar cane and maize on land which the Indian believes to be his own by inheritance. They often run the timber mills and sometimes employ Indians to work for them. There is no open hostility between the two groups; rather they live grudgingly side by side. The negro feels superior to the Indian who in turn bears deep resentment. The Indian is proud and does not intermarry with the negro, for he considers him a person apart from his own tribe. Some have retreated to the headwaters of smaller rivers to continue their lives on their own, a few who have seen Panama have moved north, others remain on the San Juan, gradually adapting themselves to a new way of life but always struggling to retain the customs which are their own.

With the negro has come commerce. Though the Indian previously existed by hunting and cultivation he has learnt the use of money. Those who work in the sawmills earn enough pesos to buy a new shirt or machete; they may sell their maize and bananas or perhaps a pig in exchange for salt, fish-hooks or a new cooking pot. The more industrious cut down trees, make large log rafts and then float them down the river to the delta, and so to Buenaventura. Among the many channels of the delta surrounded by deep mangrove swamps live a few families who have begun to readjust themselves. A certain tree, *manglé*, grows in the swamps; its red bark contains tannin. The negroes started to collect the bark, now the Indians collect it too and sail to Buenaventura with loaded boats. The journey may take as long as a week, but one Indian we met had made his fortune selling *manglé* and uncut timber to dealers in the port. He was no longer a simple cultivator, he had become a shrewd businessman. Close by lived two families who in recent years had sailed to the Río San Juan from another river, far away to the south on the Pacific coast. These people from Saija were more sophisticated and astute, and built great sailing schooners by the side of the river. We did not know where they had learnt this skilled craft; perhaps, as they said, they had copied the sailing boats they had seen in the port of Buenaventura. Each year they visit their relatives on the Río Saija and sometimes like other Noanamá they sail north to Panama to buy their precious beads and maybe a shotgun. Some remain there, for in Panama there are rivers where no strangers have penetrated and where there is plenty of good land to cultivate.

Another race of people, commerce, trade and now another religion, all have had their effect on the Noanamá. Only a few years ago a small Mission was built and today this flourishes; each morning the boys paddle their canoes to school, many with silver crucifixes intermingled with the coils of beads around their necks, to them just one more addition to their jewellery. They are taught Spanish with good intent and helped if they or their families are ill, but in adopting a new belief they must also discard their age-old tribal customs, which are slowly being destroyed. Now even Severiano chants the ancient words of Canta Haí facing a Virgin Mary which his grandson brought home from the Mission. How easily the figure can be incorporated into the world of his ancestral spirits, yet how little he understands what it means.

We left the Río San Juan with mixed feelings. Here were a people so strong and happy in their own beliefs; their lives so peaceful, almost idyllic, but Marialeeto's life could not be lived again. The timber boat chugged slowly downstream, the damp mist low over the water in a cold dawn. It was too early for the Indians to be afloat. Straddled across the bows were three of their canoes. The river waters swirled as they struck the salt of the Pacific and we turned due south, along the coast, to Buenaventura.

Part 2

Tukano

Mitú

R.Vaupés

R.Vaupés

A

B

I

Caño Berada

R.Ti

Pedro's maloca

Portage

Kuarumey's maloca

R.Piraparaná

M

Cachivera Yavakaka

Kaperwa

Cachivera Jirijimo

Ni

Bréo's maloca

— Equator — —

Cachivera
Beiju

Cachivera
Playa

R.Apaporis

BRAZIL

L

R.Miritiparaná

Boheniambo

O

Portage

R.Apaporis

Don Carlos's house

C

R.Caquetá

N

Cachivera
Cordoba

La
Pedrera

0 5 10 15 20 25 miles

Villa Bitencourt

I

El Diablo

Lying only four and a half degrees north of the Equator but eight and a half thousand feet above sea level, Bogotá is a city of cool weather – some say of perpetual spring. Once the surrounding highlands had been the home of the Chibcha who like the Inca of Peru had been overwhelmed by the *conquistadores*. To the north and south the mountains form a continuous chain, to the east and west lie the rolling grasslands of the Llanos and the valley of the Río Magdalena, from where Jiménez de Quesada, the first of the Spaniards, reached the high plateau to found the present city, followed more than three hundred years later by Simon Bolívar, the Liberator, in whose army served many Scots and Irish mercenaries.

Today Bogotá seems to retain her past in a modern setting. Aloof and dignified, she is often called the Athens of Latin America. Overlooking the city from the peak of Monserrate is a chapel, on another peak a monastery and on a third a gigantic figure of Christ. Beneath, clinging to the lower slopes are the steep, cobbled streets of the old city, and stretching towards the centre is an ever-increasing conglomeration of office blocks and banks, one skyscraper towering higher than another.

By day *ruana*-clad peasants move about in their donkey carts, the shoe-shine boys squat on the street corners and the shouts of lottery vendors mingle with the peals of taxi horns and gramophone records. From the fifteenth storey of an office building you can look down on to the red-tiled roofs surrounding the patios of the old Spanish houses, and mules carrying jerrycans of water through the streets and underneath the skyscrapers.

By night the long-distance lorries and buses rumble away, their roofs roped high with sacks and crates, their passengers bound for opposite ends of Colombia. Lights blaze from the stores and cafés; beer and *aguadiente* are served by sensuous girls in bright dresses; there is music and dancing; the brothels open and for a time Bogotá detaches herself from her mountain dignity. But by midnight, with the last cinemas over and the people streaming out, their handkerchiefs held tight to their faces for fear of catching colds, the quiet returns. In the city centre only the gigantic neon signs still flicker and, high above, the floodlit chapel of Monserrate shines white against an ink-black sky.

To us the invigorating atmosphere of the city was a welcome change. The cool fresh air, the eternal rush of people, the noise of traffic, all spurred us on to prepare for our next journey to Amazonia. For three weeks we were able to enjoy the luxuries of a modern city. Our bare attic was the store-room and we slept on the floor, while Joan the landlady with true North Country generosity fed us large meals of Yorkshire pudding and shepherd's pie. There were newspapers, films, exhibitions, concerts, parties and pretty girls, but our time was always short. When we returned to our sleeping bags we were faced by huge piles of film, cooking pots, tarpaulins and hammocks, all waiting to be rearranged and repacked for the next journey.

Each journey was to demand different organization but the one to the Río Piraparaná was to be the longest and hardest of all. We would be out of touch with all traces of civilization for three months. Even at this stage we were unable to predict our route. Neither the maps nor the information available were sufficient for us to make definite plans. Dr Schultes, the Harvard botanist, had originally advised us to go to the Piraparaná, though he had also warned us not to go too far down because of the extensive and dangerous rapids. A Colombian botanist told us to take the opposite route and go up the Piraparaná from its mouth. Our efforts to find the right solution met with many conflicting answers.

The only direct means of reaching this river in a remote part of Colombia some four hundred miles south-east of Bogotá was to fly. We settled on Mitú as our starting point, having decided to descend the river largely because of the advice of the Catholic Mission there. This settlement, close to Brazil on the Río Vaupés, was the Mission's base and the most accessible point to the Piraparaná. During the planning stages in September Brian had flown in on a cargo plane and discussed our plans with the Monseñor and the padres. Even then the Monseñor warned us that if we arrived any later than the end of November we might run into severe difficulties – there would be no water in the beds of the streams. It was now the beginning of December.

We had to find a plane to take not only ourselves but also an aluminium boat, two outboard motors and all our equipment. The regular fortnightly service was out of the question because the passenger plane could not carry our boat, and to charter an aircraft was beyond our means. So we asked the Colombian Air Force whether they could help. Our chances seemed hopeful since some troops had to be collected from another nearby frontier post. However, only a week before we were due to leave we had a severe setback. An unfortunate article about the expedition appeared in the Press, there were many exaggerations – we were even supposed to have a portable laboratory! – and mainly as a result of this the director of one of the scientific institutes withdrew his support, which meant that Nestor probably would not be able

*Noanamá **headman** with pendant silver ear-plugs.*

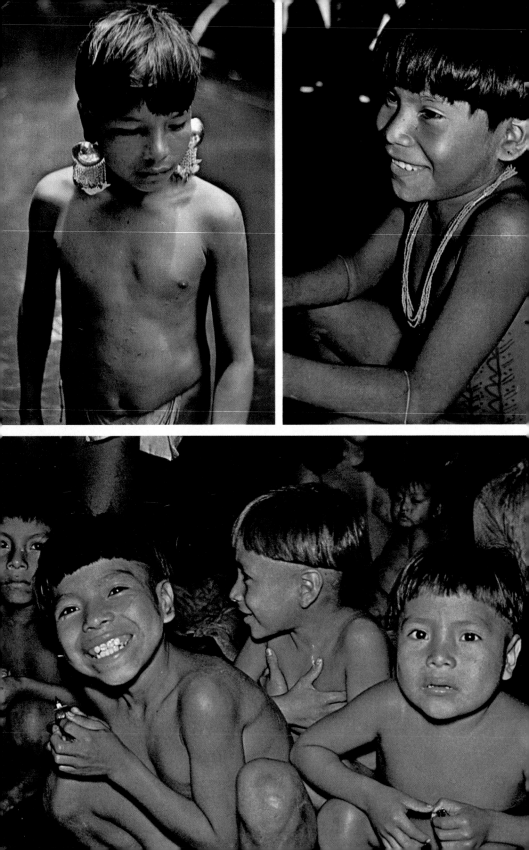

to come with us. We were also afraid that the Catalina flying boat would be withdrawn as well. We had nothing more than letters of recommendation from scientific bodies in Britain and, with no official support behind us, the Colombians had every reason to doubt our validity. They could well feel that this was work they could do just as well themselves. For two days the fate of the expedition seemed in the balance.

Fate was on our side. The Commander of the Air Force agreed to fly the expedition to Mitú on 15 December. The only restriction was that the two hundred gallons of fuel given to us by an oil company could not travel in the same aircraft. We would have to find another way of flying our fuel to Mitú. As we walked out of the Air Ministry and across the road towards the vast Tequendama Hotel we unexpectedly came upon Horacio, strolling dejectedly along the pavement.

'I've just left the bookshop,' he said. 'I had a quarrel with the boss's daughter, and now once more I'm without a job. I think I'll go back to the Llanos, find a canoe and stay down there until the rains arrive. All I need are books, some rice and beans, my hammock and my mosquito net, and I'll be happy.'

'Heavens,' we said. 'Why don't you come with us?'

Horacio's eyes twinkled and later that evening he came to our attic and said he would join us. Educated in Europe, he and his brother had both been to Bedales and later he had graduated from a Swiss university with a degree in chemical engineering. On returning to Colombia he had found a wandering life more agreeable than research or business. Now in his mid-forties he lived and worked in Bogotá as little as possible. With his wide knowledge and complete fluency in five European languages, he had been a great asset to many expeditions which he usually accompanied as a professional photographer under the pseudonym of Robinson. But he preferred to travel alone. Though always helpful, he was nevertheless a strangely remote person. Our meeting turned out to be one of the most fortunate moves of the whole expedition, for besides his vast experience and fund of jungle knowledge Horacio turned out to be a marvellous friend.

The final three days were ones of hectic preparation. The motors had to be checked, the aluminium boat transported to the military airbase; these had been loaned to us on the understanding that we would carry out a reconnaissance geological survey for an oil company. Food supplies piled higher and higher in Joan's attic, for we had to feed not only ourselves but our Indian guides and helpers as well. Colombian money would be of no use to these people. So, on Horacio's advice, yards and yards of coloured cloth were

ABOVE LEFT: *Noanamá boy, his face painted with* bija. ABOVE RIGHT: Jagua *patterns a boy's body.* BELOW: *Children listening to our tape recorder.*

bought. Pins, needles, reels of thread, mirrors, brightly-coloured combs and extra fish-hooks to supplement those Donald had already brought from England were all found in the market area. After hours of haggling we would wend our way homewards, laden with tins, paraffin lamps, rope, candles and many other items. Up to the very last moment we were packing endless supplies into plastic bags and rubber bags, inside kitbags and into tins which we had painted bright red to cheer us up in the green forest.

Early on the morning of the 15th a truck arrived; we loaded and left for the airbase, only to find the boat would not fit into the Catalina. They had been trying since six in the morning. There was nothing we could do, we had to take the flight or not go at all. So we left, without Nestor and without our boat. We had luckily sent the fuel ahead to Mitú in a cargo plane.

We slowly climbed above Bogotá and thence across the Eastern Cordillera towards the Llanos. As we landed at Villavicencio the oppressive heat seeped into the aircraft. Situated directly underneath the foothills of the Cordillera, it is the port of entrance to the Llanos and the tropical forests bordering the plains to the south. Here ranchers ride the streets, tether their horses and carouse in the beer saloons till dawn; then they return to their *fincas* deep in the plains. From here the rivers run east, to the Orinoco and then to the Atlantic.

We continued on our way southwards over undulating grasslands, then over unbroken forest. Suddenly we entered a storm and, as we bumped up and down, became lost in swirling rain. An hour later we emerged and a ridge appeared on the horizon. Beyond, the wide brown Vaupés with a straggling line of painted wooden houses broke the unending carpet of green. We landed on the white sandy strip of Mitú; once a rubber boom town, now a lonely outpost settlement and mission station, an oasis in the forest.

Earlier we had heard we might find it difficult to make friendly contact with the Indians of the Piraparaná. Very few white men had been able to enter the river, either from its source or its mouth, since the beginning of the century, when the most brutal atrocities had been committed by the Casa Arana[1]. This rubber company, financed by British and Peruvian interests, had extracted rubber from north-west Amazonia to export it down the Amazon through Manaos. The camp chiefs established themselves as potentates and were greatly feared. Their labour was entirely drawn from the Indians whom they treated not as human beings but as slaves. Women were raped, men who displeased their masters brutally murdered, those who failed to carry sufficient loads had their hands slashed off with machetes and were left to die. Many spent their lives in chains. So serious were the atrocities that in 1912 Sir Roger Casement brought the matter before the House of Commons. Many Indians retreated into the Amazon's remoter tributaries.

[1] The atrocities were in the Putumayo region – not the Piraparaná – but their influence was felt throughout north-west Amazonia.

Today the *caucheros* still avoid the Piraparaná. Only a few years previously one had entered and tried to take an Indian's wife. He was shot with poisoned arrows and savagely cut to pieces. Two botanists had travelled some distance up the river from its mouth, but no one had descended its entire course. At Mitú only Padre Elorza was able to give us first-hand information. Young and zealous, he had been the first missionary to enter the Piraparaná, one month before we arrived. He had travelled half-way down the river and then turned up a tributary to Brazil. A wooden canoe could withstand the rough journey, he said; an aluminium one would not only be too wide for the creeks of the headwaters but would get ripped on the boulders. A suitable canoe, with a hollowed tree-trunk base and sides built up with planks, was lying half-filled with water in the mud at the side of the Vaupés; it belonged to the Mission but he thought the Monseñor might lend it to us. He also told us that his Spanish-speaking guide, an Indian from the Brazilian tributary he had ascended, was still in Mitú and he advised us to take him. He knew the river and he spoke the Tukano dialects. So we employed José, a small and somewhat shifty-looking man, together with his more genial brother, Uriel. We would pay them in pesos and feed them; they would take us to the Piraparaná and from there return to their home. From Padre Elorza we also learnt that two Persian anthropologists had reached the first house on the river only the year before. They had arrived earlier in the season than ourselves, stayed two weeks with the Indians and then returned to Mitú. The headwater streams still had had water in them. We were not to be so lucky.

That evening as we drank cold sweet lemon juice with the padres, their lives for a moment seemed blissfully peaceful and remote. They showed us their museum of countless ceremonial death masks, once worn by the Indians of the Vaupés. It seemed a curious paradox that we were entering territory with the help of a mission which was doing everything to displace the culture we had come so far to see. We walked back to the wooden house of the Commissioner where our host Don Alonso, wizened and immaculate, sat listening to the radiogram beneath an old tarnished chandelier – Mitú had known better days. Don Alonso insisted we drank beer and *aguadiente* and met everyone in his town; the negro who could repair the canoe and whose wife cooked delicious mealy *tamales*; the doctor and nurses from the hospital; the mechanic to test the outboard motors; many *caucheros* and finally a young Argentinian dentist who aimed to make his fortune capping people's teeth with gold. His price was high, but he would accept crude rubber, pelts and crocodile skins as payment before he moved on to the next outpost. The evening ended in hilarity as we danced to scratched seventy-eights revolving on a gramophone whose coiled trumpet betrayed its age.

Next morning before dawn, our thick heads were stirred by resounding hymns. It was Sunday and the Mission had their loudspeakers at work to call the town to Mass. We too went inside the crowded church. Later that day the Friar Tuck Monseñor formally lent us *El Diablo*, the leaky canoe which we now had to repair. Horacio became more and more perturbed by the enormous quantity of fuel and equipment we had decided to take with us; we would be bogged down in no time, he said. Much was left behind and through fear of the rapids ahead we decided not to risk the Kudelski, the most valuable tape recorder; this after all was only the second of five journeys. We cabled Nestor to follow us with the aluminium boat as soon as he could, but to travel as light as possible; for the rivers would be even lower by the time he arrived. In anticipation we left him drums of fuel and supplies. Still we had too great a load for *El Diablo* alone and Don Alonso kindly lent us his larger canoe, *El Vencedor* (The Conqueror), with his motorman Candilo and an assistant. Time was short, we had to go now and, as Horacio aptly remarked 'muddle our way through to the Piraparaná'.

This was the most difficult of all our journeys. The past few days had been filled with worries and doubts, while our plans had had to be modified beyond recognition. Yet we had been warned to always be flexible when travelling in Amazonia, a place where 'two and two never make four'.

El Vencedor sank lower and lower into the water as we loaded, first the fifteen-gallon fuel drums, thirteen in all, then our mountain of equipment and food supplies, planned to last us for the next three months. Now we were ready to leave with the two boats lashed together fore and aft with two wooden poles. Suddenly there came a rumour that an Avianca plane would be arriving, and we decided to await the final chance of news from Nestor; perhaps the aluminium canoe was to be sent through after all. While waiting we said good-bye to the padres whose bearded faces barely concealed their obvious doubts about our future. Then we learnt that the plane had been cancelled.

The motor started and the three of us, together with four Indians, left the landing stage with a wave from Don Alonso and the villagers. They had all been more than kind to us, had in fact enabled us to start the journey when at one stage, with no boat, all had seemed lost. Now, as we travelled up the wide, 'black' Río Vaupés, we had every reason to wonder what lay ahead. Our raft-like craft moved slowly but steadily up either bank, never in midstream, for the current was very strong. We took it in turns at the outboard motor but soon realized that Candilo was by far the most capable hand, so we sat and read. Horacio, his broken glasses perched on the end of his aquiline nose, looked the ideal sage, lost in a German book on atomic physics.

The lower reaches of the Vaupés, as it runs into Brazil to join the larger Río Negro, are a series of dangerous rapids. Only recently one of the padres from

Noanamá woman cutting sugar cane.

Mitú had met his death with two of his Indians when their canoe overturned. The upper reaches of the river have a gentler gradient, passing through softer sandstones instead of the hard igneous rocks of the lower course. Nonetheless we soon had to negotiate our first rapids. To the uninitiated eye it seemed impossible to pass through, but Candilo, after one false attempt when the motor stalled, took the half-loaded *Vencedor* skilfully through the jutting boulders. Donald followed with our smaller motor powering the loaded *El Diablo*, her bows nosing into the frothing water and the waves breaking over the fuel drums. This was our first rapid; we had no idea that we would have so many more to negotiate before the end of our journey. Brian examined the rocks, chipping off pieces, looking at them through a lens and packing samples away for our geological collection. Then we lashed the canoes together as fast as possible and continued to creep along the banks, eating our lunch of dry biscuits and *farinha* – a thirst-quenching mixture of manioc flour and water, the Indian's habitual meal when travelling.

The tropical sunset is swift, with no extended twilight, and so by five-thirty each day we had to stop travelling and quickly find a break in the forested bank where we could make camp. Our boats tied and the cooking equipment ashore, we set about cutting a clearing. Horacio was a cook *par excellence*. Years of travel had taught him that the most efficient stove was to be made from a tall biscuit tin; you made your fire at the bottom and placed the pressure cooker on the top. We were eating our diet of rice and corned beef within half an hour of landing and, slinging our hammocks, were soon gazing up at the starry sky, listening to the croak of the bullfrogs.

Soon we left behind the wide Vaupés with its deserted forest banks and entered the black enclosed waters of the Río Ti. With the dry season already well advanced and with less water every day, we were forced to unlash our two canoes and continue with one following the other. The stream narrowed, the black waters shallowed and the white sandbanks crept closer on every bend. Near the mouth of the river we had arranged for two more Indians, the brothers Matias and Bernavez, to come to help us. They knew the route through to the Piraparaná and they warned us that, with our heavy loads, we were going to find the journey extremely difficult – unless it rained. Their warning was fully justified, for with the lower river level the fallen tree trunks formed one long barricade to our movement upstream. In the rainy season with the high water, one could float over them, but now every trunk had to be cut. Fortunately the Indians were experts with our axes, their muscular bodies perched precariously on a water-borne log, the axe falling rhythmically against the hard wood, the water splashing up into their faces. These were civilized Indians who could speak Spanish; they had

---

Working a trapiche, *a press for crushing the juice from sugar cane.*

originally worked wild rubber for one of the great rubber barons and they had earned their clothing in exchange for their labours. Their torn trousers were only a veneer of the civilized world, for here they seemed to come into their own element: they talked to each other in Tukano; they became alert to the forest they knew so well.

We were living in a closed world of limited horizons, on either side the thick forest, ahead the river and above a ribbon of sky. Giant emerald king-fishers with orange heads and long black beaks darted out in front of us. Myriads of white butterflies rose off the sandbanks, settling on our bodies to enjoy the salty sweat. On occasions we saw a delicate wader like a sandpiper bob up and down on the sand near the water's edge. The water had now changed colour, no longer black but a deep wine red, as it flowed over the pale sandy bed. We supposed this colour was due to the high iron content in the rock.

Our first major halt was made at Pedro's house. He had established him-self as a tradesman between the Indians on the upper Piraparaná and the civilized rubber gatherers of Mitú. He bought *farinha* from the Tukano in exchange for fish-hooks, salt and cloth. His magnificent thatched house was a foretaste of what we were to see. But the occupants with their dishevelled clothes, the sheets of crude rubber hanging from the beams and the iron cooking pots, seemed a strange paradox.

We unloaded all our equipment, sending Candilo and his assistant back to Mitú with *Vencedor* and the larger outboard motor. With him went one of our valuable cameras whose shutter had jammed during the first day, and a note to Nestor in Bogotá, warning him of the difficulties he would encounter and advising him again to travel as light as possible. Of the now depleted party, José and Uriel were to be our guides throughout the journey; Matias would ensure that we reached the first Indian habitation on the Piraparaná; while Bernavez went on ahead in his dugout canoe carrying two drums of our fuel. We were joined by one more man, old Miguez, who brought his own small Indian canoe. From now on we would have to make double journeys with *El Diablo* until we reached Indians who would carry our loads in their own canoes.

Next morning, while Donald and Horacio repacked much of the kit, Brian and José went ahead with a small load in *El Diablo*. The Ti narrowed and then divided; here our route towards the Piraparaná portage lay up a tiny tributary, the Caño Berada or Fish Bow Creek, as it was known to the Indians. With our arrival in the Berada, a mere stream flowing out of the undergrowth, our whole mode of travel changed. We could no longer use the motor; instead we had to push the boat upstream. We spent the rest of the day waist-deep in water, clambering over submerged timbers and occa-sional rocks; an Indian out in front cut a way through the fallen trees.

Christmas Day saw us cross two rock ledges where the boat had to be completely unloaded and then dragged over. That evening was a beautiful one and we made camp at an old *mitasava*, the Indian traveller's staging point, where he erects a small palm-thatch shelter. We must have been on higher ground, for it was dry and sandy while the forest had changed to small birch-like trees, with lichen and moss underfoot. Somehow this was an appropriate place to eat our wild Christmas turkey which Miguez had shot earlier in the day and drink each other's health from the precious bottle of 'medicinal' whisky.

The next day our watery struggle continued and progress became even slower. Only half the equipment reached our camp site, this time back in low-lying forest. That evening Donald and José went ahead to the next stream junction to return at dark with the news that there was barely any water at all in the stream, and that we would be pushing the boat over dried-out sandbanks. Matias, our hardest worker, departed across country to the Piraparaná. He left at dusk, his coca pouch slung across his back to ward off the pangs of hunger. He promised to return in three days with men from the first habitation on the river; he was true to his word but it took him more than three days.

That night there was a disquieting atmosphere in the camp. Horacio was even more unhappy than usual about our excessive amount of equipment. Our three remaining Indians, José, Uriel and Miguez, kept to themselves, talking through half the night. We awoke to find Miguez vanished, never to be seen again, and José and Uriel packing their own belongings on to their backs. They said they were going to join Matias and bring back more men – we knew they were about to desert us.

We made them put down their gear and then listened to their tale of woe. We were not feeding them well enough; they wanted more than just *farinha*, they needed rice as well. They were being made to carry too much, and the stream beds were so dry that it would be impossible for us to get through until the rains arrived. So we compromised, we agreed to leave behind some of the fuel if necessary and to give them the same food as ourselves; we repeated our promise to pay all the Indians who worked for us in cloth and trade goods – or even money if it was of any use to them.

During the day we pushed the boat, first down to the previous site and then, fully loaded, back towards our present camp. Once Horacio lost his way when taking a short cut; he was not well and we thought it was due to a recurrence of malaria. That night he became worse, and with him unfit we decided to go ahead on a reconnaissance with José, leaving him to guard the equipment and recover, while we tried to reach the other side of the portage; if necessary we would go overland to find the first house.

Early next morning we packed our rucksacks and left with a week's supplies. Walking over high ground with willows, lichen and moss, to our great joy we reached the western entrance to the portage after only two hours. We walked through the low scrub for half an hour, along the path over which we would have to drag our boat. Then on the far side we saw the headwaters of the Piraparaná – there was water, not much, but at least more than in the headwaters of the Ti. We knew then we could reach the main river, even if we should find it difficult to take all the equipment. Enthusiastically we returned to tell Horacio the good news. We found him lying in his hammock and reading, and to our surprise he told us that all the trouble stemmed from a fish bone which had lodged itself in his throat.

Our best plan was to take the boat forward, leaving all the equipment ready for Matias and his Indians. We pushed with renewed efforts but over such dry sands that we often had to stop, dam the trickle behind us, then wait for the water to rise sufficiently to see us over the next sandbank. At other times we had to dig down into the sand to make a channel through which we could push El Diablo. Two days later we reached the portage.

Travel in Amazonia is almost entirely by water; on the smaller rivers by dug-out canoe, on the larger ones by launch or even steamer. In headwater areas it is frequently necessary to cross from one river system to another, and to do this the Indians and *caucheros* make portages or paths, along which they can carry their canoes. Portages are also used to skirt long sections of rapids where it is too dangerous to take canoes through the river. Some may be five miles long, others only a few hundred yards. The size of the boat and the number of people at hand determine the time it takes to cross. With five of us, three pulling a rope attached to El Diablo's bows and two pushing from behind, it took only four hours to cover the mile over the watershed. On the flat pathway with the boat's hull sliding smoothly over rollers cut by the Indians, there was little difficulty. But when we had to heave the canoe out of the gullies it took us all the effort we could muster to bring the heavy water-logged craft – which weighed eight hundred pounds – out of the root-strewn quagmire on to the sandy track.

The choice of camp sites while travelling in such areas is a difficult one. Very often lack of time in the approaching darkness forces a rapid decision. Obviously it is best to find high ground above a rising river but this ground is often a refuge for thousands of ants and all manner of crawling insects – who naturally have the same idea in mind. It was such a camp that we hit that night and we found that all the kitbags, tins and crates were already a seething mass of black ants. Termites had completely covered a pair of boots which we had left lying on the ground, and we were besieged by sweat bees.

After dark there was a sudden calm. In the distance a faint hiss could be heard, gradually coming closer and closer. It was the wind racing through the forest – nearer and nearer, until it became a roar and the whole jungle was in turmoil; trees swaying, clouds of leaves flying and rotten branches crashing to the ground. In a moment torrential rain was upon us. Horacio sought safety under the plastic sheet of his mosquito net; Donald took refuge under his battered trilby and the groundsheets, while Brian dived beneath the tarpaulin and spent the night stretched over tins and kitbags.

The New Year came in with more rain. For all the discomfort it brought we could only look upon such deluges as a sign of good fortune; they were early this year, the rivers would now be higher and our descent easier. So we started on our journey downstream. *El Diablo*, lumbering along like a loaded ark, was stopped by every snag and log. She took days to cover the same distance as the slim canoes of the Indians, when they later travelled back up the river in a matter of hours to pick up the fuel drums we had had to leave behind on the portage.

One day canoes appeared gliding towards us, both loaded down with large wicker baskets of *farinha* and paddled by two men in loincloths. Strings of minute white beads were around their necks and black berry bracelets around each arm. An old man, his wizened face eyeing us suspiciously, was sitting in the bows of the first canoe.

This was our first real contact with the Indians of the Piraparaná. Their immediate reaction was not one of fear, but rather, like our own, of enquiry and interest. They said nothing until José hailed them in their own dialect. There ensued a long, almost formal exchange of greetings which we were to hear many times when travelling through their territory. Before they left we asked them to carry a message for Nestor – in case they should meet him, for they were travelling to the Río Ti.

Much depended on our guide José. That he had been with Padre Elorza was not necessarily to our advantage, for in the first place we could not be sure what effect the first contact with Catholicism had had on the Indians of the Piraparaná, nor did we know what instructions José had been given by the padres. We had to depend on him entirely both for our own safety when travelling downstream and for the information we were to get. He was not a very pleasant or easy character. From the outset he had always wanted to have his own way and if this was not granted then he became moody and unco-operative. We could never be certain what he would do next and after his attempt at desertion we could not trust him. However he worked very hard and showed remarkable common sense, and without him we would never have got through the rapids ahead of us.

His experience with white men had not only come from the Mission. Some five years previously a *cauchero* had come to his river home close to the Brazilian frontier. He had taken six boys away with him to work the wild rubber trees and one of them was José. Later he had escaped from the *cauchero*, but during those four years he had learnt how to operate an outboard motor, to handle money and had even been in an aeroplane. He had come under the Mission's wing only recently, and it may have been this combination of experiences that had complicated his character. He no longer possessed the Indian's direct simplicity.

The last days before reaching the first Tukano house on the Piraparaná were not easy ones. At one point we had to cross two formidable waterfalls where all the equipment and fuel was carried overland, while we dragged the boat over the riverside rocks to avoid the midstream torrent. At the first of these the boat was lowered over a twenty-foot rock wall by means of a crevice into which we had forced timbers. *El Diablo* began to show severe signs of weakness. The ribbing above the hollowed log hull began to give and the planking above it worked loose at the joints. Large lumps of pitch came astray and we found ourselves caulking her sides with strips torn from our trousers. On many occasions we hit submerged rocks and logs, and the further we went the more we had to bale. Once a jagged rock edge pierced a large hole in the bows and water came gushing in. One thing was certain: an aluminium boat would by this time have been ripped to pieces.

Our journey downstream was a cold, wet and dreary affair. Both Donald and Horacio had ceased to wear boots because of raw blisters. Our shins had become a mass of open sores from knocks sustained underwater. But these exposed rocks gave Brian opportunities for geology. Much to everyone's dismay – except his – *El Diablo* became more and more weighed down by samples which found their way into the used biscuit tins. José always wanted to know whether there was gold, but there never was, nor indeed were there any fossils. We were attempting to make a compass traverse of our route, but our methods at this stage were hardly accurate.

We made camp one night on the driest land available, near a junction with another tributary. It was an unhealthy spot with bats swooping low beneath the trees. Later one of our guides had his toe incised by a vampire bat and woke in the morning to find his hammock soaked in blood; these bats often carried rabies. While Horacio was making breakfast, a scorpion ran up his arm. When he yelled, José, who was standing close by, flicked it dexterously into the hot ashes of the fire.

Some days later, after an unusually long stretch of paddling, we jumped into the water to pull *El Diablo* over a fallen tree. A large boa constrictor unfurled itself from beneath the boat, shot between our legs and zigzagged swiftly through the water in front, its dark green body coiling and recoiling as it vanished down the river.

It is a mistake to think that the forest is alive with poisonous reptiles and fierce animals. The discomforts stem from ants, insects and many varieties of stinging flies. We rarely saw wild animals although birds were quite plentiful. In this higher part of the river, a particular small bird would always warn all other creatures of our approach with a piercing three-note whistle. Calling louder and louder it was answered by others in the vicinity. The noise was rending and the more we talked, the more it sang. The Indians called it the *Wa-pey-yer*, and we later heard this bird had driven some explorers mad.

For the first time in a week the sun pierced the thick canopy of leaves, catching the shining emerald, blue and yellow wings of giant butterflies. José, who had been carefully watching the passing bank, asked to borrow one of our shotguns. He soon returned with three *pava* – a type of large black-cock – which he had shot with four cartridges. Like all Indians, he was much more adept at hunting than ourselves.

The day wore on and the river widened, trees and creepers came right down to the water's edge, their leaves reflected peacefully by the calm surface. Sometimes the thick green foliage was covered in pale purple flowers, rather like lilac, whose sweet smell floated across the water as the boat moved through the beams of sunlight. It was warm and the scene had changed. We were no longer enclosed and we only once had to jump into the water to guide the loaded boat through a rapid.

Here Horacio, whose ankles had swollen to an alarming size, stumbled and fell in the rushing torrent. Perhaps this was an indication of our condition and the need to reach dry land. Sores had not healed and many had started to go septic. By contrast José and Uriel had gone from strength to strength, their bodies seeming to profit from the very hard work they had had to undergo.

Now the trees' shadows were lengthening across the river and three white egrets glided ahead of us. José's voice broke the silence: 'Only one more turn and we reach Kuarumey's *maloca*. His father was a famous chief who refused to allow any white man to enter the river – now he is dead.' As he said this we rounded the last bend.

There in front of us rising from the water's edge was a clearing of green manioc with an expanse of sky behind. We paddled the boat alongside the wooden canoes moored to the bank, while in the dusk we could barely distinguish the features of the Indians as they came down the path towards us. They carried no arms and seemed to be friendly. Soon they were helping us unload *El Diablo*. We debated whether we would stay the night by the river or in the *maloca*. The Indians however were in no two minds about this, and we found ourselves stumbling up the path in the darkness, following our laden hosts, very glad to feel the good dry earth beneath our bare feet and the warmth of the fires inside the great *maloca*.

2

A Death

Matias arrived at the *maloca* the following day with the rest of the equipment we had left behind at the portage. Without his help we would have had to abandon it. That same night he started back on the return journey with his brother Bernavez, back to their *maloca* on the Río Ti. With them seemed to go our last contact with the outside world. Now was the time to collect our thoughts, to reorganize the equipment and to decide how we were going to carry out our work. The surroundings, the atmosphere, the Indians, everything was new. Each day, when evening arrived and we had eaten, we would sit across our hammocks and read by the light of a candle, or write up the day's events in our diaries. On Friday 6 January Brian wrote:

'Did not sleep very well last night, probably because I had taken a large mouthful of coca just before getting into my hammock. Nearly choked, the fine green powder making it virtually impossible to breathe; so had to run down to the river and wash my mouth free. The Tukano must have a special method for swallowing it.

The women got up very early, long before dawn, but I couldn't tell the time because my watch was lost on the way over the portage – too bad. They rubbed down manioc and the continuous noise made all further sleep impossible. Horacio left for the river before first light to develop a film he had taken with his old Rollei, also one of mine to see whether I'm giving the correct exposure in these dark conditions. He prepared the hypo last night and has to develop before the water temperature rises.

At dawn Kuarumey opened the door and the cold air rushed into the *maloca*. I went out to the jungle to relieve myself, armed as usual with a bottle to collect a humus sample. We do this nearly every morning – all these tiny bottles. I wonder whether the American drug company will ever discover a new Amazonian anti-biotic? Lovely pale pinks and delicate blues, the mist rising in great banks off the forest, and dew dripping from the trees. It was so peaceful and cool.

We joined Horacio for a late breakfast; all of us rather at sixes and sevens with each other as to what to do. The last days have taken a lot out of us and

---

Our train of canoes on the Piraparaná – José in front.

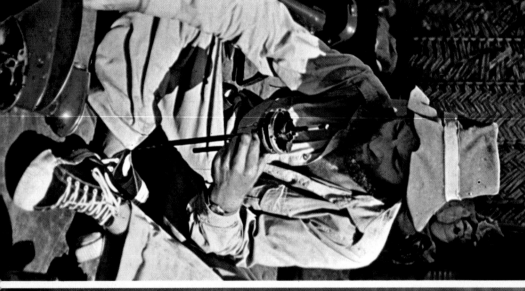

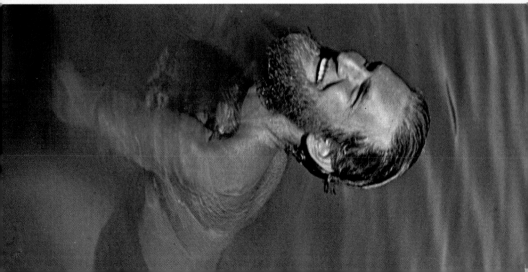

at times we are very irritable. Donald, the most silent, is by far the most understanding, while Horacio and I with our opposite points of view tend to get across one another.

Spread out the two tarpaulins on the sand in front of the *maloca*, then all the equipment on top of them, once more throwing everything to the air and the sun. Donald and I doctored our sores. Both he and Horacio have the beginnings of boils on their arms; this could be dangerous. If our sores go septic we really shall be in a mess – we had better take some penicillin. Donald dealt with the medical kit, Horacio checked over all the food supplies. With his blue and red pinstripe shirt, a Roman nose and scruffy growth, he looked just like an Arab street vendor squatting over his wares in the *souk*. We seem short of meat and Nescafé but otherwise all right. I took out all the cameras. Some of the lenses are in poor shape and neither the electronic flash nor my Japanese one is working. Spent ages trying to repair them and reached the conclusion that the filament on the electronic had broken – probably knocked as we came over the portage. Donald discovered a dud contact on the Jap flash and after much wastage of bulbs and various electric shocks got it to work.

The heat at midday is tremendous but a swim in the river refreshed me. José and Kuarumey had gone out with our two twelve-bores and returned at noon with three *pava*. Being stationary is a blessing; we can send the Indians off hunting – they love using our guns – and so supplement our rations. Have to be careful because Nestor should soon be arriving.

p.m. I slung my hammock between two trees – the sandflies never seemed to leave me alone – and wrote up my geological notes till the sun went down. Am putting all the specimens in sample bags, and it's lucky we have them, for some of the sandstones are crumbling to pieces. Horacio measured the rice into our bright-red tins – funny to think they were once green and with me in the snow and ice of Cocuy. Donald spent the whole afternoon drawing the *maloca* – beautiful, he should have been an architect. The children love watching him, and one little boy – I think he's Kuarumey's son – kept tugging his long beard, then racing over to feel mine, completely intrigued by our hairy faces.

Spent the evening editing birdsong tapes with Uriel who gave me long descriptions of each bird; we had seen very few of them. Surrounded by many overwhelmed listeners, and one boy started to imitate some of the songs amazingly. Ate rice and stewed bird and after silica-jelling the cameras (the plastic bags seem to puncture easily) climbed into my hammock. It's now late, a woman is still rubbing manioc somewhere in the darkness: they always seem so willing to help us, but Kuarumey, no ... he's sitting beneath

---

LEFT: *Horacio López.* CENTRE: *Donald Tayler.* RIGHT: *Brian Moser.*

the *bréo* flame taking coca with two other men. He is silent and has offered little real assistance; I wonder whether he resents our presence here.'

It did seem at times as though Kuarumey resented our presence, and he later had some cause for his suspicions – certainly in his own mind – when events took an unexpected turn. He was a striking man, tall and rather gaunt, with a proud almost arrogant manner. There was no doubt as to who was the head of the *maloca*, nor that we were visitors, fortunate to have his hospitality. We saw little of him during the daytime and it was some time before we learnt he was making a canoe some distance away in the forest.

Though the Tukano travel through the forest on hunting expeditions, canoes are used to go further afield, to fish or to trade with other groups. They are a river people as much as a forest people, and like many Amazonian tribes they have evolved their own methods of making canoes.

The Noanamá, we found, dug out and shaped their canoes from solid wood, and it was necessary for them to find very large trees to do this. Many tribes of the southern Amazon use the bark of a tree, like the North American Indian, while some groups of the Guahibo and the Maku living in areas remote from the larger rivers do not use canoes at all. The Tukano, however, shape their canoes by a process of heat-warping.

A tree – a hard type of cedar – had first been felled, then a twenty-foot section was cut and barked, and allowed to lie for several weeks, before Kuarumey started to cut the wood. Each day he went to the clearing, setting up a palm frond to shade himself when the midday sun broke into the clearing, through the gap in the trees overhead.

Using his *azador*, a curved hoe-like blade, and a long stick with a sharp metal end, he first shaped the outside of the log, scraping off the bark. Then he made holes along its length and began to cut out the centre. It was hard work and he would often break off to make himself a cheroot, using the rolled leaf of a palm, while his eldest son continued the work. Once he disappeared in the jungle to set a monkey trap, a ring-snare high in a tree with fruit as the bait.

He worked carefully, feeling the sides of the canoe so as not to make the shell too thin. After several days it was ready, braced with two small stumps to prevent the sides from closing. Then Kuarumey and several Indians from the *maloca* dragged the hull along the forest paths to the river bank nearly a mile away.

Now the canoe was ready to be warped by burning. This could be undertaken only at certain times of the year when there was no risk of rain, for water on the hot wood might split it. Before they obtained iron and steel the Indians used to cut the trees with their stone axes. They would only partly shape the hull and burn out the centre with fire. Now, with the canoe already shaped, the burning was quicker and it would be completed within a day.

The tinder-dry wood heaped underneath was soon alight and Kuarumey, helped again by his son, began to turn the hull, holding the canoe on rollers, first the right way up, then upside down and lastly on its side. The flames from the fire leapt five feet into the air all along its length and the men began to sweat as they watched. Soon they were covered in charcoal from head to foot. Every so often Kuarumey reached for his coca bag and shook some of the powder into his mouth. Gradually the sides of the trunk were forced open and wedges were placed along its length.

'In the Llanos they hang the canoe over the fire and there is less danger of the wood actually bursting into flames,' said Horacio. At that moment Kuarumey's wife approached us along the path carrying an earthen bowl full of *chicha*. 'And they don't let women approach during the burning for fear of the wood splitting.'

All day long they worked on the smouldering canoe. About midday they bound the ends with liana to prevent it splitting and occasionally put mud on the thinner parts to prevent further burning. The work was completed before dusk. The canoe would cool gradually during the night, and in the morning the braces would be removed and replaced by flat wooden supports. Then Kuarumey would try out his new canoe in the river. It was well built and the sides were even, barely half an inch thick throughout. It should last him for several seasons, providing he did not lose it during the winter floods.

The sun shone warmly on the russet water as Kuarumey paddled the slim canoe away from the port and down the river – so light, so strong, so manageable and in shape so beautiful, yet for ourselves unthinkable – we would have capsized in a moment; only Horacio could master an Indian craft. *El Diablo* was now on the bank drying in the sun, and Horacio and José were starting to recaulk the battered shell.

The rough passage over dried-out river channels, through log-strewn stream beds, across the portage and over vicious rocks, had jarred the joints so much that, were we now to have slid her into the water, she would have sunk like a sieve. For days we had left her on the bank to absorb the heat of the morning sun, turned her and then covered her with a tarpaulin against the occasional afternoon storms, Now the old caulking was pulled away and melted down together with the pitch we had brought from Mitú. However, this was not sufficient and José exchanged some of our fish-hooks for wild beeswax and resin, and this too was melted down.

The fragrant smell of pitch and beeswax filled the air and as the lumps slowly dispersed in the bubbling black syrup, José began to tell of the rapids which lay ahead: 'Listen to the water,' he said, and in the distance we could hear the rumbling; the falls were three bends downstream. 'Only half a day's journey away is the fall we call Piña. In the dry season it is a long series of rapids and we need help to carry everything from the upper end, through the forest to the port at the lower side. We generally take three hours along this trail, but you will take more.'

So he went on. We would need people to help us through at each major fall. Now we fully realized what an encumbrance our equipment was still going to be. But there seemed to be a *maloca* near most major rapids and with luck we could ask for help from the people living in them, though here again José was uncertain: 'Much depends on whether there are any men at home and whether they want to carry such heavy loads. There are many *cachiveras*, and Yavakaka – the Otter – one of the largest, has no one living near it.'

We counted sixteen major falls in all, but often one *cachivera* would consist of many rapid sections covering at least two or three bends in the river. José would demonstrate these by drawing with his finger in the sand. Our imaginary map of the Piraparaná became a hazardous line curling southwards. There would be at least two interruptions a day on a journey which would take the Indian in his fast canoe seven days to complete, but ourselves – we hardly dared guess.

El Diablo was due for as hard a buffeting, if not harder, than she had already had. Her hollowed tree-trunk shell was, with the exception of one hole, in perfect condition. Above, forming a freeboard, were the planks from which we had stripped the caulking. We dipped hemp – instead of our trousers – into the boiling pitch and Horacio vigorously tamped the sticky black wads into the seams and cracks. Once the outside was complete we wedged the same cracks from the inside. By early afternoon all the seams shone black, the wood was dry, and as we slid her down to the river she seemed barely half the weight we had dragged up the stream beds. *El Diablo* had a new look.

Late the same evening, after we had taken our boat and the remaining eight fuel drums below the first rapids, José came up to us as we sat talking in our hammocks. In the centre of the *maloca* the men were squatting on their stools taking coca. At the far end a woman delicately turned a cassava cake to bake its underside on the hot clay oven. José stood between our hammocks, slung in a triangle, the candlelight flickering on his face.

'After the journey to the next *maloca*, I do not want to work for you any more. My brother and I are going home to our *maloca* on the Querarí.'

This was a shock. The house was only two days downstream, and José had threatened to leave us before. We treated the matter more lightly than he perhaps had expected. He asked to borrow one of the shotguns and Brian lent him his twelve-bore. Such a move might be judged foolish, but we knew

---

ABOVE: *Negotiating shallow rapids with* El Diablo *on the Piraparaná.* BELOW: *Getting the fuel drums across the river.*

that José was the one man who could take us through to the mouth of the Piraparaná.

Throughout the whole journey the factor which played more on our minds than anything else was uncertainty. The way back over the dry channels was almost out of the question and the Indians would never have taken us; the way forward appeared to be a long succession of cataracts. Then there was the question of Nestor – would he ever arrive and how long should we wait? The longer we stayed the more insistent José became about leaving. He did not enjoy his role as an interpreter, he did not like asking his fellow-Indians questions and he seemed completely indifferent to the work we were trying to do. All this was understandable but it did not ease our position.

It was cold and wet when José and Uriel left early next morning to take a load of equipment ahead. Mist hung low over the forest and the trees dripped with moisture. 'This is white rain,' said Horacio. 'It is more usual in the winter months, so perhaps we are due for a wet spell and Nestor will get through after all.' We all had doubts in our minds and now, with José gone, we had no means of talking to the people in the *maloca*.

Suddenly Kuarumey's wife ran out and grabbed Brian's arm, beckoning him to follow her inside. From the far end of the dark interior, behind the palm screens, came strange sobs. The sounds rose and fell; across the bare earthen floor a slight figure bent over the embers of a dying fire. It was Watsora whose husband had been away on a hunting expedition for nearly a week. Her naked body, lit only by a dull red glow, was doubled up. She heaved and hardly seemed able to breathe. Only the day before she had carried her heavy basket of manioc from the plantation. Now her thin, drawn face, her sagging breasts, her dishevelled hair, aged her beyond belief. A young girl clutched her around the waist and moved to and fro with the heaving figure, quietly chanting to herself. Watsora's baby son ran to his mother's side and clasping her arm began to cry.

Kuarumey's wife implored us to help. She pointed to the black medicine chest. Only the previous night we had given the headman aspirin, but this illness seemed much more serious than a headache. We could not be sure what was wrong. Perhaps she had an internal haemorrhage, maybe it was consumption, or was it appendicitis? We couldn't know, none of us was a doctor. Horacio was firm: 'No, we must not give her any drugs, for if she dies, then what do you think will happen to us?' For a time we argued but eventually agreed. Horacio was right: no matter what we felt, we could not afford to be held responsible for her death, nor could we interfere.

A Tukano shooting fish with a long fish arrow.

The wails increased, the young girl's chant grew louder as she repeated the same notes over and over. The atmosphere in the *maloca* became unbearably tense and, while Horacio read outside, we went down to the river, trying to escape a situation which we could do nothing about. Our minds were not at rest and, when Horacio's drawn figure appeared walking slowly down the sandy track, we could guess what had happened.

'Watsora died five minutes ago,' he said and went back up the path. We said little and silently followed him back to the *maloca*. On the way we passed Kuarumey's old mother. Her normally jovial face was now serious. She avoided our eyes and continued to feed her toucan with beetle grubs. Inside all was silent, the wails had ceased, even the children were quiet and their innocent curiosity had turned to wariness. There was nothing we could do except wait and keep to ourselves. The boat was downstream and we had no means of talking to anyone. The tiny black sandflies converged on us in the stifling heat of the early afternoon. A woman came over to our equipment, undid a tin and took out a handful of rice, looked at the grains, smelt them and then carefully poured them back again, wiping her hands on a kitbag when she had finished.

Our anxiety increased. To read or write was impossible. We left the *maloca* to walk across the forest clearing. The question of giving or not giving drugs to the woman before she died had produced one dilemma. Now the question was – what next?

Returning later we noticed that the earth in the centre of the floor had been disturbed and fresh yellow clay lay on the surface. None of us had actually seen the corpse, but Donald had seen the young girl, who had been wailing at Watsora's side, take the dead woman's hammock down to the river and wash it. Later we learnt that the Tukano always bury their dead inside the *maloca*. The method is much like that of the Noanamá and the highland burials of the ancient Chibcha. They dig a trench and excavate a horizontal vault about three feet beneath the surface. The corpse, with the knees bound to the chest in the foetal position, is wrapped in his own hammock or in barkcloth and then inserted in the vault which is blocked with leaves, so that earth never touches the body. With the body are placed private possessions: pottery or a basket in the case of a woman; a bow and arrows, coca pouch or snuff-shell in the case of a man. They retain these possessions for the afterlife, the happy hunting grounds where they will travel in spirit.

No ceremony could have taken place in so short a time, and the women continued to make cassava, as though nothing had happened. Before the death they were wailing, now they were silent. The people who had once been so ready to smile, the children who normally followed at our side, were aloof and distant. Each one of us was tense and worried and it was a relief when a new face came to the entrance of the *maloca*. He seemed familiar and we recognized one of the Indians we had first met on crossing into the headwaters of the Piraparaná. He was returning home after leaving his baskets of *farinha* on the Río Ti and offered to take some of the equipment downstream in his empty canoe. The offer we accepted.

'There are *jakaratinga* in a small creek near my maloca.' he said in broken Spanish, 'and I want to borrow a shotgun and a torch to go and shoot one tonight.'

We had heard that this type of baby crocodile was good to eat, and this was another chance to restore the Indians' confidence in us. With a certain reluctance Donald lent his twelve-bore. Now only Horacio's ·22 remained. We always had to rely on their help. If they looked on us as friends, they would not steal our guns. If they did not, they could kill us just as easily, whether they had our weapons or not.

That night the men squatted on their stools, around but not on the patch where the woman was buried. As they chewed coca, they mumbled at times in answer to Kuarumey. Several times one of his younger brothers left the group and came over to our hammocks to look inquisitively at our kitbags and finger them, his solemn face caught in the failing light of the torchwood. Horacio was more worried than either of us, for only a few years before he had been attacked by a group of Aucas in Ecuador and had escaped by swimming under his raft; the same tribe later killed five American Evangelical missionaries who, in attempting to establish friendly contact, had landed their plane near one of the Auca settlements. Horacio had always preferred to travel alone, paddling his canoe along deserted rivers and slinging his hammock close to the bank. To live under the same roof as the Indian made him feel ill at ease. Our anxiety was only increased by his recollections of a journey he had made in the Llanos the year before, on a tributary of the Orinoco:

'Moving downstream late one evening, I was paddling my small canoe, when I heard voices. Rounding a bend I saw a small group of Guahibos on the bank. Before I had even drawn level with them I heard the hiss of arrows. Suddenly I felt a searing pain as one passed through my left arm and pinioned it to my side.' He showed us the great scar on his arm. 'I continued on down the river using my paddle as best as I was able, lying in the bottom of the canoe with the arrows thudding into the side.' How he had to extract the arrow from his arm and continue for days before he could get help was a grim story, all the more so in our own predicament.

It was still raining the next morning. Without any warning, Kuarumey stalked out of the *maloca* leaning on his stave, looking neither to left nor right. Some moments later two men followed him down to the river, their paddles on their shoulders and coca pouches slung across their backs. They were taking Kuarumey to the shaman who lived deep in the forest below the Piña *cachivera*. For the time being, all we could do was to wait. An old man sat humming to himself in front of the palm screen where Watsora died. Here was an opportunity to make a unique recording, but it was not the time to upset the Indians.

Donald wrote in his diary, 'José took Brian's gun with him when he left, now mine has gone too. As B. just said, "This is the sort of thing that could have happened twenty years ago – they take away your boat, then your guns, then murder you." It doesn't do to have too much imagination!'

All afternoon we waited in suspense, feeling trapped within the area of the *maloca* and the green manioc plantation surrounding it. Then, with dusk approaching, José and his brother walked up the path from the river. They carried nothing and José seemed ill at ease while Uriel remained silent. Over the evening meal we told them that we would leave early next morning and that our intention was to descend the Piraparaná, then the Apaporis, and eventually arrive at La Pedrera on the Caquetá. To return to Mitú was now out of the question. Up to now José had thought we were going to return to Mitú and he greeted the new plan with apparent enthusiasm. Still we could not be sure of his intentions. When they went back to *El Diablo* to collect the gun and their own belongings and did not return after an hour, doubts once more entered our minds. Horacio left for the river carrying his rifle and we followed, but our alarm was without foundation – we met our guides as they were coming back along the path.

That night we were able to relax a little for the first time in three days. At least our guides and the canoe had returned, though we began to think Nestor would never get through. In case he did we left detailed instructions in the *maloca*, together with a projected sketch of the Piraparaná and supplies to last him until he reached the proposed rendezvous. More important was the shaman's decision, but this we did not know, for by dawn next day we had left the *maloca* and Kuarumey had not returned.

A manioc plantation below a Tukano maloca.

3

Warpaint

Below Kuarumey's the river was wider and deeper – deep enough to use our diminutive 7-h.p. Johnson outboard motor. Frequently during a day's journey we would come to rapids or a fall where everything had to be removed from the boat and carried to a point where it would be possible to reload. Then, using ropes, slithering over the rocks, pulling, pushing and heaving, we would get the empty eight-hundred-pound shell over the rapid sections. Sometimes the canoe seemed on the point of being swept away to destruction, but José and Uriel, together with the Indians, who for the small reward of beads, a piece of cloth or nylon fishing line were always ready to join us, seemed to know exactly how to manage it, though much bigger than their own light and portable craft.

Where the rapids were long and severe or there was a bend in the river, the Indians would sometimes have made a portage through the forest. On these occasions we would disappear for long periods, pushing and heaving *El Diablo* over the twisted roots and swampy ground through a jungle labyrinth, to reappear shouting and yelling to encourage ourselves at the lower end of the rapids, ready to load and continue on our way. During the severer overland passages the canoe might get a bad knock, and in spite of the recent overhaul it would be necessary to do more caulking. Sometimes, in despair, we doubted whether the old boat would even reach the Apaporis before she finally gave up and sank. To return the way we had come – which had been our original intention – was out of the question. Our only way out was to the Caquetá, a major tributary of the Amazon. What this journey would entail we could not imagine, for all the maps we possessed had often proved incredibly inaccurate. Of the time it would take us and the route we knew nothing. We had, however, heard that the lower reaches of the Apaporis were impossible to navigate owing to a series of great falls and rapids. This knowledge certainly gave us cause to worry during the ensuing weeks.

José by now had taken over responsibility for the motor. We took it in

LEFT: *The front, painted with a design in charcoal and clay, and great eaves of a maloca.* RIGHT: *Cutting palm fronds to thatch the roof.*

turns to take bearings and to time distances for our very rudimentary compass traverse. Often we came to fast sections of the river, where we would stop the engine, raise it off the back of the canoe – to which it was lashed by a piece of rope in case of an accident – pick up our paddles and guide the canoe through the swirling waters. It was as well we had the Indians with us on these occasions, for we never knew what lay ahead, and the water swirled by faster and faster. The following was a daily occurrence: '*El Diablo* was filling with water rushing in over her stern. We hung desperately on to extremely slippery rocks, then suddenly got lost in the froth with the boat going safely ahead. The boys take it all in their stride and utter high-pitched yells as they miraculously guide us through the more dangerous parts with their paddles.' Horacio was in his element at such times; all his travels by canoe in the higher tributaries of the Orinoco had been done with a paddle as his only means of propulsion. An engine was anathema to him, something totally unreliable, which invariably broke down at the worst possible moments and wasted days in repairs – if repairs were possible – whereas a paddle provided unfailing if slow progress.

At this stage we not only had to travel down the river but also to return up it, as we still had too much equipment to take at once. Normally José and the Indians would travel downstream for several hours with the equipment, then return for us. It was on one such journey of José's that the outboard started misbehaving. It was too late to do anything when the engine finally stopped and refused to restart. The following morning we found to our dismay that it had seized up. We stripped it down and after completely dismantling it found that the gearbox oil had leaked away and the whole shaft had locked solid. Fortunately we had enough gearbox oil in reserve – later we learnt that bananas make an excellent substitute – and we thought all was well again until, as the gearcase was being replaced, the clutch sleeve snapped. This rendered the engine useless. So that day we continued paddling down river in a very despondent mood – the thought of paddling our way to the Caquetá was not a happy one. The best we could do was to make for the next *maloca* and if possible effect a repair.

We arrived at the *maloca* that afternoon. Not a single Indian was within sight, not even a dog. At first we assumed the house had been abandoned, but a smell of wood smoke lingered. Puzzled, we noticed the fires had only recently been left. This was the first time we had encountered such a breach of hospitality, for the Indians must have known of our approach. We assumed however, they would return at nightfall, so we set about hanging our hammocks and preparing our beans and rice.

The Indians did not return that night or the next, and the deserted *maloca* seemed strange and forbidding. Horacio was certain that these were unfriendly Indians and that this was their way of showing it. We should therefore be cautious and move on as soon as possible. But the broken engine enforced a stay. We tried wood, then Perspex to replace the broken sleeve, and it was several days before we found that a section from one of our aluminium eating plates was the answer.

One day, while we were waiting in the deserted *maloca*, we were suddenly surprised by shouts. Outside a fierce-looking Indian with a carved redwood club in his right hand stamped and grunted his way round the bare sandy ground in front of the *maloca*. He was followed by three younger men, each carrying a machete, all with their faces covered in red warpaint. Mario Capitan, who had been made a 'chief' by the *caucheros* wore a long white feather in his ear-plug; he seemed annoyed. Probably he had come out of curiosity or to demonstrate his authority, or he may have heard of Watsora's death. His father had had great influence over the lower Piraparaná, murdering all whites who entered. Mario, we reflected, could well do the same. Then suddenly and silently he and his small band of warriors departed to the river, to their canoes, back to their own forest home.

It was with some relief that we set off again from the deserted *maloca* to continue downstream. At night we would clear an area near the bank for a camp site, put up the tarpaulin for the equipment, then sling our hammocks to the nearest trees. If it started raining we would have to huddle under the tarpaulin till dawn. It was much pleasanter when a *maloca* was close by at the end of a day's journey, as there we were assured of warmth and a roof over our heads.

During the course of our journey we visited fifteen *malocas*; in some we only stayed overnight, in others several days. They extended a distance of about 250 river miles – from Kuarumey's to the last rapids on the Piraparaná, about 100 miles from its mouth.

Though at times we were angry with José for always hustling us on with threats of desertion if we did not continue downstream, it was for the most part only through him that we could talk to the Tukano: only those who had worked rubber knew any Spanish. It was during these visits that we became better acquainted with the Indians, though they remained remote, perhaps because they distrusted us, true 'Sons of the Forest', their personalities hidden as deep within themselves as they were deep in Amazonia.

4

The Forest Addicts

The Tukano are small: a man rarely exceeds five foot six and the women are often no more than four foot ten inches. To see a cripple or deformed person is unusual. They are healthy and immensely strong. A man wears no more than his loincloth, today cut from a piece of trade cotton but formerly a strip of beaten barkcloth. Around his neck are three or four coils of minute white porcelain beads, which are among the most valued objects of exchange; a tight string of black berries is strung on *cumare* palm fibre above each elbow. The ears are often pierced with a short cane jutting out from the lobe; sometimes a feather is put into the cane, or a flower replaces the earplug. With their short, cropped hair and well-proportioned bodies they stand out as strong figures, beautifully adapted to the forests in which they live.

Their gait is jerky rather than slow and relaxed, indeed they almost run; whether the Indian is out hunting or carrying heavy loads he always moves in the same way. We could only look on amazed as our fifteen-gallon fuel drums were carried for two- or three-hour stretches with no apparent difficulty. They only showed any signs of wilting in strong sunlight; an Indian would rather travel by night than on an open river in the midday sun; his home is in the cool forest or under the dark eaves of the *maloca*. His face painted red with *karayuru*, a bow and a quiver of curare-tipped arrows in his hand, he has little sympathy for strangers and would rather remain undisturbed. It is therefore not surprising that the Indian's face tells you little. When he stares at you with his black eyes, it is as though you were peering into the cold unknown, and there is little warmth in his expression. We very seldom noticed any demonstration of affection among the older people. Husband and wife live together rather as a matter of arrangement than through love, and tenderness was only shown to the younger children. The old people, once unfit to go out hunting or to work in the plantation, may be neglected in times of shortage and even left to die. They are no longer of any use to the society, so it is best they go; for theirs is a harsh world where only the fittest can survive.

Although the Tukano seem outwardly reserved, lacking in affection and often proud, they are invariably very courteous. Their greetings are formal – just as we shake hands they always exchange a lengthy stream of words. It is as though the visitor to a *maloca* is explaining his reasons for arrival while the host answers him in short phrases of affirmation. They do not look at each other during the greeting, no matter whether they are in a *maloca*, on the river or in the forest. We were continually impressed by their simple yet perfect manners. Cassava and perhaps a newly-caught fish would be brought to us when we first arrived at a *maloca*, then, without our asking, we would be shown where we could sling our hammocks.

The men have an easier life than the women. Their short, clipped speech has, like their gait, a matter-of-fact sense of urgency about it, but is punctuated by high trills of laughter when they joke and make fun amongst themselves. They are born with a sense of humour, and it is the old who suffer at the hands of the young. In one *maloca* a little boy consistently refused to let his grandfather take his afternoon siesta. To everyone's great amusement he would tickle the old man with a piece of grass, pretending a fly was settling on his body.

It would be impossible to say whether the early push of the Jesuits up the River Amazon towards the end of the seventeenth century, and the more recent incursions of the *caucheros* and the Roman Catholic missionaries on the Vaupés and Caquetá, have had an influence on Tukano thought. Certainly their beliefs are very complex. Moreover, the Tukano live in an area as far from the Amazon as the Hebrides from London, while the first direct missionary contact with the Upper Piraparaná had been made by Padre Elorza only the month before we arrived.

Besides believing in some vague all-powerful good spirit or god, the Indian believes in many lesser spirits, both good and evil, all of which have a great influence on him and to a large extent rule his life. The good spirits can be recognized in the pleasant things of the forest. They are represented by fruit trees and plants – bananas, pineapples and other edible fruits, and coca too; the various trees used in making the *malocas*; the cool and clear forest streams. Whereas the poison in manioc, the twisted creepers and roots which trip weary hunters, and the jagged rocks in rapids which split canoes – these are evil spirits.

Apart from this animistic belief, the Indian believes in an immortal soul – at least in some cases, for he acknowledges the existence of spirits of the dead, usually his ancestors. The spirit of a living man wanders only when he is asleep. The shaman on the contrary can divest his body of the spirit at will and glide through the jungle in the guise of a puma.

Indian life is greatly influenced by this fourfold world of the spirit – the monotheistic spirit or god, the animistic spirits, the ancestor spirits and the detached living spirits, and it is the evil ones who hold the greatest sway over a man's life.

Usually the men are called after birds, and the women after plants and nowers, but when asking a Tukano his name we would be given a Spanish one or nothing at all. Possibly the reason for this was that by saying his name aloud an Indian might call back the spirit of an ancestor who had the same name, or worse, by telling us he might have given us power to work evil over him. Incidentally they would usually ask ours, which we would give them – to their obvious amusement, possibly owing to the strange sound which they would find almost unpronounceable.

An Indian will show a stoical indifference to a wound in fighting or an accident while hunting. On one occasion a man was brought to us with his hand full of gunshot. He had been carrying his old carbine through the forest by the muzzle! We spent nearly two hours cleaning the wound and picking out the shot, while he chatted away to his brother seemingly unconcerned. Yet when suffering from a less obvious ailment an Indian is often convinced that someone has worked evil on him. Should death occur, his relations must seek revenge on whoever is responsible. On the occasion of Watsora's death our own position was extremely unsure, particularly when Kuarumey departed on the following morning to visit the shaman.

It seems in retrospect extraordinary that we were ever allowed to continue our journey. For the shaman once consulted has to find a victim on whom he can place the blame for an ailment or death – in this case both, in the same house, the one in which we were guests. What better subject could he have had, the visiting white man, regarded with suspicion by the Indians, and uninvited? Barely two decades earlier the Indians of the Piraparaná showed no compunction in killing *caucheros* who interfered in their lives. Surely their views could not have changed so radically, in so short a time, to make ourselves an exception to the rule.

Perhaps the most noticeable thing about Watsora's burial was the speed with which she was buried and the fact that this was done within the *maloca*. This could be accounted for by the fear that the body might be whisked away and eaten – some of these tribes were once cannibals – and then the spirit could never escape to the afterlife. Also, once buried, there was no indication as to where they had placed the body.

Like most of the Amazonian tribes the Tukano have no real central authority or clan cohesion. The authority, such as it is, is invested in the heads of families. These composite families seldom number more than twenty to thirty people, usually far less. In the past clans have united to fight a common enemy. At the turn of the century one chieftain south of the Apaporis organized a small army of clans to fight the encroaching white *caucheros* and to kill any Indians found collaborating with them, but this was an exceptional case.

Even the head of the clan or family has only a semblance of authority, though there are exceptions, and often less power than the shaman. This lack of leadership combined with a preference for isolation – which may be partly explained by the environment in which they live – has resulted in the small unconnected settlements typical of the Indians of this region.

A headman is responsible for the provision and organization of the household. He arranges the building of the great *malocas* when it is necessary to move. He also oversees festivals and councils. In some households his actual power appeared to be slight, and it seemed to us that the average Tukano did more or less exactly as he pleased.

In the event of a headman dying, a festival is normally held in his honour after the burial. A new headman is then elected, usually the eldest son of the chief, though this decision depends on the council of elders of the household.

If the headman is the secular authority, the shaman is responsible as a spiritual one, in that he is always counteracting the influence of the evil spirits. He also cures the sick and diseased and in the event of death names the person responsible, so that revenge may be exacted. Living in a world apart, he keeps somewhat aloof from his fellow tribesmen and to enhance this sense of separation he may wear distinguishing marks.

Tukano families are small, there are seldom more than two or three children. Why more do not survive is difficult to explain, but life in the Amazonian forest is rigorous and the Indian believes that if a child cannot stand hardship at the moment of birth, it will not be able to stand that of later life. The normal custom of washing the new-born child in a stream is sometimes fatal. Moreover, should the child have any blemish or disfiguration – signs of evil to the Indians – it is all too easy for the mother to hold the infant beneath the water till it drowns. Should she have twins, this will also be the fate of the second-born, or it will be left in the forest to die. For to have more than one child at a time is to be like the animals of the forest – a terrible disgrace. In some *malocas* a dearth of children was very noticeable, especially in the lower areas of the river where the *caucheros* had greater influence.

The children assume adult responsibilities at a very early age. When we were waiting in the deserted *maloca* we noticed a small thatched shelter close to the women's entrance. It was bare and empty, and Horacio told us that this was probably a menstrual hut. They were common among the tribes in the Llanos and the women also retired to them during childbirth. Perhaps the Tukano had the same custom, but we learnt no more.

We saw no puberty rites though we did hear of a ceremony called Jurupari[1]. At certain seasons in the year the men leave for the forest to collect baskets full of chrysalises, *mojojoy*. When the women hear the men returning to the *maloca* they run screaming to the nearest plantation. Here they remain while the ceremony takes place, for they believe that the men have brought Jurupari, their god, with them, and if they or their children should see him, they will die. The men play long seven-foot flutes. One of these trumpet-like

[1] Jurupari in fact seems to be '*lingua general*' for god – and is not peculiar to the Tukano.

instruments, the largest of all South American flutes, was later obtained by Nestor and given to us to bring back to England.

While the men are alone, they carry out a trial of strength to establish the strongest members of the clan. Each man scourges the other on the back, between the head and the waist, with whips made from lianas and monkey hide. There is no fighting, but the women become more and more afraid as from the plantation they listen to their men's cries. With nightfall the sacred Jurupari flutes are carried away from the *maloca* and buried underwater in a secret stream bed. The women and children can return now, and they dance and drink *chicha* throughout the night. The feast is open to everyone. It is said that no outsider has ever witnessed this strange masochistic ceremony which is the nearest thing to initiation known among the Tukano.

As a boy grows up, he takes his place with the men. He has his own bow, arrows and curare. He takes cocaine and can wear the full feather head-dress in the tribal dances. He soon chooses a wife from a neighbouring clan, and brings her back to live in his headman's *maloca* and share in the work of the plantation. Though the headman may have two wives, monogamy is the normal rule. Should a young man wish to be independent, he may leave the house of the headman and go off into the jungle to cut his own *chagra* and build his own house.

The forest offers no incentive to communal living. There is always room for more people and other *chagras*, and independence or friction often breaks up the family before economic necessity rules it. On his new land a young Indian will cut the forest for his *chagra*, build a *maloca* and hunt when he has to. But he will do no more than that. It falls to the lot of his wife to provide the daily food: she plants the manioc, harvests and prepares it. She is responsible for the young children. She does the pottery, plaits the *cumare* fibre and makes the hammocks. She is the producer and to her falls the hardest work in their daily lives.

Unlike many of the Amazonian Indians who live in village communities, the Tukano live isolated in their *malocas*. A *maloca* is the only centre of human life for miles around, separated by a clearing from the surrounding forest and placed sometimes a mile or more from the river, away from the sandflies, mosquitoes and other insects that plague the banks, and from the prying eyes of enemies and strangers. The only signs of life are the moored canoes, and it may be as much as an hour's walk before the *maloca* is reached along a narrow, almost indiscernible path, which at times seems to fade away into nothing – as indeed it is meant to.

A *maloca* is built to vast proportions, often eighty feet from end to end and

Tukano hunting with blowpipe, bow and arrows.

sixty feet wide, with the ridge of its roof thirty feet above the ground. This ridge is supported by six great posts, three on either side; the central space extending down the length of the *maloca* is like the nave of a church. The roof is thatched with palm fronds overlapping to a depth of four inches and extending almost to ground level on either side. These fronds may have to be brought from a great distance and vary in quality – the best lasting for years, while others rot quickly and require frequent patching.

As the sun rises each morning over the surrounding forest it lights on the striking clay and charcoal designs which are painted along the whole width of the front wall. Slivers of light find their way through the palm screening and form patterns on the floor and the walls inside. The only other light comes from the men's and women's entrances at opposite ends of the house, entrances which are often kept shut to discourage the flying insects that are usually at their worst during the middle of the day. From these doorways bars of sunlight cross the hard earth floor, lighting the main posts of the house. Beyond, just discernible, is the *chicha* canoe, the great vat which quenches the thirst of the dancing guests at festivals. Near by stands a forked pole where hang coca pouches, fruit-husk ankle-rattles and fretworked gourd *maracas*. On the floor are calabashes, some with coca inside, others with tobacco, and the wooden stools on which the men squat, passing half the night over their stories of past deeds in tribal wars and great hunting expeditions.

Overhead the smoke-blackened thatch is hidden in the gloom. Hanging from a beam is the most treasured possession: the barkcloth-covered palm box containing ceremonial feathers, monkey-fur belts and puma-tooth necklaces – all the precious adornments for the tribal dances, the greatest occasion of all in the lives of the Indians. The palm-woven screens, which divide the quarters of the women and the head of the house from those of guests, reach from floor to thatch. Near by are the great, flat, pottery cassava ovens. Hosts of baskets and *cumare* hammocks are strung from the house posts around the fires, and the hard earth floor is kept spotlessly clean by thousands of tiny scavenger ants.

Why the *malocas* should have been built on such a vast and gloomy scale remains a mystery. It is possible that their very size gives the Indian a sense of protection from the surrounding forest. It may also help to keep the interior cooler. But it is most likely a sign of depopulation, the breaking up of the clans through rubber exploitation and disease; where once a hundred or more people lived, now there are twenty.

José once told us that his father spoke of tribal wars on the river, when

---

ABOVE: *Coca leaves are put into a cooking pot before baking.* BELOW: *Curing a hangover by inhaling green pepper.*

many more people lived there. We are told by Robuchon that sixty years ago the Indians of north-west Amazonia, round the Caquetá and to the north, were extremely warlike. Tribal warfare was rife and no one trusted his neighbour. *Malocas* were attacked and burnt down and prisoners taken; of these only young children were allowed to survive as slaves. The remainder were knocked to the ground with wooden clubs which the Indians still have today, their bodies hacked to pieces, their forearms used to stir the *chicha* and the armbones later made into flutes. Hands and feet were a delicacy and the sexual organs were eaten by the headman's wife to ensure brave offspring. even the bones were boiled into broth and the orgy continued until the cannibals had completed their spoil and the *chicha* had run dry.

Such a description of warfare and cannibalism would not fit the Indian who lives in the Piraparaná today, and certainly bears no resemblance to the daily life we saw in their *malocas*. We found the Indian's day measured by a peaceful regularity.

Slowly the great house comes to life. Smouldering fires are stirred into a blaze, for the hour before sunrise – even inside the *maloca* – is always the coldest. A baby cries, a young Indian moves from his hammock to the palm-screen door and eases it up to its hook like a portcullis, then saunters leisurely out into the dawn. Others follow. The women move at the far end of the *maloca*, still only vague shapes in the gathering light as they prepare cassava, pick up the water pots and go down to the river to bathe.

The men returning from the river squat on their haunches on the low stools in the centre of the *maloca*, and without any ceremony consume their breakfast of cassava bread, manioc juice and probably some leftovers from the previous night – boiled fish or a piece of bush pig. The women, who have eaten separately with the children, collect their large manioc baskets and leave for the *chagra*, the forest clearing where they grow their crops. The baskets are slung from a strip of sapling bark across the forehead; they hold their babies on their hips, walking rapidly, almost awkwardly – the Indian woman's gait is not a graceful one. Children run along beside them, some affectionately holding the hands of their mothers, others playing. A few of the elder children return to the river to fish, and some of the men go off in pairs to hunt and fish, while others move off to collect coca leaves from their *chagras*.

The Piraparaná has always been an area of coca cultivation and today the river and its tributaries are one of the few remaining strongholds of the drug in north-west Amazonia. Carrying no more than their small coca pouches and the basket for the leaves, five or six men, led by the headman, go down to the stream, perhaps taking a drink and washing themselves before they climb up the far bank. They move along a path through the thick vegetation of an old *chagra* fallen into disuse. Although an occasional banana or *pupuña* palm survives, the cultivated plants have been strangled by weeds and secondary growth.

The *cacique*, the *maloca*'s pet bird, accompanies the Indians, flying from bush to bush and cawing raucously as she glides low over their heads, her olive-green breast almost brushing their hair. She perches on a charred tree-stump, looks at them as they leave the old *chagra* and enter the forest, gives a loud 'caw' and flies back to the *maloca* to see what edible scraps can be found.

In the early morning the tall forest is dank and cool, a place of silence broken only by the occasional chatter of the Indians as they move rapidly along, their sure footsteps delicately gliding over the mass of roots which forms a base to the pathway. Few birds and no animals are about; the sun's rays piercing through the thick leaf vault give life to what might be a dead world. Suddenly they come to a wide expanse of cleared land. There is a chaotic mass of fallen trees, black from recent fires, surrounded by the forest wall. It is as if a great explosion had occurred leaving behind only the charred remains.

Every year or two, when the dry season comes in late November or December, the men cut down an area of forest, and about two months later, just before the rains return, they burn the fallen timber to make a new *chagra*. With each new *chagra*, the men, who do all the clearing and burning, move further afield, so that eventually, after some five years or more, the *maloca* too will be moved to be near the plantation.

This system of shifting agriculture, the men as it were preparing the ground for the women to work on, is carried on incessantly. Partly owing to soil exhaustion, partly because of weed strangulation, the areas of cultivation must be constantly changed, and so the moving Indian population covers wide areas of otherwise untouched Amazonian forest.

It is now January; the smell of the fire still clings to this battlefield of black charcoal. Soon, with the arrival of the rains in March, the women will plant out the manioc cuttings and by late October the first crop will be harvested; so for two years they may expect to get reasonable manioc yields from their *chagra*, after which they must move again.

The men run over the fallen tree-trunks and from the new *chagra* they move into an area partly overgrown by weeds and secondary growth. Here, placed almost mathematically across the *chagra*, in contrast to the haphazard cultivation of other plants, are the avenues of coca shrubs.

Perhaps the ritual associated with the taking of cocaine during festivals and tribal ceremonies, apart from its daily use, explains the attention given not only to its later preparation but also to the planting and picking of the leaves. The common coca shrub, always tended by the men, stands about five feet high when fully grown and may last five or more years. It is the most important of the stimulants taken by the Tukano, some of whom are heroic addicts taking as much as two ounces a day. Their life is partly geared to their addiction, and their daily practice is to come to the *chagra* and spend the greater part of the morning collecting the leaves which they pre-pare during the afternoon and evening. It is a serious task and one which each man undertakes with a strange air of concentration. Each coca plant is selectively stripped leaf by leaf before the next one is tackled. The headman carries the basket with him and gradually it fills with handfuls of pale sage-green leaves. The younger men collect the leaves almost reverently in their right hands before emptying them into the basket, their faces serious, their crouched bodies shining in the strong morning sun, their short, clipped speech broken occasionally by a high-pitched laugh.

In the distance small ribbons of smoke rise in a misty cloud. The women are just visible, their squat figures crouching among the manioc plants. They can be heard laughing; occasionally a baby cries and the children romp and play among the bright-green manioc plants whose tall spindly branches stretch skywards some six feet, terminating in clusters of long, thin, starlike leaves. With their babies straddled across their backs the women spend the morning cutting out the long potato-like roots from the sandy soil and putting the waste foliage into piles to be burnt. It is hot with the sun stream-ing down, the fires crackling and the smoke enshrouding the working bodies. There is little time for rest, though a woman will stop to swing her child around and let it suckle her breast; a mother may give a fat yellow beetle grub to her child to eat, having detached the head – a great delicacy, tasting like butter. Soon large baskets are filled with roughly peeled and half-cleaned roots.

The sun is high overhead and the men leave for the *maloca* with their basket full of coca leaves; on top they place large dried leaves from the *yarumo* (Cecropia) trees which grow like weeds in the *chagra*. The women too load their heavy baskets on to their backs, the headbands taking the greater part of the fifty-pound weight. The whole group hurries through the forest in silence, passing the old *chagra* where the headman's wife leaves the other women to collect pineapples, then down to the stream beneath the *maloca*. At this point comes one of the noisiest and most amusing incidents in their daily life. Not only the manioc roots are washed in the water but the babies too; the mothers vigorously shake their large baskets of roots, then stop to splash water over the backs of the children. For a short time there is cacophony, with screaming babies, splashing water, continuous chatter and laughter, and even barking dogs. But soon the stream is left to myriads of white and brimstone-yellow butterflies which circle everlastingly over the sandbanks, and the women, refreshed, their long black hair glistening in the sun, return up the path to the *maloca*.

Tobacco plants are nearly always grown in a little patch directly in front

---

A graceful Tukano canoe.

of the men's entrance. Boys carefully pick the tobacco leaves one by one and lay them out on cane matting to dry. An Indian sits in the shade of the *maloca's* overhanging eaves and starts to make string from strands of tough *cumare*. His graceful movements as he rolls the fibre with the palm of the hand on his shining thigh, the string looped around his right big toe, are like those used in the making of Venetian glass. An older man sits near by, deeply engrossed in the construction of a large, shallow cassava basket, a maze of cane strips almost hiding his wizened face.

The women file through their entrance, their great loads of manioc white and clean after their river washing. They pause for a moment or two and eat some cassava or the pineapples and wild fruit which they have just brought back, but soon they are working again, pulverizing the manioc on the shield-shaped wooden grating boards which have minute flints or tough palm spines set into their baked-clay surface. They work as a team, some grating, others washing the manioc in vast basket-sieves slung between wooden tripods, while yet others extract the poisonous prussic acid by placing the grated manioc flour in a snake-like *matapí*, a long squeezer of plaited cane. With the upper end looped over a pole, a woman stretches its mesh by sitting on a second pole placed in the lower loop. The *matapí* contracts and the poisonous juice runs out.

When the flour from the *matapí* is ready it is placed on the large flat ovens to make rough cassava pancakes, the Amazonian daily bread, which they eat at every meal together with fish and meat brought back from the forest. The starch from the washed manioc is also baked to make wafer-thin toasted biscuits to add to the *chicha*. Some of the flour is spread thinly on another oven to make the nutty grounds of *farinha*, and the liquid from the washing and squeezing is boiled to neutralize the poison, then poured into the long canoe-trough to make *chicha*.

The noise of grating and the creaking of the tripods lasts all afternoon. A girl feeds her pet parrot some insects, then, taking a strand of *cumare* and winding it around her toe, she starts plaiting string for a hammock to replace her old one. Squatting on the ground, an old woman kneads clay and wood ash. She rolls the clay mixture into coils on a flat board and between the palms of her hands. Then she places them coil upon coil about a clay base, smooths the clay with a pebble and leaves the completed pot in the shade of the *maloca*. Later it will be put on a fire and surrounded with wood bark and ash to bake. Occasionally we saw an iron pot, which at some time in the past must have been traded up the rivers from the Caquetá or the Vaupés. These were sufficiently few to be highly treasured and hadn't affected their own

---

ABOVE: *The shaped but unfinished canoe is dragged down to the river.* BELOW: *Then it is warped open over a fire.*

pottery making, a craft which has been all but forgotten among many of the Indians of Colombia.

Throughout the afternoon the women continue with their tasks while the men prepare their tobacco and smoke it wrapped in long cylinders of banana leaf, or take snuff, lying in their hammocks or crouching on small wooden stools. The snuff, kept in gourds or large snail shells, is made in most cases from ground tobacco; it is first placed in the palm of the hand, then a small quantity is poured into a hollow V-shaped deer bone, and is injected into the nostrils by inserting one end of the V in the nose and the other in the mouth and blowing.

During the afternoon an Indian burns the *yarumo* leaves from the coca basket in the centre of the *maloca*, the ash being carefully raked into a neat pile on the earthen floor. Earlier the coca leaves from the basket had been baked in a large earthenware pot over a hot fire, all the while being stirred with a hooped stick. The toasted leaves were then powdered inside a short wooden cylinder. They are further refined by being put into a barkcloth bag wrapped round a heavy stick, and beaten inside a large cylinder. The *yarumo* ash is added to the finely ground powder – this ash takes away the bitterness, and perhaps also the worst effects of the drug – and once again the mixed coca and ash is beaten in the long cylinder to the consistency of dust. Often this involved procedure goes on far into the night, and we became quite accustomed to go to sleep with the monotonous thudding noise still reverberating around the *maloca*. With the final process completed the powder is emptied into a half-gourd or into small barkcloth pouches, ready for the next journey or hunting trip, during which an Indian may live solely on the drug, going without sleep, food and drink for days.

The inscrutable nature of the Tukano may in part be due to his addiction to cocaine which deadens his senses and affects the eyes so that the pupils often appear dilated. This may also account for a lack of individuality among many of the men who often appear listless and resigned.

At dusk the hunters return and sometimes a monkey or a wild turkey helps out with the evening meal of cassava. The only light in the *maloca* after dark comes from the fires, but on special occasions, such as a festival, the head of the house places a chunk of beeswax taken from a wild bees' nest in the forest on a large post in the centre of the *maloca*, lighting it with a firebrand. But the flickering light barely penetrates the gloom. At other times a strip of slow-burning resinous wood is put in a fork of the same post. It is this wood – a type of cedar – which the Indians use to travel with at night, allowing it to smoulder and blowing it into flame when needed. As night comes the doors are secured and, except for the sporadic mumblings of a few old Indians squatting around the fires, all is silent.

The Tukano is a hunter. From his early childhood he develops the ability to track wild animals in the forest and the sense of location and direction which enables him to do this. The deprivations of the jungle, its innate hostility, its snakes, wild animals, poisonous plants and insects, its daytime silence and oppressiveness are nothing to the fear of being lost. To be lost in the forest is slow, inevitable death. This is a fear which is common to the traveller, the explorer and the *cauchero*, but to the Indian does not exist. He may be forty miles from his *maloca*, yet he will know his way back without faltering, as the Cockney would know his way across London in the black-out, forty miles over half-tracks or no tracks at all, across deep ravines, balanced precariously on slippery logs. He will find his way, perhaps by a glimpse of the sun, the movement of birds overhead, or the track of a tapir. Between dawn and dusk, he has only his bag of cocaine to sustain his quick jogging walk.

During the time we passed in their *malocas* the Indians would often disappear in groups for hunting expeditions. Sometimes they would go at night and ask to borrow our torches to dazzle their prey. They carry hard *macana*-wood bows and sheaths of arrows tipped with curare, a black strychnine poison, or a long ten-foot blowpipe. Also beautifully-woven palm cases filled with poisoned darts secured in kapok, as though stuffed into a pincushion. These are slung across the back and carried upside down with the beeswaxed end uppermost, so as to prevent the rain washing off the curare and to enable the hunter to extract the dart quickly.

With the hunters go their dogs, thin wiry beasts like whippets, usually pale buff or fawn in colour and well cared for by their masters. Their lives are short, and more often than not they go totally blind within five years; for the tiny red *majiñal* fire-ants drop on their eyes as they run through the undergrowth and inject formic acid. There is seldom game near the *maloca*, but further afield, beyond the *chagras* in the forest proper there would usually be waterside rodents and *agouti*, small rabbit-like forest dwellers. There were peccary as well, the black jungle pig which the Indian fears because, if wounded, it sometimes cries for its companions who turn on the aggressor with their small sharp tusks and inflict terrible gashes. These small pigs are strangely affectionate and are sometimes adopted by Indians as pets.

Their bows, five feet long and strung with *cumare*, will launch an arrow two hundred feet, but to be certain of a target the Indian will approach to within twenty or thirty yards. The arrows, without feathers and unnotched, are made of cane, with a hard *macana*-wood point dipped in lethal curare. Some tribes carry a pot of this poison round their necks; when about to shoot, they dip an arrow in the black gum and cut the head just above the point with the razor-sharp tooth of a *piraña*. Thus the poisoned point will break off in the wound if the arrow falls out.

At that time we assumed that the Indians made their own poison, but we learnt many weeks later from a *cauchero* that there were specialists in this art. The Maku, he told us, are the expert curare makers in this area. They boil the scrapings of a liana together with two herbs, then strain the liquid through leaves and boil it again until it forms a black glutinous mass. This they place in small pots and trade it with other tribes, often for food and shelter; for the Maku are nomads. Though strychnine is always the base, various ingredients are occasionally added, from ants to putrefied animal remains. The most deadly poison, which was once reserved for human beings, is said to paralyse the victim in a matter of seconds.

The monkey is the most common of all the animals hunted for the pot. These are hung over a fire and smoked for days. The first time we were offered monkey, we were given the head, which we thought we were supposed to admire. But the brain, we learnt, is the greatest delicacy, like the head and eyes of a fish. The monkey often grips a branch as it dies, and for this reason the Indians would shoot many more than they ever managed to retrieve.

We never ventured to go with the Indians when they went hunting, as we would have made more noise than them and frightened the game. Moreover, we felt we could never keep up. One morning the children came to a *maloca* we were staying in to say that a *capybara* had strayed along the river bank close to where they had been bathing. Immediately an Indian picked up his bow and arrow and quickly made for the river. It was unusual for an animal to stray so close to the house and we followed at a distance hoping that we might see the hunt.

Half-crouched, with his bow and curare-tipped arrows gripped in his hand, he began to stalk the large water rat. Getting as close as he dared, he put the small beeswax quiver head down on the ground, with the arrow shafts upright. He placed one arrow in the bow. Twisting one leg around the shafts, his toes braced against the base of the quiver, he drew back the bow waiting for the *capybara* to move into the open, ready to take a second arrow from the sheath should the first miss. He held the bow fully stretched, crouched lower, hesitated for an instant, then released the arrow. The rodent rolled over without a sound. No second arrow was needed. That night we boiled the *capybara* which tasted like pork. The poison never taints the meat; it only affects the nervous system through the bloodstream.

The tapir is the largest of the forest mammals hunted by the Indian. It is the size of a cow, with a long snout, small eyes and slotted feet, and its only defence is camouflage. Speckled brown and black like the sun-dappled forest floor, when young, and turning to a dull slate-brown when fully grown, they gather at their watering places to drink. They were hunted relentlessly by the

A Tukano shaman in festival regalia with his kurubeti *pebble stave.*

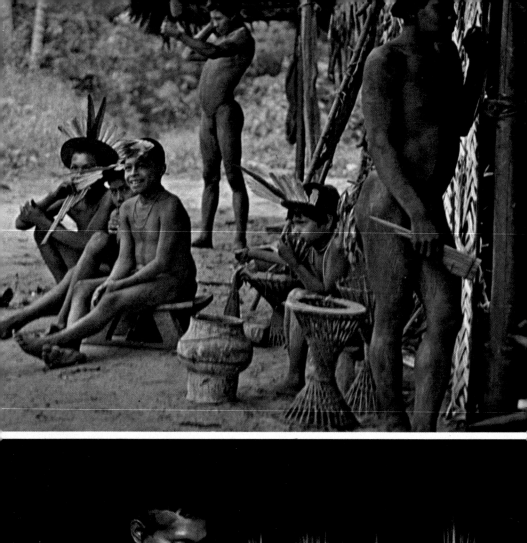

early rubber gatherers, who on occasions would shoot dozens at a time, more for sport than to supply meat. They are now nearly extinct in many areas.

Having killed such a large animal the difficulty is to keep the meat. The *caucheros* build great platforms over the fires and smoke it for days. This is the only way it can be preserved. It is not possible to eat very much of the rich, sweet meat at a time, and the Indians believe that at certain times of the year it is bad to touch it, for it is almost inedible and causes skin blemishes. Though the Indian professes to despise tapirs, he nevertheless assigns human characteristics to them; he believes they dance, drink *chicha* and even build *malocas*. He also believes that by eating a particular animal he may acquire some of its characteristics. From a peccary he can gain faith and resolution, for the wild boar's habit of going to the rescue of a wounded companion has left an indelible impression on the Indians. Just as the puma is credited with human characteristics, the *agouti*, like the legendary African hare, is attributed wisdom and wit.

The blowpipe is of as much importance to the hunter as his bow and arrow. The Tukano make their pipes from a small palm. A length of from eight to ten feet is cut and allowed to dry. The pith is removed and an inner bore put into position and polished with tree roots. The outside is bound along its whole length with bark and covered with a resinous wax. A small pig-bone sight is fixed on one end and a hard wooden mouthpiece on the other. The Indian will travel through the forest all day long, looking for birds, small monkeys and squirrels, and carrying his match-thin ten-inch darts, perhaps thirty at a time, in wicker holders.

He constantly watches the trees overhead; he may suddenly see a parrot on a branch ahead of him. He moves forward slowly; if he can stand directly beneath the bird he has less difficulty in steadying his aim. He raises the pipe cautiously and places the cupped lower end over his mouth. He reaches behind with his free arm and draws a poison-tipped dart. Inserting it in the shaft with its cotton wad, he aligns the pig-bone sight on to the bird and inflates his cheeks. There is a barely discernible puff. Seventy feet over his head the parrot squawks, starts to fly, falters and crashes through the branches to the ground. Sometimes there are other birds near by and the Indian will kill three or four before he begins to look for them lying somewhere in the dense thickets, but he never loses one. Parrots are the most common target and the most easily approached, but unless cooked for many hours they are quite inedible. We would occasionally make a soup from them. Macaws, toucans and egrets are sought after, more for their feathers than as food. Pigeon, turkey, duck and geese are far more palatable; while frogs, snakes and various grubs, ants and beetles are considered delicacies.

ABOVE: *Preparing for the festival.* BELOW: *Bréo unpacks the festival feather head-dresses from their boxes.*

5
Ni

It was on the rapids of Kaperwa, while Brian was searching for fossils, that we came across the first rock engravings (see p. 74). These man-like figures, no more than two feet high, extended along the face of an ancient deposit of volcanic ash exposed just above river level. All seemed to be in grotesque dancing postures, their outlined figures carved half an inch into the face of the rock, their webbed hands and feet splayed out and the face portrayed in relief with indentations for the eyes and the mouth. There appeared to have been more which had been almost completely eroded away except for a hand or a foot. We found a similar set of figures extending along the rock on the other side of the channel, equally strange but portraying the same subtle vitality of movement, as if caught in some prehistoric dance.

In all we counted thirty dancers at Kaperwa. How long they had been there was impossible to say. The rock was a hard volcanic tuff. With a high river all the engravings would have been completely submerged. Those on the south bank were sheltered from the sun and mostly covered in moss. There was no pigment or colouring matter and, even had we known the period of time for which they had been submerged, the rate of erosion would have been mere conjecture. Certainly the Indians could explain nothing about them.

Later we came across many such engravings on the Apaporis and the Caquetá. Some on the Apaporis depicted human figures of obscure abstract form with the body shown as a triangle or a square and with foreshortened arms reminiscent of Chibcha art in the Colombian Andes – a civilization contemporary to that of the Incas. Near by on the same rock were two forms representing a crocodile or snake. These were the only animal designs we ever saw. On the Caquetá we found engravings of a more formalized type, seldom depicting human beings but coiled, spiralled and fretted designs; many were very elaborate and covered five or six square feet of the rock face. Some were etched half an inch or more into the hard sandstone, others were mere chipped designs on the surface.

It has been suggested that as these engravings occur mainly at rapids they are more than likely the work of passing canoe men. But it is usually only at these rapids that there are rocks on which these petroglyphs could be drawn. Moreover, many are of such elaborate design that they would take weeks to carve into the hard rock. It is possible that some in the past represented boundary marks. The Indians do not appear to recognize territorial areas within the forest, but they may have rights to fish over certain sections of the rivers.

It is unlikely that the engravings can be ascribed to any one period and there seemed little resemblance to contemporary Indian art. Certainly Tukano design is mostly limited to triangles and crosses, and relies more on colour than form. The most striking example we saw was the Tatuya *maloca* on the Piraparaná, the bark front wall of which was covered with a series of cross, square and triangle designs coloured with brown, yellow and white river clays and a black charcoal compound. But this is by far the most dramatic example of Tukano art, with the possible exception of the elaborate body painting and the magnificent head-dresses used during the festivals. Their pottery, though finely made, bears no design, except for a pot containing the narcotic *yajé*, used only by the elders during certain festivals and curing sessions. This is covered with different coloured clays, charcoal and red *karayuru* dye. Similar triangular coloured designs are also found on the *yarumo* dancing-staves.

The most common type of engraving is the fretted design on the gourd maracas used during tribal dances. One end of the pebble stave, a lance-like rattle used by the shaman, is also carved with lines and triangles together with a pattern of bird feathers, said to give it greater magical power. This stave and a drinking gourd with an elaborate circular design of triangles, loops and chevrons, we tried to obtain for our collection, but without success. Certain articles were so highly regarded by the Indians that they would not part with them, no matter what they were offered in exchange.

Of all the rock engravings we saw, that of Ni the river god (see drawing on p. 31) was by far the most striking. Travelling on from Kaperwa, we came to an unusually long set of rapids through which we guided the boat with our paddles. We were concentrating so hard on the rapids and the water swirling around the boat, that the unexpected sight of a pyramid of rock jutting massively out of the river in front came as rather a shock. Even more unexpected was the grotesque figure cut deeply into the granite face of the giant boulder. With arms and legs outstretched he seemed to dominate the river, to embrace it with a hypnotic spell.

Unlike the other carvings we saw, Ni was engraved in granite. The finely-drawn lines, carved half an inch deep, gave symmetry to the life-size figure which must have taken an Indian craftsman months of labour to create. Our own steel knives were easily blunted by the hard crystalline rock.

Ni faced upstream into the setting sun. Behind, on the east slope of the rock, were suns and a quarter-moon. The suns, some with emanating rays, were composed of a series of three or four concentric rings up to two feet in diameter.

Hitherto José had remained silent and appeared to know nothing of these engravings nor had he given us any indication of their whereabouts. This was surprising, for, being himself a Barasana, of a Tukano clan, he was presumably aware of their existence. Then one evening, perhaps encouraged by our curiosity, he told us the following anecdote:

'The Barasana have always lived here, they were born here. They and the Taiwano have always been friends and had common enemies in the Tatuya, Karapana and Ureti whom they used to fight with bow and arrows. They both have the same god who has power over all things. It is he who made Ni, in his own likeness, the drawings have been here for ever, and this is the only place where they occur. The other Indians do not have them.' He pointed to a great natural pillar of granite called the Bee, which stood in the river upstream of Ni: 'That rock was once a pile of manioc, which the people had placed there. Ni turned it into stone. Below the rapids is the under-water cave, his palace, where the god sings to the drawings and the spirits.'

6

Panpipes and Don Giovanni

In early February we started to make a small collection. For exchange we had brought rolls of coloured cloth, cigarettes, combs, thread and beads, fishing line and hooks. When we arrived at a *maloca* we would give presents to the headman and his wife, then to the rest of his family. There was never any hesitation in allowing us to sling our hammocks in their houses, but our giving gifts perhaps assured them of our friendly intentions. Moreover, in return they would often give us *farinha* which would help out with our own food. Of all the trade goods, small beads, and cloth especially in primary colours, red, blue and yellow, were the most popular. They preferred white beads and were prepared to exchange many of their own possessions for them. But even if we had lived with the Indians for some time, so that they knew us, they would have been loath to part with certain things. In order to obtain one of their magnificent head-dresses, which may have taken a man months to complete because of the scarcity of the feathers, we had to give them one of our shotguns, nothing less. A shotgun was as good as a bow and arrow. For the Indian it had the advantage that you could shoot more than one bird at a time and it had a greater range than an arrow. But for years their gun would probably be useless because of a lack of shot and powder. Also the gun made a great noise and this frightened the game away. The only three we saw were ancient hammer guns, probably taken from *caucheros* they had killed.

In one of the last *malocas* of the Piraparaná we obtained a canoe. This proved extremely useful as it could be loaded with some of the lighter equipment, such as the collection, and towed from the back of *El Diablo*. Unfortunately it was narrow and unstable and on one occasion as we passed through some turbulent water, it swung sideways in an eddy and over-turned. Before we were able to do anything several pieces of our small collection had already disappeared. As a result of this we learnt to keep an Indian in the stern of the canoe to guide it.

The rivers of the Amazon are usually termed black or white, to differen-tiate between clear and muddy water. Because of the amount of suspended sediment, white rivers are said to have many more fish. There were however a variety of fish in the 'black' Piraparaná. When we travelled on the river we would often see large gate-traps at the mouths of the smaller creeks. The fish hooks and line we carried for bartering were greatly sought after, though José for some reason sabotaged much of our exchange. He told the Indians that our nylon was not as good as their own *cumare* line and he broke the barbs of our steel hooks on the house posts to show that their own were better.

'That is barbasco, a poisonous liana.' José pointed to several bundles of saplings lying on the floor of a *maloca* we were visiting. 'Soon, in late February or March, before the first rains, all the Indians near here will gather for the fish poisoning. They will build small dams in the streams, and the *barbasco* will be pounded and thrown into the water above these dams. All the fish float to the surface and, with nets made from *cumare*, or long spear arrows with forked metal ends, they will be caught in great quantities and carried to a *maloca*. Usually a particular house is chosen each year and, when enough fish have been collected, the festival will start. This may go on for days with *chicha*, panpipes and painted *yarumo* dancing-staves, and many people – and more fish than we see at any other time in the year.' This was a festival we wished to see, but we did not expect to be in the Piraparaná in March. Besides they might have been reluctant to let us watch a ceremony on which the abundance of fish during the following year depended.

Four days below Ni we came to the great falls of Beiju, and there, as we dragged *El Diablo* over the portage, we met some Indians who told us they were going to a festival at a Makuna *maloca* belonging to a headman called Bréo. It was two days' journey up a tributary, but we decided to go.

The Tukano have many festivals throughout the year; among the most important are the Fish Festivals and the Harvest Festivals for the pineapple, *miriti* palm and *guamo* fruits, and for the manioc. At all these they dance, sing and play their instruments. But to the Indian, music is also a form of relaxation and enjoyment. Often as the men laze in their hammocks they happily while away the time playing on their bamboo panpipes. Blowing across the eight- or nine-stemmed pipes two men may accompany each other for hours on end, ascending and descending the same scale, rhythmically counterbalancing one another in tuneful but repetitive melodies. They continue, apparently oblivious of repetition, and the panpipe tunes soon became imprinted on our minds. Each clan has its own variations; most of the tunes are based on their dances, though some are in imitation of birds. At night the young boys play their pipes crouched around the central posts of the *maloca*, and the clear notes carry across the still forest like church bells ringing on a cold winter's night. Only occasionally do the Indians actually sing for enjoyment; one headman uttered a staccato war song as he pounded coca leaves and occasionally the women hummed as they rocked their babies to sleep. Their instruments are more important to them; of these the snail-shell and deer-bone flutes, the tortoise shells and the clay horns are the most unusual.

It is hard to believe that a river-snail shell no more than three inches long can produce a most haunting tune. This tiny flute, the three-holed *sihoo*, is more often played outdoors than inside the house. Its clear rippling notes mingle with the forest calls, perhaps imitating a bird drawn closer and closer to the Indian hunter. The deer-bone flute, in contrast, has a harsh, piercing, eerie sound. It is made from a deer's tibia and three holes are drilled into the bone with a *capybara's* tooth. A little slit is cut into the head of the deer-bone, down which the man blows. Small lumps of beeswax are melted into the apexes and shrill notes come flowing out – bizarre perhaps, but melodious. This instrument is generally heard during the *chicha* ceremonies between the dances. The tortoise shell, too, is an instrument which has a weird, almost hypnotic tone. It is played by a man who squats on the ground with the shell gripped under the knee between thigh and calf muscles. Rapidly he rubs, almost jerks, the palm of his hand over the beeswax-coated head of the shell. Sometimes two men will play two tortoise shells and a pair of panpipes at the same time, and the continuous reverberation of the *goos*, as the tortoise shells are known, together with the syncopation of the panpipes produces an amazing effect. The high muffled tones of the *goos* echo round the *maloca*, driving the Indian's coca-bemused senses into a semi-hypnotic trance. To us this was not an unpleasant sensation and on listening closer we could pick out what was in fact a highly sophisticated rhythm. Each panpipe entered just off beat in an exciting, almost modernistic manner, more reminiscent of a modern jazz quartet than four primeval instruments of the Amazon.

Our recording equipment intrigued the Indians – those small boxes with wheels which turned, lengths of 'string' with weird metal objects on the end, held close to their faces or hung from the ridge poles of their *malocas*. It was all beyond their comprehension. At first they were frightened but once they had listened to their own voices and music, they were astounded and could not wait to hear more. We all too soon found ourselves using as much of our precious battery power to play back as we did to record. Sometimes they were intrigued by Western music – Beethoven piano concertos, Brahms and Gershwin had little effect, but the Bach double violin concerto drew many eager faces, a Haydn trumpet concerto brought smiles of approval and on hearing the Commendatore's deep voice in the last act of *Don Giovanni* the whole *maloca* drew near in wonder. Perhaps this really was the white man's shaman.

We waited four days at Bréo's while the women brought in baskets and baskets of manioc to prepare for *chicha*, and the men pounded coca leaves incessantly. During this time the *maloca* filled with families who had travelled by canoe from their distant forest homes along the winding river courses. Some had already been warned by messengers of the coming festival to celebrate the manioc harvest, but on the afternoon before it started Bréo left for a high knoll of ground, and stood blowing a clay horn – perhaps to warn the people that the festival would start that night. The low booms rang out across the forest like blasts on a ship's foghorn. To the south, near the Caquetá, giant wooden drums were slung on a slant from two central poles of the *maloca* and beaten in a secret code as warning signals to other members of the tribe. The *mangwaré* drums were the jungle telegraph of Amazonia and their signals could be heard over twenty miles away.

More and more families arrived at the riverside port, where they left their canoes moored to the bank or tied to each other with thin strands of liana. Some thirty canoes formed a series of star-like patterns with the water rushing down between them, haphazardly tied, yet buoyant and secure. Each family made its way up the steep sandy path to the *maloca*: the men with their paddles, some with fishing rods, and many with panpipes strung to their hammocks; the women bent low under heavy loads of manioc and their babies on their hips. Here the head of each family was greeted by Bréo and shown where they could sling their hammocks around the sides of the house. The women handed the manioc to Wanina, his young wife – he had two, but the elder could no longer bear him children.

The amount of time it takes for the festival to be prepared depends on the amount of *chicha* to be consumed. With over a hundred people present, four days were barely enough for the manioc roots to be rubbed down, the poisonous juice extracted and then boiled to form the basis of *chicha*. The starch sediment was baked over the clay ovens into giant wafer-thin biscuits. The boiling liquid was poured into the long *chicha* canoe which lay on the floor between two of the central posts; the toasted cassavas were broken into the liquid and fermentation began. The *chicha* gained rapidly in potency and the canoe was covered with an exquisitely woven cane mat like Japanese lattice. One ceremonial canoe was not enough, and another was brought from the river to be filled with yet more fermenting *chicha*.

In the evening the men sat chewing cocaine. Led by the shaman they consulted the spirits and their subdued mumblings continued far into the night. Their crouched bodies, lit only by the flickering of the resinous *turi* torchwood, reminded us of the semi-human rock carvings of their ancestors.

The *chicha* had fermented, the coca was prepared, the *maloca* was now a seething mass of people. The afternoon before the festival began, Wanina and the shaman's wife began to paint the bodies of the men. First deep red *karayuru* was smeared down the front of the torso, the thighs and along each arm with firm strokes of the fingers. A black liquid, the boiled juice from the leaves of a tree growing in their *chagras*, was painted on to the body with a three-pronged piece of cane. The hands and feet were totally blackened to above the wrists and ankles, and the arms and legs patterned with a lattice of

---

A head-dress made from the feathers of the royal crane.

diagonal lines. Then the women painted their own faces with *karayuru* and blackened their hands and feet.

As the sun's last rays filtered into the *maloca* and the mumblings of the council of elders died down, the shaman left the dark interior and stood in front of the men's doorway. In his hand he carried the *Kurubeti*, the sacred pebble stave. Intricate circles of blue and purple humming-bird feathers adorned one end, a swollen spearhead formed the other. This swelling was produced by soaking a bulge in the wood in water, then inserting this into a banana stem and heating the spearhead over a fire. The swollen wood is cut open and three pebbles are inserted. During cooling the wood shrinks and the pebbles are locked in the cavity. The shaman stood pointing the stave away from the *maloca*. He hit it with his right hand and the stave swayed from side to side in front of his body. The rattling of the pebbles prevented the evil spirits from entering the *maloca*. In the days of tribal war, we were told, among the people living further to the south, each warrior carried one of these staves and after victory would dance himself into a frenzy, beating the stave against his shoulder.

With darkness the festival began. Bréo carefully rolled back the cane mat from the *chicha* canoe and the women handed round gourd after gourd, full of the bitter drink. More and more *chicha* was handed round to groups of people sitting contentedly by their family fires. Some of the younger men began to play their panpipes, but as yet there was no cohesion; the groups seemed rather to be competing with one another and different tunes came from all sides, one drowning the other. Many of these men had put sprigs of sweet-smelling leaves under their loin-cloth strings and berry arm-bands. The scent from the leaves was curiously sensuous, like sweet lemon, and used as an elixir of love by the Tukano during their festivals.

The same confused cacophony of dancing and panpipes continued well into the night; it was the young men's duty to keep the shaman awake, for not once during the course of the festival was he allowed to sleep. Small groups moved up and down the *maloca*, joyfully playing their panpipes as they danced, then they retired to their family fires and drank more *chicha*. The shaman remained apart, sitting on his stool in the centre of the *maloca*, gazing as if in a trance. At his side lay a calabash of coca and the sacred pot of *yajé*, the most powerful narcotic used by Amazonian Indians. Prepared from the boiled juices of a jungle creeper, the red liquid gives the shaman hallucinations and he is able to predict the future progress of the festival. Suddenly he summoned Bréo to his side. All the men came to the centre of the *maloca* carrying their wooden stools and sat down near him. With heads bent low the men started a muffled chant, answering in unison the solo

---

Tukano profile and festival head-dress.

monotone of the shaman. At intervals the coca calabash passed from hand to hand and each man threw a deer-bone spoon of the sage-green powder into his mouth. He stored it in his cheek and gradually the coca, mixed with saliva, filtered down his throat. Louder and louder, faster and faster became the chanting, echoing between the walls of the vast dark interior. The shaman worked himself into a frenzy, waving his arms out in front of him, his hands moving in wild gesticulations, his voice a rapid series of falsetto monotones; he was expelling all evil spirits from the tribal precincts to the heads of the *caños* and to other lands. The incantations continued for nearly two hours and then in the early hours of the morning there was silence.

The time had arrived for Bréo to unlock the precious box of plumages and he lowered it to the floor. He unwrapped the barkcloth cover and took off the lid of the beautifully woven palm box. Item by item he distributed the contents to the waiting figures, eagerly clambering to adorn themselves. First the smaller boys were given their simple crowns of red and yellow macaw and toucan tail-feathers, and they dashed away to adjust these on their heads. Underneath lay monkey-fur belts, ancient quartz pendants, puma-tooth necklaces and the most important items of all, magnificent feather head-dresses. These Bréo carefully selected and gave to the elders of the tribe. Crowns of toucan feathers woven on *cumare* frames adorned their heads, brilliant gold and red, ringed with white duck-down. Majestic royal crane plumage, stuck into a banana stem which projected down the back, jutted vertically up from the back of the head. The white feathers were woven together in a *cumare* mesh and stood out like quivering spindles of spun glass, gleaming in the darkness. Behind was a single red macaw tail-feather, a deer bone bound to the banana stem with monkey fur and last of all the wing plumage of an egret.

Many of the men wore giant quartz obelisks dangling from their necks. They make them no more, but their ancestors used to spend days rubbing down large chunks of quartz in pebbleworn channels in the river beds. Others had necklaces of wild boars' tusks, pointing concentrically outwards. There were many monkey-fur armlets with glistening beetle wings which jingled as the men moved. Around the waist was another belt of monkey fur with puma teeth attached; below the knees finely-woven *cumare* garters, rubbed yellow with river clay, and above the right ankle dried *watcha* nut rattles. This, with the fierce red facial paint and black body design, made up the splendid dancing regalia of the Tukano. The women had no adornments; south of the Caquetá they stuck rings of white duck-down to their ankles with mud, but here they only painted their faces and bodies.

Now the dancing proper began. Since it was the manioc festival only the ceremonial *Nahubasa*, signifying the complete cycle of manioc from the time it was planted to the time it became cassava, was danced. Each man carried a long cane stave in his right hand and they joined in a line across the centre of the *maloca*, facing the women's quarters. Dazed from the *chicha* and coca they gazed in front of them and sang a slow dirge, beating their staves on the ground. Slowly they moved off in a clockwise circle inside the four central posts. The tempo increased, but the chant remained the same, the voices grew louder and combined with the hollow thuds from the staves and castanet-like rattles. The whole atmosphere changed, no longer were there rival groups competing with their neighbours, instead everyone took part in the dance. The women joined in, slipping their small bodies under the linked arms of the moving men. The circle increased, the women with their right hand to the small of the back of one man, and their left to the hip of another. Only Wanina, the headman's wife, accompanied by her small children and carrying Bréo's youngest son under her arm, did not join the circle. She moved slowly round the centre, her eyes fixed constantly to the ground, uttering a high-pitched wail as the dancers moved solemnly about her.

The manioc dance continued through the night, but with the approach of dawn the younger members became impatient for a change of rhythm. To them such festivals were an opportunity for amusement, heavy drinking bouts and the possibility of finding a wife. One or two started to play on their panpipes, they were joined by others and soon the whole *maloca* became alive with young couples and trios weaving happily across the floor, in between the posts and along the sides of the house. Their young bodies gliding through the darkness, their feet delicately stamping the time on the ground, they seemed completely lost in the lovely panpipe tunes of the *chiruru*, the Tukano courtship dance. All too soon the thuds of the bamboo staves were heard and the elders again took control.

Throughout the entire festival the dominating figure was the shaman. Existing as he does in complete detachment from the rest, he sat alone, occasionally taking snuff from his snail-shell box. It was he who influenced the festival which, without him, would not take place. Every few hours he summoned the elders about him and as coca was passed round the mysterious chanting began. No one would tell us what was being recited, we could only gather that the tribal ancestors were being consulted and evil spirits exorcized. They did not like us to record this part of the ceremony, for quite understandably they believed we might take away their magic power.

Day and night the people danced, their plumed bodies glistening with sweat, caught in the beams of the sun or the dull glow of the torch-wood. There was continual sound – of panpipes, of cane staves, nutshell rattles and people's voices. Gradually the *chicha* canoes were drained. Gallons of the liquid had been consumed and the men had to rid themselves of their hang-overs. Nonchalantly they poured boiled green-pepper juice down their nostrils from funnels made of leaves. With grunts and snorts they cleared their heads and staggered down to the river to bathe. Inside the *maloca* those that remained were asleep; many of the women had already left for the *chagra* and the visiting families began to leave. They moved quietly in single file down to their canoes, unleashed them and paddled away. Life returned to normal. The plumages stood in the sand, shimmering in the sun, before Bréo meticulously packed them away, and with them remained the memory of the dancing figures, resplendent as birds of paradise.

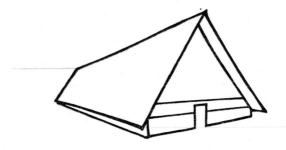

ABOVE LEFT: *An Indian taking snuff; round his neck a quartz pendant and a necklace strung with jaguar teeth.* ABOVE RIGHT: *Boy playing panpipes.* BELOW: *A headman lights a torch of beeswax.*

7
Missing Links

Until we had passed the last rapids on the Piraparaná we were always anxious, as we were never sure how long José would stay with us. Had he left us we might have found it difficult to get other Indians to help, and certainly we could never have managed *El Diablo* ourselves. There were many occasions when he had threatened to leave, but so far he had been persuaded not to. So it was with some relief that we passed these rapids, though there was nearly disaster, for José determined to take *El Diablo* through fully loaded. We watched aghast from the bank as for a moment the boat completely disappeared from view in the turbulent water. But somehow she stayed afloat.

Now the river was anything from thirty to a hundred yards across. It wound sluggishly this way and that between low banks covered in dense forest and bordered with *miriti* palms. There were no houses, for most of the land was liable to flooding during the wetter months. We saw no Indians on the river, nor any canoes moored to the banks. At times the river meandered forming giant oxbows, where, through the sparse jungle, we could see a bend in the river that we had passed perhaps an hour before. At one of the bends a low cliff rose sheer from the water's edge. It was formed from clay and shales of Tertiary age, and in the beds Brian found deposits of lignite, tree-trunks and plant remains. To the west of us lay the Apaporis, to the east continuous forest as far as the Río Negro, the home of strange, seldom-seen foresters, the nomadic Maku.

Since leaving Bréo's *maloca* we had been troubled less by flies and insects; the jigger worms, which had laid their eggs in our feet when we walked barefoot about the *malocas*, no longer bothered us. Only the *nutchis* remained as they took some days to incubate. One night after an exceptionally large one was removed from Donald's shin, he wrote, 'A rather painful process. However it had its reward for it was definitely a record breaker – fat, furry, and fully half an inch in length....' They could only be extracted by using nicotine to poison them, or rubber latex to block their breathing holes where they lay under the skin. We never learnt how we got these painful worms.

ABOVE AND BELOW: *Dancing at the festival to celebrate the manioc harvest.*

Probably they resulted from a small fly or mosquito injecting the egg into the bloodstream. Horacio had come across them in the Llanos, but only in cattle and dogs, never in humans.

Though seldom bothered by mosquitoes we occasionally ran into a belt of the *pium* fly which could give very irritating bites. At night when we found a sand-spit, or dry ground in the forest where we could sling our hammocks in the trees, we would first inspect the ground to ensure that our equipment would not be covered in termites or ants by the morning. Fish, which the Indians caught for us, was now our main food. One type looked and tasted almost like salmon; another, a flat fish, was very similar to the *piraña* with its razor teeth and protruding lower jaw. Even in February, towards the end of the dry season, many days were overcast. When the sun did appear, it was usually followed by a heavy afternoon rainstorm often accompanied by a cold wind, so that in spite of our nylon jackets we found ourselves shivering with cold. One day we passed very close to a green water snake. It coiled itself and thrashed the water with its tail, its head out of sight, until it finally disappeared locked in the jaws of its invisible assailant.

Along the river banks and high in the trees overhead, we saw herons, ibis and egrets, a brownish bird similar to a bittern; king-fishers, not so brilliantly coloured as the British kind, and duck would rise off the water in front of the boat. The varying shades of green were broken by white hibiscus, the crimson flowers of the chocolate tree, the flashing blue wings of the giant morphous butterfly or the wasp yellow of a swallowtail, beautiful butterflies which sting like fire-ants as caterpillars and live on blood, offal and manure. Sometimes the transparent glinting wings of a dragonfly passed by, while at night shadowy nightjars flitted over the river between the pin-point glows of the fireflies.

On the evening of the second day after leaving the rapids we sighted the Apaporis, a river of strange contrasts with its great width, muddy banks and putty-coloured water. We had decided to reach the falls of Jirijimo. They were alleged to be a magnificent sight when the river was in full spate. A few people had seen the falls from the air, though in the days of the rubber boom the river was used as a highway, and the *caucheros* had made ramps through the forest as a portage. But this movement up and down the river had always been during the wet season, and we were travelling during the last month of summer, when in fact the river was at its lowest ebb.

For two days we moved up the Apaporis after making a dump of all our equipment, including the Indian canoe which we hid in the forest, for we knew we would have to return the same way. On the evening of the second day we reached the falls of Playa, somewhere below Jirijimo. In the winter it would have been possible to have hauled the boat on to the great sandstone slabs and pulled it up the ramps, which, though terribly overgrown during the last thirty years of disuse, could have been cleared sufficiently. But now to our dismay we were confronted with the magnificent but daunting falls. The river tumbled a vertical forty feet over the lip of the basin into the turbulent water below, with a roar and a mass of spray, while all around were sheer walls of rock.

We tried to find a solution. We spent a day walking up the river only to find more falls above Playa. Somewhere behind, further up the river, lay Jirijimo, but how far away we did not then know. Should we try to walk through the jungle to the falls, even if it meant several days' journey without any certainty of finding them at the end? This might have been our best chance. Should we return to pick up our small Indian canoe, and carry that over the falls? It would take too long and we did not have the reserve of fuel. Could the five of us manage to pull *El Diablo* up the vertical face and, once over that, find our way up the next falls? As the boat was already in a flimsy condition, it seemed unlikely that she would remain in one piece. She would have to survive the return journey as well, and we did not relish the thought of walking to the Caquetá.

That night Brian, who had remained the most undaunted, wrote in his diary, 'We clambered over the rocks and through the very overgrown and at times almost vertical ramp – this will prove a hellish problem with only five of us and a boat which is semi-rotten, held together by beeswax and old trouser legs....' The following day: 'We all seemed in a bleary state, probably because *a fondo* all of us knew this would be the furthest we would get ... I still think we could make it, but the time factor and the risk involved to the whole expedition just do not make the attempt worthwhile.'

Realizing the futility of continuing, we prepared to spend another night below the falls. Over the river a tern circled, hovered, dived into the water with a splash, came up, then dived again, on and on till the dusk turned the greens to black. The moon rose high, the colour of straw changing to a white so brilliant that we could read in our hammocks. The water moving down from the falls was covered with a froth of giant bubbles, making the surface look like an ice-floe, dazzling white in the moonlight. The following day we turned back the way we had come. Some hours after starting Horacio found that he had left his rifle behind, so we had to return to the falls. That night we all seemed a little despondent; we still had a long way to go and we did not know what lay ahead. There was no need to build a shelter or raise a tarpaulin, the sky was clear and the sands still hot from the day-long sun. Earlier we had washed our clothes in the river and bathed, sliding our feet along the muddy bottom; for there were rays, and by doing this there was less risk of stepping on one. Along the edge of the sand-spit were the cloven-hoofed slots of a tapir, and the rounded pad marks of a puma. Perhaps that night we had disturbed many forest animals at their usual watering place, the only sandbank for many miles along this side of the river. Overhead hung the Milky Way and Orion's Belt – with the binoculars we could see the nebula in his sword. Sirius stood out a pale electric blue and later we could see the Morning Star in the east.

The river was wide and very shallow, and we got into difficulties: 'José went to sleep on the engine and we hit a rock in midstream – a horrible grinding noise as it passed under the boat, then a crash as it hit the engine. She is letting a lot of water in, though it does not seem to have damaged her seriously. We are lucky; if this had been an aluminium boat she would have ripped from end to end.'

Two days below the falls we reached our dump again and reloading our equipment set off downstream, waving goodbye to Uriel who set off for his *maloca* on the Querarí; only José now remained. *El Diablo* was fully loaded again, she began leaking badly and Horacio made running repairs as we moved down the river. Soon a wind got up, the water became very choppy and we found ourselves baling continuously as the water slopped over her two or three inches of freeboard. She was not going to last very much longer.

All along the banks the forest presented a solid wall. There were seldom any breaks where there might have been a habitation. A clan of the Tukano, the Letuama, had lived here before the advance of the rubber barons early in the century. A few still remained and we visited one of their houses. The *maloca* was shaped like a pagoda, quite unlike anything we had seen before, round at the base with a steeply slanting thatched roof, terminating in a ridge about thirty feet above the hard earth-baked floor. Inside, every sheaf of each section of thatch seemed to have been measured and the whole had an appearance of amazing symmetry. The light came in through two roof aper-tures and inside, though cool, it was nearly as bright as outdoors. This was surprising as the darkness of the Amazonian house is a deterrent to flying insects. In strange contrast to the house were the old aluminium pots and tin trunks lying inside – a sharp reminder that we had left the Piraparaná. The headman and his family had deserted the house and it was now used by the occasional passing Indian as a resting-place.

We met two *caucheros* who had their houses on the river bank. One of them, Alirio, was half-Indian by birth. His father had been a European-educated official of the Colombian government, who in his later years had preferred the life of the forest. Alirio had known no other life; he had married an Indian girl and now spent his days collecting wild rubber, selling it to another *cauchero* further down the river. He was talkative and eager to help; he told us of a botanist – Dr Schultes – whom he had accompanied beyond the first rapids on the Piraparaná. When he knew we had come all the way from the Vaupés he seemed almost disbelieving. He told us on no account should we continue all the way to the Caquetá on this river, for there were many rapids; moreover, nearer the mouth of the river there were falls, one nearly as big as Jirijimo. Our only way was by a portage which led through the forest to another river, the Miritiparaná. From there it was possible, he said, to travel all the way to the Caquetá without encountering more rapids. We would have to leave our boat behind on the Apaporis, as it would be impossible to take it across without the assistance of many Indians. We would have to get help from the Miritiparaná, and a boat, in order to continue our journey to the Caquetá. This was the first time that we knew exactly what lay ahead of us; from then on we would follow Alirio's instructions. He kindly sent his son and one of his workmen to help us over the rapids which we had to pass before the portage. That night we came to Lugo's house where we had a less friendly welcome. Heavy-set, urbane and gold-toothed, Lugo offered us little. We asked if we could sling our hammocks in the house and he grudgingly consented; so Brian asked him to join us in a meal. Horacio was furious. 'Why?' he said. 'Why should we offer him our hospitality?... It is for him to invite us.'

The following day, as we continued down the river, we wondered why Lugo should have been forced to live out his life in the forests of the Amazon. Surely it could not have been his wish; and what did he fear in strangers? Perhaps it was better than a lifetime in gaol. Later, while we were collecting rock samples, we came across the rock carvings called Boheniambo. Scattered over the flat sandstone island in the centre of the river, these formalized carvings, none of them more than two feet long, seemed to be imitations of Chibcha art from the Andean highlands. The figures, with stylized triangular head, square body and foreshortened arms crossed in front of the chest, were a contrast to the more natural art of the Piraparaná.

There was no moon that night and the rain clouds were heavy, as we tried to find the small hut which would show where the portage lay. Flashing our torch along the bank we became anxious. Somewhere below us lay more rapids and we were afraid of being swept away into them. Suddenly the beam of the torch showed up a small grass-roofed shelter – it was the portage. We knew the worst of our journey was over. The same night Horacio went ahead with José to see if he could make contact with a *cauchero*, Don Carlos, whom Alirio had spoken of. We unloaded *El Diablo* for the last time, for here she had to be abandoned.

Don Carlos greeted us as if passing travellers were an everyday occurrence. Tall, slim and proud, like a Bogotano, he was the last person we would have expected to find here. Though he wore a pyjama top and had a towel round his neck to flick flies and wipe the sweat from his forehead, he looked as if he might be equally at home in a dark suit, with white collar and furled umbrella.

In no time our great heap of equipment was whisked away by Indian helpers across the portage. The difficulties we had foreseen seemed to vanish. Five hours later we were sitting down to a magnificent meal of chicken and rice in Don Carlos's wooden-frame house, surrounded by green banana palms and manioc plantations overlooking the muddy Miritiparaná.

That evening the conversation turned to rubber, the exploitation of the Indians and the atrocities. There had been two booms in the area. The first died out with the end of the First World War and the increased production in Malaya. Then with the Japanese occupation of South-East Asia during the Second World War, attention again switched to the Amazon and this continued into the fifties. Now only small interests remain and although the Indians are well paid and housed, the old fear of the *caucheros* is still there and many prefer to live their own lives.

Carlos told us that he had sixteen Indians working for him. Most of them only worked during the summer months – from November to March – when the forest was drier. If there was rain the latex from the wild rubber could not be collected. During the winter months the Indians returned to their homes to attend to their *chagras*. The men cut traces through the forest at fifty-yard intervals within easy shouting distance of one another, so that none of the trees are missed. Each morning they place small wooden cups beneath a fresh slash in the bark, returning later to empty the latex into rubber bags slung on their backs. A different section of the forest is covered each day until the cycle is completed and they start again. When the rubber is brought back to the house formic acid is added, though any organic acid can be used, even lemon juice. This coagulates the rubber which is then rolled into sheets, some of which Carlos showed us hanging from the roof-beams of his house.

At the end of a season's gathering the rubber is shipped in bales up the Caquetá to Araracuara. From there it is flown to the merchants in Bogotá – usually in May and June – and Carlos added, 'This is about the only time in the year when I see civilization. To save costs we arrange that the plane brings all our supplies and merchandise for the next year on its inward journey. These are mainly for the Indians, for there is nothing he can buy with money here, so I keep a small trade store.'

Later Carlos spoke of the Missing Link or Loys' Ape, which he maintained lived in the area. Three years before, one of his young workers was out in his rubber trace when he was suddenly attacked by a beast, which held him fastened to the ground all night. The boy who had fainted from fear, was found the next day and brought to Carlos's house where he took forty-eight hours to recover. He was thoroughly washed but the foul smell of the beast was impossible to remove. Several rubber gatherers claim to have seen the ape in the area of the Miritiparaná. Something very similar has also been reported from the Llanos, in the wooded river valleys near the Orinoco.

Stories of the half-human ape are as common as those of lost cities, the Amazonian women and the tribes of white Indians who hunt by night. All occur in the myth and legends of the tribes. But to hear a first-hand account of this ape-man from a reliable witness was unusual.

Before dawn we set off down river in Carlos's long, narrow, shallow-draught Caquetá boat, faster and more graceful than the stouter ones of the

Vaupés. Horacio said that every river he had known on the Orinoco and Amazon had something different about it. Each had its own character, its individual appearance; in the same way you could almost tell a river by the boats on it and the way they were handled.

As we travelled down the twisting river we passed an old covered launch going up to the Mission Station. A rotund and bald padre standing at the wheel gave us a cheerful wave as the boat chugged on its way. Close behind him came a canoe full of tin-helmeted anti-malarial workers. We reflected that one day they might reach the Piraparaná and daub their black DDT stamps over the *maloca* entrances. That night we camped on a long sand-bar and, armed with shotgun and torches, we dazzled the crocodiles. Few of them were more than five feet long. Carlos shot at them before they could run off the spit into the water. One was half-stunned by the roar of a near miss; his back glistening emerald-green in the torchlight, he glared defiance at us as we slipped a noose about his belly. We had had a request from Dr Medem, the zoologist in Bogotá, to bring a crocodile back, alive. Luckily, perhaps, he escaped a few days later.

The Caquetá seemed like a great lake studded with sandbanks and wooded islands. It was impossible to tell at a glance which way the water was flowing. We learnt the reason for this as we came to the rapids of Cordoba. These acted as a dam and funnelled a river over a mile wide through a channel no more than a hundred yards across. Keeping well to the right bank, we passed through the swirling white water and rocky projections without mishap. Two days later four convicts escaped from the national prison at Araracuara; being unfamiliar with the river they took the left bank of the rapid in their flimsy raft, only to be swept into a whirlpool. The two who survived were taken prisoner by the frontier-post guards. They had been less than ten miles from the Brazilian border and freedom.

Two hours below the rapids we saw a white statue of the Virgin Mary overlooking the river and, behind, the green sward and grey huts of La Pedrera, the military border post. There we could put through a radio call – a Catalina would pick us up and we would be back in Bogotá in forty-eight hours. It was an incredible thought. On the bank where we moored the boat there was an old wooden bandstand, like those you find in an Oslo park. Inside was a barber's chair and a broken mirror. We looked at our three-month-old beards, our sun-blackened faces – and laughed.

But that evening as we glumly surveyed the pile of equipment and the collection, we pondered on the Commandante's words: 'No plane will land here on the river, there have been too many accidents in the past. Besides, we have no means of communication, the transmitter has broken down. I am sorry ...!'

What were we to do? It was better that one of us should make contact as soon as possible, so Brian travelled down river to the Brazilian frontier post.

A week later an Air Force Catalina flew in from Belem and he was allowed to travel on it to Leticia. There he notified the naval authorities of our plight, and requested passages on a Colombian gunboat which was to call at La Pedrera if the low river level would allow it.

We paid José his salary but he seemed angry that it was so little. Someone found Brian's lost watch in his baggage and he was put in detention by the soldiers. Before we could intervene he had escaped and returned to the forest. A week later the gunboat got through, and Donald and Horacio travelled down river again on the Yarrow-built *Cartagena*. Twice she went aground in the shallow Caquetá and had to be moved by manpower. All on board had to stand up to their necks in water for hours on end. In the early days of March we reached the Amazon. After travelling upstream for four days and nights, we arrived in Leticia with all the equipment, including the Tukano canoe.

And Nestor? He had decided, perhaps wisely, not to join us. We had already left Mitú before he could get any communication through to us, and after that it was too late. So maps, food and fuel await the next traveller to pass the same way, over the portage to Kuarumey's and the *malocas* of the Piraparaná.

Part 3

Kogi and Bintukua

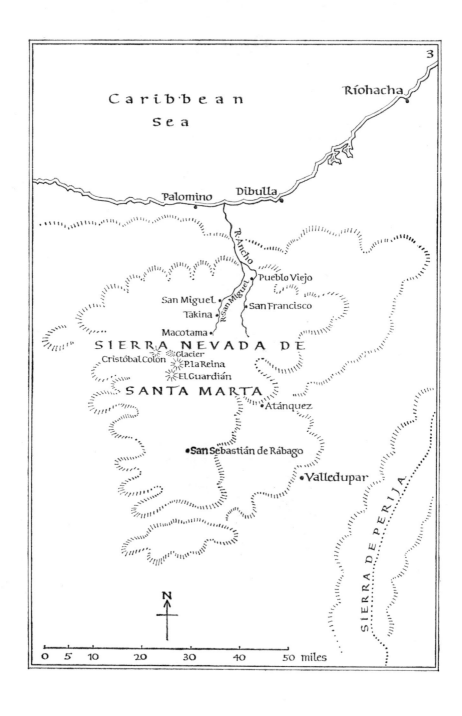

I

Beasts of Burden

'If you want to visit the most interesting people living in the Sierra Nevada, I advise you to go to the Kogi on the northern slopes. They are a suspicious mountain people, ruled by their *mamas* or priests and inhospitable to strangers. I don't think you will find out very much about them in the month you plan to stay, but still you may record some music. Oh yes, don't forget to take flea-powder, or you will be bitten to death in their huts.'

With these words Dr Reichel Dolmatoff warned us of the reception we would be given by the next tribe we were to visit: We hoped to go first to the Kogi in the north and then to the Bintukua in the south of the Sierra. We also planned to climb La Reina, 18,155 feet, one of the highest peaks in Colombia. This was perhaps over-ambitious, for only Donald had mountaineering experience and already one anthropologist in England had raised his eyebrows at the thought of trying to combine a mountain climb with the study of an Indian tribe. However, with the Amazon behind us, we had nothing to lose, and a climb into the snows would be a complete change from our jungle existence. After a month in Bogotá we were re-equipped and reorganized. Erwin Kraus, the well-known mountaineer, had told us of a new route we might take to reach the peaks. So on 4 April with a motley selection of ice-axes, crampons, rucksacks, kitbags and crates, which caused both amusement to travellers and consternation to the cargo authorities, we once more left Bogotá Airport and flew northwards towards the Atlantic coast.

The three of us – Horacio was teaching English in Bogotá but Nestor had rejoined the expedition – spent the night in Barranquilla, the largest port in Colombia, at the mouth of the Río Magdalena. By air it is only a three-hour journey from Bogotá; the paddle-steamer meanders sleepily downstream for a week; we were, as usual, in a hurry – this time to beat the rains, not the drought. A strong sea breeze blew down the wide modern streets, cooling the sultry air. Men gesticulated outside bars in open-neck shirts, the women wore bright cotton dresses. All too soon we were flying eastwards to Ríohacha, the capital of the Guajira, the northernmost peninsula of the country.

In the morning haze the foothills of the Sierra rose abruptly from the coastal plain, but we could not see the snow peaks. They were well covered in cloud, the cloud we were afraid might enshroud us during the coming weeks. Below was the blue sea; a ribbon of white marked the shore; behind, the flat scrubland suddenly turned to sand – we landed at Ríohacha.

Here we bought our provisions, with the help of Axel Kloch, a Dane who had come to Colombia in the 1920s as an engineer, turned to gold prospecting and was now starting a hemp business. Though the shops of Ríohacha were reputed to have quantities of contraband, we were to be disappointed, unless we thought we could climb to 18,000 feet on whisky, American canned foods and cigarettes! While searching the town we met a young farmer of German origin who had a ranch in the foothills. He said he would take us to the river valley where we would have to transfer to mules. Early next morning we were about to leave when two men in uniform informed us we were wanted by the Special Intelligence! With a contraband ship in port two nights before and our beards arousing cries of 'Fidelista' perhaps this was not surprising. We produced our passports, Nestor explained in professorial tones that we were scientists and we were allowed to go on. We hurtled in a dusty bus towards a small village, back across the desert and scrub over which we had flown only the day before. Dibulla, a fishing settlement at the mouth of a small river coming down from the hills, had a curiously sleepy air. In the late afternoon warmth the surf beat against the sandy shore, a man jogged homewards on his donkey and in the distance a naked negro cast his net into the sea with all the grace of an expert. The three of us sat in the sand, each one lost in his own thoughts; it was a rare moment as we forgot about time.

The moon was still shining and the rats rummaging beneath our hammocks when Brian left on the nine-hour climb to Pueblo Viejo, the last village in the foothills where mules could be hired; he returned the following afternoon with five beasts and two muleteers. The loads were difficult to lash to the pack-saddles, so the journey was hindered by frequent stops to readjust the equipment on either side of the mule's back. Each animal had a different capacity and one had to be completely unloaded; no matter what oaths the boys shouted or the sticks and stones they threw, the poor beast could go no further. We travelled through flat dusty scrubland; in the river valleys were banana plantations, their great green leaves bent heavily towards the ground. Occasionally we passed a small palm-thatched ranch inhabited by people, no longer pure negro but *mestizos* with Indian and Spanish blood. They eked out a living from their bananas, maize and *panela*, crude brown blocks made from sugar-cane juice which they boiled into syrup and left to solidify. We too ate *panela* as we climbed higher, leaving the plantations and entering a scene of parched grassland, changing to forest where watercourses flowed. A haze shimmered over the lowlands behind us; in front clouds obliterated the hilltops; at times we followed the mules, at others we went ahead, listening to the shouts '*Mula, mula! Macho, caracho!*' echoing through the valleys beneath.

Pueblo Viejo was once the site of an Indian village. Today the Kogi have retreated higher into the mountains and only *mestizo* inhabitants live in the small mud houses, transporting *panela* and vegetables to Dibulla on the backs of their mules. Beneath the wooded hills the nights are cool and bands of howler monkeys can be heard moving through the trees. The *mestizos* lead a hard life, and to them the Kogi Indian is just a man to be exploited. We were to be treated like them, it seemed, as they raised their prices to take us on the next leg of the journey to San Miguel. For a whole day we searched for animals and haggled until eventually Don Cerafin, the negro Comisario of the village, lent two oxen and another man two mules. Alcibiades, a rotund and talkative settler who spoke Kogi, agreed to come as our interpreter and his horse was to be the fifth beast of burden. He was the son of a Guajiran mother and a Panamanian seafaring father who on his travels no doubt heard and liked this incongruous Greek name. Alcibiades had lived part of his life in Barranquilla but assured us that his present existence was more peaceful and far more profitable. He had been to San Miguel quite often and some years before had accompanied an American woman botanist to collect plants from the high and desolate *paramo*. He spoke with knowledge and authority, but we knew he would do little work. 'That's for the Indians,' he quickly told us.

At dawn the next day we loaded the backs of our zoo, but not without more trouble: the owner of the two mules decided to withdraw his animals; our loads were too heavy and we were going too high; besides, he had a better offer to take *panela* to Dibulla. This was a last-minute effort to raise the price, but it failed; we left under a cloud of swear-words and made our way up into the highlands. Parched by months of sunshine, the bare grass slopes were cream against the cloudless sky, as we wound our way along the narrow path cut into the hillside. Once an ox wandered off the track, and there was another delay when a load jammed between two boulders. The oxen seemed such clumsy beasts as they swayed from side to side, their wooden pack-saddles laden with our gear; yet the ox is the true beast of burden in mountains, he can carry more weight than a mule and he is sure-footed on muddy tracks. We only once met someone – it took us by surprise. An Indian family dashed past us without a word, they did not even look up as their white-cloaked figures ran rapidly by.

We came to a saddle and dropped down to the valley of the Río San Miguel. We passed through a Kogi village of round mud huts with conical grass roofs; again the people seemed frightened, the women and children running inside and the men eyeing us with suspicion. Here Alcibiades talked to Antonino, the shrewd Kogi *cacique* or chief of the valley, his face half-hidden by long strands of black hair. His wizened old body twitched as he watched us through dark slit eyes. He did not seem pleased to see us. He spoke a little Spanish and said there would be no one in San Miguel, all the Kogi were here in the lowlands looking after their sugar-cane plantations.

We continued along one side of the valley, and entered a barren land of dried grass and stone. In the grey-blue misty light of dusk, the roof-cones of San Miguel pierced the horizon. The path curled upwards between giant boulders and then across open grassland to an immense wooden doorway, the only point of entrance to the hillside village. We felt as though we were entering an ancient Inca capital, fortified against hostile strangers.

The village was deserted; in the darkness it was like a conglomeration of beehives outlined against a cold starlit sky. In the centre were two rectangular mud-walled houses, and inside one we strung our hammocks from great wooden beams which might have stood for hundreds of years. Next day as we unpacked the equipment, a family ran past with a little boy dragging a pig on the end of a rope. They did not stop or look up. Later Antonino's son arrived; he had been sent by his father to stay with us. Wherever we went, he came. When we left to swim we saw we were also followed by six men, all in long white cloaks: they all constantly rubbed little sticks inside a peculiarly shaped gourd, then poked the sticks covered with a white powder into their mouths which bulged noticeably on one side. We were never allowed to leave their sight and for two days we waited in these weird surroundings, planning the route and packing mountaineering equipment into our two rucksacks. During the two weeks we expected to be away, Nestor and Alcibiades would stay with the Kogi, in the hope that one stranger would have more success than three.[1]

[1] In these chapters we owe much to Dr G. Reichel Dolmatoff's work on the Kogi, in particular as regards their religion.

2

The Queen of Ice

On Friday 14 April we left San Miguel with three Indians as guards and our lone ox loaded with rucksacks, crampons, a kitbag of provisions and two ice-axes. The early morning mist threw a blue light over the barren slopes strewn with granite boulders; in the distance jagged rock pinnacles rose to 15,000 feet through the haze. Much of the dry grass had already been burnt, only sparse shrubs emerged through the charred remains and an occasional giant cactus spiked heavenwards like a solitary minaret, somehow managing to extract moisture from the arid soil. We passed two more villages, much smaller than San Miguel, and were told their strange names – Takina and Macotama; they were the priests' homes and we were not allowed to stop. Twice we wanted to examine small mounds of earth at the side of the track, but no, these were sacred to the priests and we could not touch them. In Macotama an old Kogi sat silently on a stone slab; there were four more slabs outside a circular grass house, but we were forbidden to go anywhere near. We might have been prisoners of war.

We left the San Miguel valley and climbed westwards along a smaller track, clinging to a steep slope scarred by gashes which soon would turn to rushing torrents. The sun was high above our heads when we stopped to bathe in a freezing green mountain stream as it cascaded over dazzling white boulders worn smooth by rushing water. While we bathed, the three Kogi perched on the rocks to wash their long straggly black hair. Then we continued through a rockier but greener landscape with delicate pink alpine shrubs glinting against the blue sky. There was no feel now of the sultry lowlands, we had entered a rarefied atmosphere, our heads felt tight, ears popped and eyes seemed sore. At 12,000 feet we reached the highest Kogi hut, used when they tend their cattle in these high pastures, and stopped for the night.

Under the grass roof through a haze of smoke we watched the three guides who were intrigued by us but always attentive to their leader's guttural words. Next morning before dawn he had vanished, taking the ox with him. The two others were eager to climb the rock slabs behind the hut; they refused to wait while we heated porridge and in a moment were running up the mountainside without any of the equipment. Climbing steeply over the slabs, we watched the two Indians cross the valley and ascend the other side; they shouted to us and then sat down and waited till we arrived. A deep blue lake lay far beneath and through a saddle in the rock wall ahead we could see the snow. The two Indians pointed and turned away. This was the land of Nabulwé, the land where the mother goddess ruled supreme among the snow-clad peaks; where the spirits of the dead eventually arrived, whence no one could ever return. They would come no further, they were frightened, and while we were still gazing at the snow they started back to San Miguel darting down through the boulders.

Plans had to be altered; we could no longer rely on help to reach the base which we wished to establish at the glacier gap and would have to carry everything through ourselves. That night we pitched the tent above a small blue lake edged by reeds; at the side of the corry lake far below was a Kogi shrine – a flat boulder covered with granite chips set in individual pyramids. Maybe these were the offerings each Indian made to Nabulwé. The only hope of making the ascent was to cut down our loads and go through as fast as possible before the bad weather came. We allowed ourselves two complete changes of clothes and rations for ten days, only two cameras now, and, as our one luxury, a minute transistor radio which had little difficulty in picking up such far-flung places as Caracas, Puerto Rico and New Orleans. A small-scale map constructed from aerial photographs was our bible, but the route had to be determined by ourselves.

The next four days were spent in arduous back-loading of supplies from Blue Lake Camp to the eventual Glacier Gap Camp. We accomplished this in a series of leap-frogs, establishing one camp and a supply dump in between. It was a barren, silent world of rock wastes, precipitous gullies, glacial valley bottoms and sphagnum swamps bordering the moraines. To the south, on our left, was the rock wall rising three thousand feet above us, capped in snow and dominating a glacier which we skirted. To the north a veined pattern of narrow valleys fell away towards the coastal plains, hidden in perpetual haze. Only in the morning were there cloudless skies and clear vision, by midday we were enveloped in cloud which billowed up from the valleys below. In the mornings the view before us spread to the mighty summits of Cristobal Colon and Simon Bolívar, behind us were the jagged silhouettes of lesser peaks and in the distance the hills which formed the frontier with Venezuela. There were no animals; we had seen the last wild cattle as we climbed away from the blue lake; our only companions were a small bunting, a rock pipit and once a tiny crested humming bird which hovered among the *frailejones*, tall almost primeval ferns. Once near the ice we seemed to leave nature to enter another planet; only the sounds of falling rock and rippling ice streams broke the silence.

The manioc dance round the wife and small son of Bréo the headman.

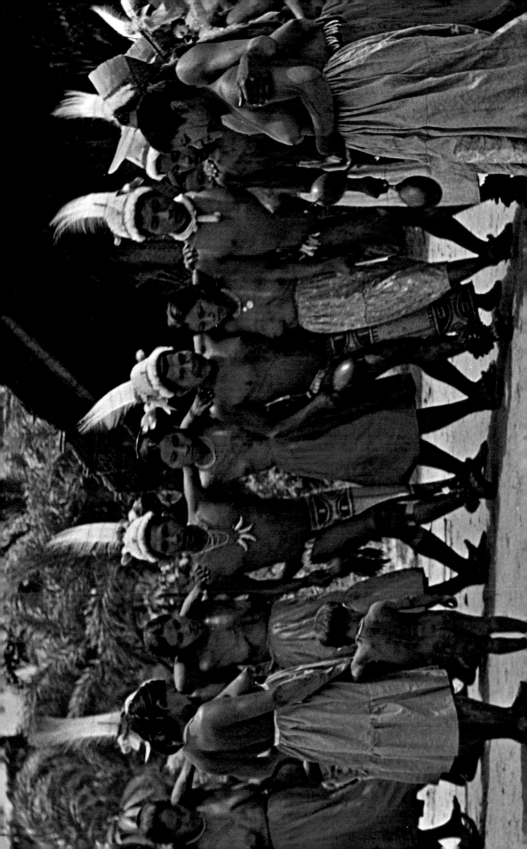

Our way forward through a dense blanket of white mist was often slow. One afternoon a steep gully barred our way and we were forced upwards on to the glacier. Here the rock fell away in a precipice, so we pitched the tent on a bare slab of granite and waited for the cloud to lift. It only cleared at dusk; in front, over a sea of snow and ice, stood Cristobal Colon, cold, black and jagged against an orange-tinted sky. At 15,000 feet, this was the highest point we had reached and already altitude was beginning to hinder Brian: 'Feeling somewhat ill, altitude sickness or *soroche* as it is called out here seems to be having its effect . . . not much fun leaving the tent in a bitter gale with the wind blowing straight off the ice. Donald appears much fitter than me and is setting a tremendous pace. Still, this is the only way we can get forward. To sleep with the wind battering against the flimsy tent walls.'

By the evening of 20 April all the supplies were in Glacier Gap Camp, where we had pitched the tent on the moraine overlooking a minute lake at the foot of the glacier. All that afternoon we had brought the second load through thick cloud. When we descended the final gully, clutching to the wet rocks, a giant condor suddenly swooped through the mist to herald our arrival: an enormous, almost ominous bird, with what must have been a nine-foot wingspan and finger-like pinions at the tips; its cruel yet majestic head ringed by white feathers showed it with reason to be the king of Andean birds. That night the mist turned to snow and our sleep was spasmodic as Donald's diary shows:

'I put my hand to the roof of the tent to see what the weight of the snow was – it is still remorselessly coming down – may have to clear the fly again soon. That is hell because here inside the igloo it is comparatively warm, but outside it is bitter and the fine snow seems to drive to the bone. Occasionally through the dull silence one can hear a crash as another rock makes its way down the mountainside. Tonight the frogs are silent and there are no stars. Just the snow, the wind and a half hull-down mountain tent on a bleak moraine.'

The future looked bleak when next morning, with the snow still falling, the pressure stove broke. The solder around the safety valve came away and petrol spurted out. Gutta percha brought in case a filling came loose in our teeth was useless, and besides the stove was dangerous. We discarded it and filled a quarter-pound tea tin with sand, piercing holes in the top. The petrol burnt smokily from the sand, blackening everything it touched, but for the next week this patent 'Brooke Bond Burner' warmed our food. Though the snow continued, visibility improved and we made a reconnaissance journey

LEFT: *Patterns in palm thatch.* RIGHT: *Rock engraving on the Piraparaná – a dancing figure at Kaperwa.*

to the glacier to see how we should cross. For the first time we put on our crampons; roped together with Donald leading, we cut steps into the steep ice wall to progress towards the centre of the glacier, carefully prodding our way through a maze of crevasses. Once more cloud enveloped us and we returned in the hope that the morrow would provide better weather. We knew we were now within striking distance of La Reina but we also knew the snow would soon set in for good. We packed our rucksacks with the minimum we would need for five days: emergency-ration bars, oats, packeted soups, Horlicks mixed with powdered milk, sugar, chocolates, sweets and raisins; a spare set of clothing and two pairs of socks; a single camera, a small plastic box of medical supplies, one water bottle filled with petrol, two bowls, two spoons and – a flask of whisky. These, together with our tent and sleeping bags, were the only things we took, for we had to travel light and fast.

On Friday 21 April we crossed through the gap and Donald wrote:

'After quite a struggle we reached the lip of the glacier. Snow on the rock-scree approach made going difficult. As we reached the glacier slight snow started, accompanied by a swirling mist, cutting our vision to a mere ten to fifteen yards. After some delay I found the steps which we cut yesterday, and within half an hour we passed over the deep crevasses on the crest of the glacier. These were rather dangerous, being partly hidden by the new fallen snow ... the mist gave an eerie effect. All we could see was the ice cap and the occasional boulder held fast in the moving ice.'

We moved down off the ice, along a valley of mist. Even though we could see little we felt as though we were passing through kinder surroundings; the ground was spongy and green, there were fewer rocks and the pinnacles above were hidden in cloud. We were travelling faster than we imagined and were surprised when a valley opened out in front of us; there was a lake; around it were cows' hoof-prints and myriads of peeping black frogs. According to the map we expected a lake, but this was too large; we skirted its brown water ringed by moraines and then the cloud lifted – in front was Pico El Guardian, the highest peak in the southern part of the range; behind and somewhere to our left was La Reina. We had come too far, but if the next morning was clear we could make an early attempt up the north face of El Guardian.

Our efforts proved fruitless. First, the crevasses were impossible for only two men to cross, then we found that a rock wall which from a distance we thought could be scaled was precipitous and coated in thin ice. We turned back but not before looking north on to all the highest peaks in the Sierra – Cristobal Colon, Simon Bolívar and Simmonds stood together, and to the east Reina, a massive block of rock capped in ice, towered alone; we would try to establish a base at the foot of her glacier that night. The clouds crept up from the valleys, the sky had a cold moisture-laden look, and yet high as we were it was extraordinary to find that the one sign of life was a group of black flies scattered sleepily on the snow. We must have been well over 16,000 feet, but these flies could still exist in the intense cold. By midday we had left El Guardian, and as the snow came down we retraced our steps up the same valley to climb a steep gully and come face to face with the mountain we aimed to climb. The cloud lifted and in front was La Reina, her huge glacier flowing away from the peak almost to our feet. In an icy gale we pitched our tent close to a lake and for a moment, with the wind lashing waves and weed to the shore, the broken wall of ice rising from the water, we might almost have been on the fringe of the polar icecap.

With three days' rations left we decided to give ourselves one day's rest; tomorrow, Sunday, we would make a reconnaissance of the best route on to the glacier and then on Monday 24 April we would attempt the summit. Fortunately Sunday morning was fine. The snout of the glacier was a glowing mass of white pinnacles and unscalable pale-blue cliffs, so we climbed a rock gully deep in snow and came upon more pinnacles, like an army of ice men set against us. Crossing on to the ice we made our way towards the centre of the glacier. This was the route Erwin Kraus had shown us, but in front were vast gashes. Our best way seemed to keep to the right, the side nearest the summit. Then the cloud came down. As we made our way back we discovered an exquisite cave with long silver icicles at the entrance and inside an enthroned ice queen surrounded by palest blue. That night Donald wrote:

'It is now ten days since we left San Miguel. One suspects altitude and de-hydrated rations are having a debilitating effect. For the last week we have been at an altitude mostly in excess of 14,000 feet and with the work of double loading we both feel a little weak in the legs. Brian has headaches and his eyes are bothering him; I suffer occasionally from shortness of breath, a fairly common ailment at this altitude. On the whole we seem remarkably even-tempered with very occasional lapses.'

Disagreements we obviously had, but on an expedition – and especially now, high on a mountain – we could not afford to quarrel, we were a team and we had a job to complete. Our temperaments were very different: Donald was constant, quiet, restrained but determined, while Brian was impetuous, unpredictable, equally determined but often over-ambitious. Perhaps such a combination was to our own advantage, but above all we were friends and because of this we found ourselves at the foot of La Reina.

After a restless night with the tent leaking and the fear we might not wake up, we left camp at five-thirty on the morning of 24 April. It was still dark and misty as we crossed the route we had explored the previous day, but by seven we were on the edge of the glacier and making our way towards the centre over deceptive corrugations, often thigh-deep in snow. Here small crevasses were treacherously hidden by recent falls and we traversed to the right where we had to cross three larger ones by thin ice bridges. This was dangerous, and Donald was unhappy about the risk involved, for one of us only had to slip and the other would have found it very difficult to hold him on the far end of the rope. By eight o'clock the mist lifted, the sun came out and we passed into an unbelievable world of dazzling white snow surrounded by pale-blue crevasses, a deep blue sky, almost black, and La Reina emerging before us like a huge lump of icing. All was silent and everything shone, but as we moved along a steep slope our talking seemed to dislodge the new snow from the ice, and it slid downwards in rumbling avalanches. By ten we found ourselves at the foot of a steep ice and snow wall; its seventy-degree slope looked almost vertical, and as we rested in an ice cave we thought this must be the final ascent. Chocolate and raisins fortified us and then we started:

'Donald leading extremely efficiently on the rope, and I following in his footsteps some twenty yards behind. The snow often came away from the ice and rumbled terrifyingly down and down the slope, into the crevasses at the base. I was very cold, my feet numbed senseless and my hands in a similar condition. Both of us had the knuckles of the right hand badly cut as we jammed the ice-axes into the slope, leaving a red-brown trail of blood behind us.'

For two hours we cut our way, step by step, up this eight-hundred-foot slope and then with the mist swirling over the lip we reached what we thought was the summit. To our dismay we could just see the land rising along a razor-edge of snow and ice. We continued with precipices on either side until at last a snow plateau spread out ahead of us and we reached the peak at 1.20 p.m. It was now snowing hard and bitterly cold, so we returned at once to the top of the ice wall. Here Brian's feet were too numb to get the crampons to hold. An alternative route had to be found and, retracing our steps towards the summit, we moved out on to the glacier in search of a way through the crevasses:

'I was for trying an ice bridge over a crevasse or for jumping the near end of the same crevasse; my feet were so numb that I had no confidence in descending the same seventy-degree slope and dragging Donald down with me. Donald however was emphatic that at this late hour – 4 p.m. – we must return by the route we came. So, in the sleety snow and mist we returned to

---

Light streams through the thatch of a maloca as an Indian pounds coca leaves.

the ice wall and Donald went ahead, on a very short rope of only about ten feet, cutting steps into the ice and magnificently guiding my feet into them. He certainly saved my life.'

By six-thirty we reached the ice cave. It was dark and as we drank the last drop of whisky it looked ominously as though we would have to stay there the night. Luckily the moon came up through the mist, our footprints and especially the ice-axe holes were just visible, and we recrossed the moonlit glacier to reach the edge at eight-thirty. As we stumbled back across the rocks, still roped together, we might well have been two drunken men. Indeed, so exhausted were we that we could not find the tent. Only at ten o'clock did we discover our camp – it had been a very long day.

The climb was, as Donald later remarked, 'a very close shave'. The effect of high altitude had made Brian think he could jump impossible crevasses, we had very nearly been benighted on the mountainside, and then in our exhaustion we had completely lost our sense of direction. What was more the snow came down relentlessly for the next two days, and as we returned fully loaded along the north face, against a driving blizzard, we often found ourselves clambering waist-deep through snow. Our rations could not have lasted a day longer, our bodies were weakening and the weather broke. We had climbed La Reina only just in time.

A Bintukua playing an embra *flute.*

3

A Tenacious People

The snow lay behind as we jumped from boulder to boulder across the great granite slabs which stepped down in unending ledges towards the little blue lake. In contrast to the shining ivory of the granite a deep green dyke of basalt pierced the older rock and ran straight across this wilderness to become twisted, contorted and finally lost in the bare peaks which formed the eastern end of the north ridge. Our route was down past the first camp site and back to the stone hut where two weeks before we had been deserted.

Much of the hillside was now scorched black by fire, the lake levels had risen, the streams were fast becoming torrents and drizzle took the place of misty sunlight. Alone but for three highland cows and a tiny black and white calf, we forded the last stream and made our way through the mist to the hut. The entrance in the circular stone wall was barred by a gnarled tree-stump, so was the doorway, but inside the earth was dry and grass strewn over the floor showed that someone had been there since our departure.

For the first time for days we were able to dispense with petrol and sand for cooking and became enveloped in wood smoke, stifling yet wholesome after the fumes in the tent. Fresh onions and potatoes from the patch surrounding the hut, rice and meat were a luxury to stomachs which had somehow contracted after their diet of oats and emergency ration bars. As we were eating, we saw a piece of paper jammed between two boulders in the wall. It was a note from Nestor dated only the day before and written in Spanish, for Nestor nearly always conversed with us in his own language. It read:

> Dear B. and D. .... How are you? I thought I might meet you, but Alcibiades and I are so cold up here that we must return. We'll send two Indians to help carry your equipment back to San Miguel. While you have been away we have been to San Francisco and recorded some music on the Kudelski. All goes well. Saludos.

It was grand news to know that Nestor was making some headway with the Kogi, while to have used the tape recorder was more than we had ever expected. As we lay in our sleeping bags, spread on the springy mat of dried grass, we talked of the future, of our chances of working among these uncommunicative people and then of the distant plans for the expedition.

The blanket of smoke hung low, field mice scuttled in the grass roof above and one descended to run lightly over Brian's face. Strangely enough it was a pleasant sensation, a change from the unfriendliness and cold of the higher peaks.

The morning was clear as we washed in the stream. Suddenly two children, a girl and a small boy, dashed up the river-bed over the boulders. There were no houses higher up, so where the children were going we did not know. Perhaps this was their family's hut. Certainly they were surprised and extremely frightened, and in a moment they had vanished. Usually the children were the most approachable members of a community, so this was hardly a good omen for the future. As we moved down the narrow valley of the Río San Miguel we sometimes saw people far beneath us, close to their upland huts, but they ran away to hide when they saw us.

The sun beat down and the rucksacks seemed heavier than ever as they swayed from side to side, piled high with extra equipment. In the heat we could not resist drinking quantities of the cold, almost salty, green water which rushed down between the boulders. Some of these were enormous and only when we were above them did they stand in true perspective, dwarfing everything, even the huts which lay near them. Plucked from the highest peaks, embedded in the slowly moving ice and then deposited in the valleys which the glaciers had carved, they were the remnants of a past ice age, a once frozen world. The desolation still remained.

Ahead, two large thatched houses rose from the parched ground; the first was old and the thatch had turned a dark grey-brown, but the second was new and blended with the dry grass from which it sprung. Conical and covered with esparto, they had no windows, only an entrance facing north down the valley and guarded by a protective eave. We were at Macotama, the highest and most isolated home of the priests, and the two houses were their 'temples'. Projecting from the apex of each roof was a great rack of straw-bound staves, in which were hundreds of broken potsherds, sacred sherds which belonged to the priests. At first all seemed deserted, but as we approached the older temple, a robed figure emerged from the dark interior, followed by a small black terrier-like dog, and walked awkwardly towards us. He wore a white toga-like garment with long hanging sleeves covering his brown arms, and on his short legs baggy trousers. Across each shoulder was slung a bag woven from the beaten fibre of the *maguey* cactus and striped with bold brown lines of bark dye. In his left hand he carried a small bottle-shaped gourd.

The *mama* – the name given to all priests of the tribe – came closer and stopped. He looked at us but said nothing and made no movement. Thin strands of long black hair flew out in the breeze behind his stern head. He was a noble figure, but his wide-set brown eyes appeared full of suspicion. The lines from his nostrils curved scornfully away from a straight nose down to a tightly-closed mouth. Occasionally he blew down his nostrils, as if in anger, and his dog snarled when we tried to walk closer. Still the *mama* stared, rubbing his lime stick vigorously inside the gourd and showing no sign of friendship. We watched him sit down on one of six slab seats erected in a line outside the old temple. He looked fixedly into the distance, all the time rubbing his stick around the gourd to add yet more substance to the yellow encrustation on its rim.

As a child the *mama* had been chosen as a future priest. For twenty years he had been taught the dances, myths and legends of the Kogi by the elder *mamas*; he was never allowed to set eyes on a woman nor to see the light of day. He only knew the paths of the Sierra by the light of the moon.

When a boy reaches puberty, Nestor had told us, he is initiated by the *mama* into the use of coca and given a *poporo* or gourd. This is the most precious object a man possesses, it represents woman and, more than that, it is linked to the supreme being, the mother deity. Then the *mama* tears the youngster's tunic away from his body and presents him with a new, adult cloak with sleeves. When he pierces the *poporo* with the lime stick it is in imitation of ritual defloration, the stick represents his penis and the rubbing movement inside the *poporo* copulation. He is taught that all sexual activity must be repressed and expressed only in the use of the *poporo*. All necessities, all frustrations are henceforth concentrated in this tiny gourd from which he becomes inseparable.

At first the young man's mouth is burnt by the continual chewing of coca leaves and of the lime which releases alkaloids in the coca. For fear of the *mamas* and loss of prestige amongst the other men he dares not stop. Instead he rubs concentrated tobacco juice on to his teeth in the hope that this will ease the pain. He keeps this syrupy mixture inside a small close-fitting double calabash, rather like a Victorian snuffbox, scoops a little out with his thumbnail and as he closes the calabash licks one edge to ensure that the two portions fit tightly together. Partly from the tobacco juice and partly from the stain of the coca leaves, his teeth become blacker and blacker as he grows older. Very occasionally when a young man gets married he stops taking coca but this is due to the influence of his wife. No woman is allowed to take the drug, they live in separate houses from their menfolk and believe their husbands will be reduced to eventual impotency. So they try to stop them chewing cocaine, but the *mamas* prevail and the man will be outlawed unless he agrees to conform again.

Here, much more than among the Tukano of the Piraparaná, a man's senses appear wholly deadened; his life is to a great extent governed by his belief in the power of cocaine and the *poporo*. Wherever he may be, whether travelling or just contemplating, he clutches the gourd and rotates the stick in it or round the outside. As he grows older the yellow encrustation of lime around the rim becomes thicker, for the constant rubbing continues until he reaches a stage of complete obsession. Yet it is this very obsession and the overruling authority of the *mamas* which have held the Kogi together against centuries of foreign infiltration. With coca there is no need for sleep, their minds are clear and they can communicate with their ancestors for days and nights on end. To accomplish this is the ultimate aim of every Kogi man.

The Kogi are an intensely religious people. They believe in one supreme being, the goddess Nabulwé. She is a symbol of fertility. Her realm is in the snows of the Sierra Nevada, and that is where all the dead eventually go. All her sons and daughters became the first lesser gods, the heroes and founders of their ancient lineages which date back for hundreds of years. These are the good spirits; evil is personified by the spirits of the dead, or their ancestors – not that they are considered evil in themselves, but if the Kogi do not continually appease them with gifts their anger can be very destructive. This belief goes back to their Tairona ancestors and, archaeological evidence suggests, far into prehistory.

There was no open hostility, only this fear, suspicion and secretiveness. Perhaps by climbing into the land of Nabulwé we had infringed on the most guarded of Kogi beliefs, in which case the *mamas* must have ordered their people to have nothing to do with us. The path, a mere ribbon on the rocky hillside, curled steadily downwards round each spur towards Takina, the next priestly village in the valley. In one section were two temples, old and blackened, identical to those in Macotama. In the other a group of people stood on the bare ground between the small grass houses. As we approached they retreated to their doorways, but two of them, a man and his wife, remained close to a gnarled tree-trunk, a tethering post for their oxen. The man was dressed in the normal threadbare garments and wore only one striped bag across his shoulder. With wrinkled face and unkempt hair he appeared much older than his plump and pretty young wife. Fair brown skin, serious dark eyes and long flowing black hair gave her a quiet attraction. She was wrapped in white homespun cloth, her arms were bare, round her neck were long coils of bright red beads and round each wrist a single string with two black seeds. These last were to ward off illnesses but the coils about her neck were a sign of great wealth. She was shy and remained behind her husband, but he was friendly and, unlike the other Kogi we had met, spoke a few words of Spanish. They were on their way home to the Río Donachui on the southern side of the Sierra; the journey across the Pass of Surlibaka would take them five days as they shrank from the ascent into the land of perpetual snow.

'Each year I come back to Takina to visit my family. I was born here, but my wife comes from the south and her family own many oxen. Now we have built a house there and I too own oxen, but here in Takina everyone is poor except for the *mamas'*, and he pointed to the two temples.

We asked him his name. He gave us a Spanish one, Andrés, and offered us some *panela* which he was taking with him for the journey. He was intrigued to see us break the block with an ice-axe, but travellers had quite often come to the Donachui and in spite of his lime gourd he seemed civilized by comparison with his remote relatives. We said good-bye and soon reached the *mamas'* settlement. Standing by were four women, each adorned with coils of wine-red beads. They looked at us, but there was no question of getting any closer; an old man strutted out from the dark entrance, stopped and waved angrily with his right hand. Takina was the chief centre of the *mamas* and it became increasingly obvious that they would do all in their power to stop us getting to know them.

Alcibiades had told us that in Takina and Macotama at the solstices there are special ceremonies which no outsider is allowed to see. The *mamas* post sentries at the heads of the valleys to warn of any stranger's approach. If anyone comes near the ceremony is stopped. The *mamas* are supposed to dance outside the temples wearing exquisite masks of engraved gold.

The heat increased as the track fell away from parched plateau to tangled scrub and prickly pear. Rounding each spur we eagerly hoped to see the clustered roof-cones of San Miguel, but it was not till late afternoon that we arrived. Nestor and Alcibiades were amazed at our rugged and windswept appearance and we sat talking in the semi-darkness of the tall wattle house which the Kogi had lent us. The village was still deserted, but as we recounted episode after episode a figure appeared silhouetted in the doorway. It was Antonino, the old *cacique*, with a live chicken in his arms. He handed it squawking to Alcibiades and then squatted attentively on the floor. The old man barely understood a word that was said, but occasionally he asked Alcibiades a question, then pondered and slowly moved his hands in amazement.

'This is a present,' Alcibiades said as he plucked the chicken, scraped roots of *arracacha* and peeled plantains to prepare a *sancocho de gallina* (chicken stew). 'Many Kogi will not eat any animal or plant which civilized man has introduced; they are forbidden by the *mamas*.' To a *colono* – the term applied to men who worked the land bordering on Indian territory – such a custom was incredible and to be treated with scorn. Alcibiades was a rotund and jovial man with an ever-present smile. He always tried to oblige us, but with the Kogi he, like other *colonos*, was out for what he could get. They were the people with whom one bargained, from whom everything was extracted and as little as possible given in return.

The steam from the stew rose and filled the house with a delicious smell. Soon we were listening to Nestor's story of their journey to San Francisco:

'With great difficulty we persuaded Antonino to lend us an ox, and then followed the track which climbs eastwards from here, first up the steep ridge, then down into the valley of the Río Ancho. The path was so narrow that we did not dare put the tape recorder on the back of an ox for fear it would bump against the jagged boulders on either side. The village was spread along a terrace on the valley floor, larger than San Miguel but with just the same small beehive houses. As we went down the winding track, Alcibiades showed us a cave where he had once found some engraved figurines of stone, but we found nothing and the guards refused to let us stay.'

The house was now dark but for the flickering of candles perched precariously on top of various kit-boxes. By now there were four figures squatting patiently on the floor, their cloaks dangling between their knees, their hands constantly moving as they rubbed the sticks in and around their gourds. Two of them ate the stew we gave them and they listened uncomprehendingly as Nestor continued:

'When we entered the village we were taken to the house of a very old man, the *cacique* of San Francisco, indeed the civil head of the whole region. He wasn't at all friendly, but gruff and unwilling to co-operate. For two days I tried to get information, but it wasn't easy and the old man was always asking me when I was going to leave. On the second night we told him we wanted to hear some music. At first he was adamant in his refusal, but after hearing a recording of his own voice he brought us a long cylindrical wooden drum. Oxhide was stretched over one end of the hollow trunk and kept taut by small wedges. Standing it on end, he struck the skin with a stave and added a softer, more rapid beat with his left hand, the rhythm remaining constant. The *cacique* said the drum would be used during the ceremony when they pray for rain for their crops. This will take place in three weeks' time but he won't allow us to see it.

'Next day, for no accountable reason, he came up to Alcibiades and told him that we would have to leave. He had asked me for rum, the local brew they make in Pueblo Viejo. However we had none, and anyway I would have refused. In any case, all visitors like ourselves are intruders, and usually one of the first questions they ask in their strange guttural way is "When are you going?" '

As we moved about San Miguel we gradually got used to our guards, who never let us out of their sight. What we did to incur their suspicion in the first place we never really learnt. Perhaps all people who visit the Kogi are allotted guards. Certainly when we left to climb the mountain, the snow peaks where the mother goddess lives supreme, there was some debate and amusement – as if such a thing were possible anyway! To our knowledge no one had climbed to the peaks from the San Miguel valley, the usual approach has always been from the south. Thus our reappearance after two weeks may have caused some consternation and concern, certainly among the *mamas*. For if we had climbed into the snow with our strange pointed metal axes and iron spiked feet, we must have been in the land of the dead. Why then had we been allowed to return? – that was a question we might well have asked ourselves. Certainly in the eyes of the priests we were highly suspicious, to be guarded and asked to leave at the first possible opportunity.

We soon learnt that there was little to be gained from questioning them and what little we did learn was thanks to Alcibiades. Often all four of us would talk far into the night before the biting Sierra winds penetrated the thatch and doors and forced us to retreat into our hammocks and blankets.

We lived during those weeks in San Miguel, in a hut called the 'government house'. Opposite us was a Roman Catholic chapel, locked and bolted and long deserted. All around us, grouped on an old river terrace perched on the side of the steep valley were eighty round thatched houses and the large *Cansa Maria* – the Kogi temple.

The houses in the village, like those lower in the valley, were mud-walled, thatched with mountain grass and raised on rock foundations. There was barely room for three people to stretch out and sleep. With a fire in the centre and no outlets for the smoke save through the thatch, the interior was well protected against the cold nights. The blackened beams were evidence of the perpetual smoke which made it impossible to stand up without suffocating. The conical roofs sloped steeply to allow the torrential winter rain to run off quickly. On the apex of the roof broken potsherds placed over a vertical stick kept the rain from passing inside.

One day we were lucky to see the Indians making a house. The framework for the walls had been completed and the men were making the conical roof separately on the ground, ready to be placed on top of the house when the women had completed the wattle walls.

Some of the houses higher in the mountains were not only roofed with thatch but grass-sided. Perhaps this was due to the scarcity of good clay for walls. In the highest huts we stayed in the walls were made entirely of stone, but at 12,000 feet there was little else they could use, even grass for the roof being scarce.

The building, like all work, was done on a communal basis; the paths were usually kept clear by the different villagers in whose locality they lay, as were the high log bridges, carefully bound and railed, which spanned the streams from stone platforms. Though the men wove cloth, the women spun the cotton.

The Kogi are monogamous, except for the priests, and though each family has two or even three different dwelling-places throughout the year, they never live together. The man's home is always separate from the woman's; the young children live with their mother. If a child is conceived inside a

---

A Motilon girl applies make-up to her nose.

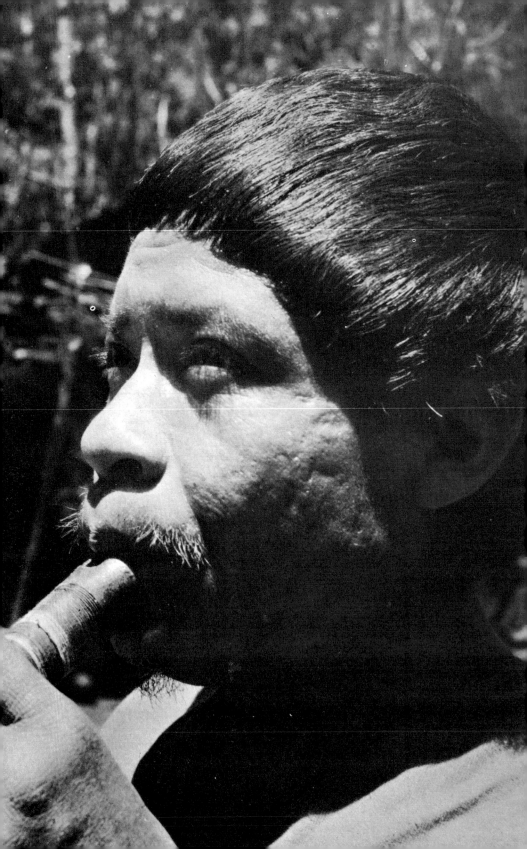

house, or in darkness, it is believed that it will be blind or at least lazy for all its life.

It was hardly surprising that our own efforts to record while we stayed in San Miguel were fraught with difficulty. The village was virtually deserted and only the men designated by the *mamas* to keep watch over us remained. All day long they followed and at night they crouched on the earth floor by us. One night, Asinto, one of the guards, hearing the recordings of the drum, arrived with two flutes. A little over two feet long, they were made from single lengths of cane. At one end was a strange beak-shaped head of beeswax melted on to the cane, and projecting from this head was a long feather quill, the reed. One flute had five holes, the other only one.

'These are *kuisi* flutes,' said Alcibiades, as we examined them. 'The one with five holes is the *embra*, signifying woman, the other is the *macho*, the male flute. The *embra* calls and the *macho* answers; the Indian playing the *macho* always waves a *maraca* in his left hand.'

The *maraca* was very different from any we had seen before. True it was made from a gourd and filled with dried fruit-seeds, but the circumference was pierced with minute holes. At first, Asinto refused to play, demanding rum or, failing this, pesos, for our beads, wool and needles were of no interest to him! We paid each flautist two pesos – Asinto had brought a companion – and they began. Asinto held the *embra* vertically in front of his body, the fingers of his two hands covering the five holes. The younger boy opposite him covered the single hole of the *macho* with the index finger of his right hand and waved the *maraca* in his left. It was a solemn, almost belligerent tune of piercing trills, ascending and descending the minor scale. Strange and haunting, it was both advanced and beautiful, and at the same time savage and primitive. As the two men played their long strands of black hair at times completely hid their faces and their bodies swayed to and fro in time to the music. The determined rhythm persisted, the notes rose and fell and the two men became apparently oblivious of all about them.

When the two flautists eventually stopped they showed little interest in hearing their music on the playback. On the contrary Asinto seemed annoyed that we had made any recordings at all. Usually the Indians begged us to replay their tunes, but not the Kogi, they believed that we were robbing them of their knowledge and that their power would be lessened. Everything the white man knew had been told to him by the Kogi's ancestors, but the meaning of their music was to remain secret. They would not talk about it and soon departed. Yet the strange trills continued to float through the cold night air. Later the flute-playing changed to singing. Their voices rose

---

A Maraca playing a flute made from the tibia bone of a missionary killed fifty years ago.

and fell like the flutes, somehow restrained and muted in an effort to sing continuously for hours on end. To recite the tribal traditions, sometimes for days and nights, is the object of every Kogi man. Physical prowess is of no significance to him, but the pursuit of wisdom and knowledge is of the utmost importance.

The lower hillsides were still streaked by slow-moving ribbons of fire; an orange glow and a crisp crackling sound filled the valley of San Miguel. Each year, just before the rains were due, the hills were burnt, yet nothing was grown on these barren slopes where only occasional cows or oxen roamed. Cultivation was confined to the river terraces and alluvial soil along the valley floors. Higher up onions and potatoes grew within stone walls encircling the mountain huts, but here, less than five thousand feet above sea level, the scene changed.

An avenue of tall mango and avocado trees went down to the river, the leaves shaded the pathway from the hot sun overhead. In a month's time, at the end of May, the fruit would be ripe and there would be avocado pears in profusion, but all would rot for the *mamas* forbade them to be eaten. Lower down were the thick green fronds of plantains, and we recalled how the guides who took us into the mountains brought no more than rock-hard dried bananas to eat on the journey. Among the plantains and also closer to the river grew sugar cane. There seemed little organization in the Kogi system of cultivation, though running among the tangled mass of cane stems were some rudimentary irrigation channels. Perhaps this was a remnant of the techniques used by their Tairona ancestors. Sugar cane and plantains had, however, like many other plants, been introduced here in more recent years. With the advance of the *colono* their agriculture was changing, often to suit the needs of the newcomer. A large sugar press stood in a cleared patch; the wooden structure supported three vertical grooved rollers and above them, projecting horizontally over the ground, was a long pole.

'They harness an ox to the pole,' Alcibiades explained, 'and then drive him round and round, putting the stems of cane between the rollers. Later they boil the juice in an iron cauldron and pour the molten sugar into wooden troughs where they wait for it to set into blocks of *panela*. We taught the Indians to do this and we buy the *panela* from them to use when we are making rum, or to sell when we take our mules down to Dibulla. The Indians with whom I do business mainly come from Santa Rosa and Santa Cruz, the villages lower down, where it is hotter and more humid, and the cane grows much faster. There the people are more friendly. Many of the families also own a house in San Miguel and a mountain hut higher up where they pasture their cattle. They sell onions and potatoes as well, but it's the sugar cane and *panela* I'm really interested in, and I repay them in rum. You know the five-gallon jerrycan you are using for paraffin ... when you leave why don't you give it to me as a present? It would be ideal for carrying rum.'

Small family groups constantly on the move would often pass through San Miguel; in front the dog, followed by an ox led by the father, the mother knitting a new *mochila* or shoulder-bag as she walked and finally a small child being dragged by the family pig on a string. They never stopped and usually tried to avoid us, as they travelled between their three levels of cultivation.

We wondered whether the Kogi had always had to struggle so hard. Looking up the hillside we could see the remnants of a vast terrace system, now overgrown and untilled like wrinkles in the grass slope.

'Yes,' Nestor exclaimed, 'it might almost be a miniature Machu Picchu. Once the hills were covered by forest but the ancient Tairona felled the trees, built these amazing earthworks and sowed maize. The Tairona and the Kogi, who are descendants of Tairona artisans, were once skilled maize cultivators and you can sometimes find huge millstones where they ground corn. Then, with the push inland of the Spaniards and the advent of the *colonos*, maize was slowly discarded and the terraces became overgrown. Now the *mamas* forbid anyone to use them, for they believe that the spirits of their ancestors live there and are displeased with the surviving members of the tribe.'

We climbed up the hill, away from the valley bottom and soon emerged on this series of uniform steps progressing one above the other in unending regularity. Each step was about three feet high and each terrace from three to ten yards wide. They were covered with grass and the original walls could barely be seen. On some were giant boulders, so large they could not have been moved by the original builders, and on one of these our three guards sat down. Silhouetted against the falling rays of sunlight – for the sun left this deep valley quite early in the afternoon – the three long-haired men methodically rubbed their gourds, looking like remote herdsmen from the high Himalaya. Occasionally they uttered a few short, sharp words to each other but they did not like us to come close to the boulder. On it was a sprinkling of white powder and at its base the remains of broken sea shells.

'This must be one of the sacred boulders where they make lime for their *poporos*,' Nestor continued. 'Each year some of the men go down to the coast, generally to a village west of here called Palomino. They fill their *mochilas* with sea shells and then bring them back into the mountains where they trade them with other members of the tribe. The shells are extremely valuable and the Kogi will walk miles so that they can exchange the shells to make lime. It's an intricate process: they weave two criss-cross meshes of esparto grass, place the shells between these mats on top of the boulder and set fire to them. The esparto burns away and only the disintegrated shells remain. They pound these to a very fine powder which is then poured into the small hole of the *poporo*.'

The three guards continued to scrutinize our movements. Occasionally one of them would dip his right hand into his *mochila* and pull out a smaller cotton bag, and from this he would take a handful of dried coca leaves. He put these straight into his mouth to form a wad in one cheek, or exchanged his handful with one of his companions. This custom was peculiar to the Kogi: whenever two men met, whether on a track or in a village, they always exchanged coca leaves as the natural form of greeting; as we might shake hands.

Near the village the path wound through rows of coca bushes which often ringed the houses. At this time of year they were covered with bright red berries and seemed much taller than the plants we had seen in the Piraparaná, though the leaves were smaller. Between the rows were shallow irrigation channels and as Nestor collected cuttings from some plants he told us that the women pluck the leaves and give them to the men who toast them inside a thick earthenware urn in the ceremonial house. Before anyone is allowed to grow coca he has to get permission from the *mama*. Coca and the *poporo* are at the centre of the Indian's life. With them he can live, without them he will die.

Nestor carefully prepared the plants he had collected. Sitting beside the black and battered medical trunk with a candle balanced precariously on one end, he leant over the stems of coca. He meticulously cut the branches so that they would fit inside lengths of plastic. Then, sealing one end by running a candle along its edge, he poured spirit alcohol into the bag to preserve the specimen and sealed the other end. With his spectacles perched on the end of his nose, the lenses steaming over from the heat of the candle, he pored intently over his notes. Only a neat goatee betrayed the suave Bogotano. Once there was a yell as the flame jumped up and singed the projecting whiskers.

As we watched him Alcibiades, in answer to our questions, explained the difference between the social and religious festivals which the Kogi held. On the one hand were secret rites when young men who reached the age of puberty were initiated to sexual intercourse with old widows, and when the *mamas* prayed to their mother deity in the land of Nabulwé. On the other hand were agricultural feasts celebrated in the large villages of San Francisco and San Miguel, when oxen were sacrificed.

'You have seen the tall poles stuck in the ground in the open space at the lower end of the village. They tie the oxen to these and then slit their throats. Some never eat the meat, others maintain the intestines are the greatest delicacy. The festival in San Francisco will probably last a week and when the drinking and dancing stops everyone goes down to the river, the men carrying their flutes; and just as the men and women never dance together, so they wash on opposite sides of the water.'

One evening we asked Alcibiades what the large circular house at the end of the village was. Earlier in the day we had managed to enter it unseen.

Inside were long benches, many fireplaces and several smaller benches placed as if it were some form of community centre or meeting-place. With only the light from the two doors, it took some minutes before the eyes were accustomed to the interior. Some of the excavations around the Sierra had revealed the foundations of temples, much like this building, used by the Tairona; one had been a hundred and fifty feet in diameter, more than twice the size of the one we visited. Perhaps this was a temple. 'It is used by the men,' said Alcibiades. 'Women are never allowed to enter it. Here in San Miguel it is used mainly as a rest-house where they weave cloth and bake coca leaves. After dark they usually retire there to chew coca and to talk. Sometimes they recite and sing. But the religious centres are up where the *mamas* live.'

From a distance the Sierra Nevada had always seemed shrouded in mist. Only once did we glimpse the range in its entirety, from the plains to the south. The clouds at the head of the valley cleared and, through the trees and across the wide plain of the Magdalena, from perhaps forty miles away we looked for fully an hour at the Sierra standing clear, almost black, as if some giant spoon had been placed in a plain of molasses, drawing it skywards. This must have been the sight which had greeted the Indians for thousands of years as they moved to and fro across the plains, perhaps migrating north-wards, but more likely moving southwards from Central America to the Andes.

Perhaps the very first people to reach the South American continent saw it and decided this would be a place to settle in. Later migrations influenced by the Maya and the Aztec came to settle around the slopes of the Sierra – only to be overwhelmed at the beginning of the sixteenth century by the new invasion from Europe. The Spaniards were in pursuit of new lands, con-versions to the Catholic faith, slaves and the gold of the Tairona, the Chibcha and the Incas of Peru.

For hundreds and perhaps thousands of years, the Sierra has acted like a magnet. Rising to nearly nineteen thousand feet from the shores of the Caribbean, it is the highest coastal mountain range in the world. Its lower slopes are forest land, changing to savannah, to rocky tundra and finally to ice and snow-capped peaks. Its tumbling snow-watered streams were a source of fish and a means of irrigating the plains lying on all sides.

It was here in the hundreds of years before the first Spaniards came that a complex culture gradually evolved, culminating in that of the Tairona. It is only these last inhabitants of the Sierra of whom we have any knowledge. Archaeology has yet to tell us of earlier peoples who lived around this mountain.

During the few weeks we were with the Kogi we were constantly re-minded of their ancestry. Unlike any of the people in the Amazon, here we felt was the remnant of something so very different. Here was a strange, withdrawn, intensely religious people who lived in the past. Everything about them and their life seemed almost as old as the forested valleys and jagged peaks about them. What was the past? Who were these people from whom they claimed descent? Why had they isolated themselves in this way high in the mountain?

In 1501 when Rodrigo de Bastidas carried out a reconnaissance for the King of Spain, he moved westwards from the bleak desert coast of the Guajira, until he saw the snow-capped Sierra Nevada. All along the coast he encountered natives and in his reports he noted the great numbers of people who lived around the lower slopes and plains of the mountain, of their large townships, their irrigated lands, and their prosperity. These people whom Don Rodrigo had seen were the Tairona.

Once, like the Indians of the Amazon, their ancestors had been nomads gathering fruit and hunting wild animals in the forest. Then perhaps, like the Tukano, they had begun to cultivate the land, cutting large areas of the jungle, sowing *yuca* and plantain and building permanent houses, appointing chieftains and fighting other tribes.

At some stage maize may have been introduced, and like the Noanamá they began to cultivate it in their riverside jungle clearings. But maize grows better on higher ground and gradually the maize cultivators turned to the highlands, and new crops were adopted. In the folds of the mountains the people thrived and increased, but land was more restricted, unlike the jungle where there had been no limit to their expansion. Soon, as with the Motilon Indians whom we were to visit later, there arose warrior chieftainships. Land being at a premium, they had learnt that to expand or even keep it they had to fight. From such a society arose a class system of chieftains, warriors and shaman-priests. By irrigating where there was no water and by terracing where the land was too steep they learnt to live on it. With the increasing population, the shortage of land and the possibility of famine, the people turned more and more to the *mamas*, and the civil power of the warlords declined. These were the people the Spaniards first saw along the coasts of the Caribbean on the slopes of the Sierra Nevada, people similar in their way of life to the Incas of Peru, and the Aztecs and Mayas of Central America to whose influence it seems they owed much. They were proud and reserved, though friendly; soon they were trading with the Spaniards. They wore cotton-weave cloaks, often encrusted with gold ornaments and precious stones. The women wore gold necklaces, bracelets, ear-rings and nose-rings. Sometimes the men were seen with beautiful feather head-dresses inlaid with gold and bronze. Their fields were well irrigated and they had learnt to work metal, bronze and gold. Stone-masons built the foundations of the houses, constructed dams, built bridges and even made paved roads. They traded with tribes further afield exchanging gold and cloth for salt and fish. In all the townships were great temples in which the high priests worshipped the sun, the moon and perhaps the spirit of Nabulwé.

At first the Spaniards were content only to trade. They established ports along the coast, in spite of pirate attacks from French, Dutch and English, among them Drake and Hawkins. The settlements expanded and conflicts arose between the Indians and the soldiers. The Spanish priests were horrified to witness the paganism of the Indians and did their utmost to change their way of life. The Indians resented this and retaliated; thus began a war which continued throughout the sixteenth century and ended only when their townships had been burnt to the ground and their priests hung or burnt. But the Spaniards who had wished to colonize the fertile land themselves soon found that it was impossible to maintain the irrigation, to keep the fields fertile or to keep the jungle back. The roads, the only means of communication, soon became unusable, and within a few years the land of the Tairona was once again abandoned to the forest.

It is difficult to conceive that the many thousands of Indians living about the Sierra were killed. What then happened to the survivors? Perhaps, like the survivors of the Incas who fled across the Andes to the headwaters of the Amazon to escape the *conquistadores*, some of the Tairona moved over the Andes, across the plains of the Llanos to the tributaries of the Amazon. There had been migrations in the past. Many of the rock carvings that we saw in the Amazon seemed to bear resemblance to those of the Andes. Could these have been carved by the emigrants as they journeyed eastwards into the rising sun, perhaps in search of another great mountain, to the mouth of the Amazon and the island of Marajo where they could go no further? The funeral urns found near this island show a marked resemblance to those of the Tairona in the Sierra Nevada.

Many of the Indians were forced to live in the new Spanish towns and settlements, as slaves to new masters. The remainder, it seems, withdrew into the folds of the Sierra Nevada and perhaps among them were many of the priests who survived the Inquisition. Of these people there remain today only three distinct groups who still maintain a semblance of the early Tairona culture: the Sanka, a group numbering less than five hundred, who are rapidly losing their way of life, living on the south-eastern slopes of the mountain; the Bintukua, still numbering more than three thousand, living along the southern slopes of the mountain; and on the northern side, less than two thousand of the Kogi, of all three groups the one which for four hundred years has remained the least affected by outside influence.

The two forces which could have been most destructive to them, the *colonos* and Christianity, have had little effect, the former because the land which the Kogi occupy and cultivate is poor even for the *mestizo*, and too far from the markets of the coast; the latter, because the Church, in spite of the chapels it established, has been able to achieve nothing: the Kogi *mamas* who can count their predecessors through tens of generations, still have supreme influence over the people.

In San Miguel nearly all the houses had heavy wooden doors secured by a chain lock. Only a few were left open and in one of these we found a great wooden chest inside which were many official papers dating back to the mid-nineteenth century. It seemed very strange to find these in this remote village, but it brought to mind the efforts made by the Government and the Church to control these mountain people, with apparently so little success. Certainly when we arrived we told Antonino that we were an official expedition, that we wished to record their music and that we had the support of the Government. He was not very impressed, if anything it seemed to make him more determined to see us leave.

'We have often in the past tried to trade with these Indians,' said Alcibiades. 'But they will have very little to do with us. Their priests keep them so isolated. The padres had been coming up here, they say, for decades. But look at it now, a deserted church and never a padre since I can remember!'

It was Alcibiades who had suggested that we should take rum with us when we visited the Kogi. This he told us was the only means of bargaining with them. For rum they would do anything for us. This we had rather doubted and we felt that as Alcibiades made and distributed his own liquor, he was perhaps just boosting his own sales. Nestor was adamant, he said no. Later, we met some Kogi who had been drinking the *colono* firewater, made from fermented sugar; they were rendered insensible by the alcohol, incoherent and barely able to stand on their feet. Then we understood Nestor's reasons. Rum could be the greatest threat to these people and the one way the authority of the *mamas* could be undermined; for the life of the Kogi necessitates an intense self-discipline. His religion is his discipline. He has a set code and ideal: 'To eat nothing but coca, to abstain totally from sexuality, never to sleep, to speak all his life of the ancestors, to sing to them, to dance and to recite; to live a good life and to return to the realm of the great mother at death.'

Such an ideal would be hard to live up to, if not impossible. In the long run it seems inevitable that he will begin to assume the mode of the Christian. The Sierra Nevada is a classic example of the stages of integration. But the *colono* spirit seemed a very short cut to disintegration.

It was undoubtedly the *mamas* who were responsible for the Kogi's inhospitality, though we rarely saw them and their orders were relayed through the local *cacique* Antonino, who persisted in asking us when we were going. So even in our enthusiasm it eventually dawned on us that, though they would never offer us violence, we would gain absolutely nothing by staying.

In the Sierra Nevada: Brian before the final climb up La Reina.

It seems that these mountain people gave up weapons a long time ago. We never saw one of any kind. Their approach to us was one of purely passive resistance. A photographer we met later, when filming the Sanka, had for some reason unknown to himself infuriated them to such a degree that they had resorted to stone throwing. It was all he could do to save himself and the camera from being badly damaged. Perhaps in our persistence on occasions in recording music we were fortunate not to suffer a similar fate. At times we felt like trespassers, everywhere about us were sacred places where we were forbidden to go. Once when we had been taking photographs of the terraces on the opposite side of the valley the guards had again become very agitated.

'You see,' Nestor told us, 'to the Kogi everything is imbued with the spiritual. Their fundamental belief is that all this land belongs to their ancestors. It is only as it were on lease to them. That is why they don't cultivate the terraces any more, it belongs to the ancestors. If they did use the terraces, they would be afraid of their wrath. The spirits of the ancestors manifest themselves everywhere, in streams, on hills or rocks like those you have seen in the terraces; in the lakes in the Sierra and even in caves, like the one that Alcibiades and I saw on our way to San Francisco.'

'But they don't believe in that sort of thing any more,' interrupted Alcibiades. 'At least that's what they tell me.'

'They must, otherwise why should they be so concerned with our presence? Why do they ask us to leave certain places? Why did the old *cacique* ask us to leave San Francisco a week ago? Why was Brian's guard so concerned when he discovered the inscribed tablets near the Cansa Maria below San Miguel, and tried to make him turn his pockets out? Why for that matter do they feel obliged to put offerings of cotton thread on the graves of the ancestors if they do not fear them, or rather fear their wrath if they don't?' Nestor was swinging in his hammock as he spoke. Lighting his pipe slowly, he replaced his glasses on his nose and looked towards us. 'You know, many people have come to see the Kogi, some just out of curiosity, others to try and christianize them; some, like yourself, Alcibiades, to trade with them, and yet others to study them. Perhaps over the centuries they have learnt to ignore all these people, to tell them nothing, to give them nothing. Perhaps in that way they believe they will be left alone. Few people have had any success with them. What have I learnt about their narcotics and stimulants? Very little. What have you learnt about their music? Nothing. They have hardly let you record any. You cannot expect to learn about them in so short a time. It takes years and great patience. One or two people have learnt something about them. Preuss knew something of their mythology. Mason, the American archaeologist, was probably one of the first to find out about their past and their Tairona

---

ABOVE: *Glacier Gap Camp*. BELOW: *Donald moves towards a crevasse.*

ancestors. But you should read Dr Reichel and ask him about the Kogi! He knows more than anyone alive. He spent many years in the Sierra Nevada.'

We sat listening far into the night.

'No,' Nestor continued, 'you can't hope to understand them. They believe in the supreme god, their mother deity. They believe in their ancestors. The taking of coca and all its implications, its representation of food, woman and memory, the power of the *mamas*, are all an integral part of their belief. Without that belief or force, they would never have lasted for four and a half centuries of European influence.'

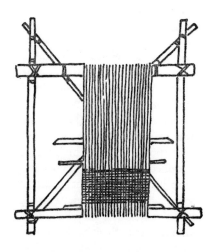

4

The South Side of the Mountain

At one time we had thought it possible to travel from the Kogi across the Sierra to the Bintukua on the southern side. Erwin Kraus, the alpinist who lived in Bogotá and had given us so much advice on the Sierra, had told us that we might be able to cross the glacier bringing oxen as high as possible on the northern side, then to carry the equipment over the ice on our backs into the valley on the far side, where we could have arranged for another team of oxen to meet us.

We had thought at the time that this sounded simple enough. It was only when we were encamped at 15,000 feet at the foot of the same glacier, its ice face disappearing far above us into the swirling mountain mists and snow, that we realized that the plan was impractical. The Kogi bearers we had taken had deserted us several days before. All around us the snow lay thick and extended far down into the valley below. The winter had really set in. We knew then that we would have enough on our hands to get across ourselves on our own two feet, without trying to bring teams of oxen up and struggle over the glacier with the heavy equipment. Reluctantly we decided that to reach the Bintukua we would have to skirt the mountain by road and mule.

If the northern side of the mountain had seemed inhospitable with its deep-forested lower regions, its bleak savannahs, sunless ravines and valleys, the southern side seemed in contrast much gentler, though even here the high savannahs were equally bleak, swept by the north-easterly trade winds, coming in from the Caribbean over the dry desert Guajira Peninsula; the valleys, however, were broader, more fertile and somehow less savage.

As everywhere on the Sierra, game was scarce. On the lower slopes there used to be agouti, peccary and even tapir. Rodents of all kinds abound, particularly squirrels in the forests, and it is still possible to see the occasional deer. We never saw a bow or a blowpipe, though the Indians sometimes had very old-fashioned shotguns. One of the first Bintukua we met carried one slung across his back, the leather strap crossing his chest like a cavalryman's.

We thought at first that they must have been Kogi. They were dressed almost identically; only their woven cotten cloaks were without sleeves and they wore a strange sort of helmet made from *fiqué* fibre. But apart from this their manner gave them away. They seemed friendlier, more willing to talk, in their guttural Spanish.

'Where are you going?'

'What do you want?'

'Where have you come from?'

We noticed that they did not ask us when we were going!

After a short discussion amongst themselves they gave us a friendly nod and moved off down the twisting path, sunk deep and brown in the side of the savannah, winding towards the wider valleys below and the *mestizo* villages bordering the Sierra.

As we climbed higher, the pack mules we had hired from one of the villages jogged along the trail in a cloud of dust behind. The sweeping savannah showed signs of erosion and from green the slopes took on the colour of a pale lateritic pink. At first we thought this must have been due to over-grazing. Perhaps in the past the Mission had kept too many cattle on the land.

'It probably started a long time ago when the Indians who used to live here in great numbers first began to cut the timber over these slopes,' suggested the *colono* who had come up with us in charge of the mules. 'Except for the heavy showers during the rainy season, it is for the most part very dry.'

Certainly it is thought that when the Tairona moved into the highest Sierra they forced the plains Indians to abandon their irrigated fields. This was caused first by the silt coming down the streams, then by the gradual drying up of the streams themselves. Once unbroken forest had extended around the mountains. By cutting it the Tairona had upset the ecological balance.

But it was only parts of the high savannah that were affected. As we moved down to the Mission of San Sebastian a wide green valley lay before us, with conifer forests along the bordering hills. On one side of the valley we caught a glimpse of the tin-roofed Mission, with its glistening white walls and heard the echo of a bell being slowly rung.

Half an hour later as we moved up the cobbled roadway and entered the inner courtyard through a big stone arch, the rain which had been threatening suddenly came down with a roar. We walked down the hallways, our boots clattering on the stones. The Mission seemed completely deserted, like a medieval castle. We passed through latched doors till finally we came to the chapel. There must have been a hundred children, all it seemed Bintukua, all singing Christian hymns. But what a strange sight! What would the Kogi have thought of such a scene!

The service over, a padre came towards us, brown-cassocked, cloth-capped and bespectacled, with a silvery beard reaching to his chest. Behind him the children passed silently, shepherded by black-robed nuns. He motioned us to sit down on the wooden benches in his office. Over the door was a vast painting of the Virgin Mary, in one corner a big radiogram, and on the wall, framed photographs of the Mission and groups of priests.

'How long has the Mission been here?'

'For several decades now, since the beginning of the century. That is, in these buildings. There was a mission here as early as 1750 but it was abandoned during the last century.'

The old father introduced us to some of the brothers: a shy wistful monk from Valencia, who had not returned to his country for twenty-five years, and a jolly, dark Guajiran Indian.

Nestor gave the old father a note of introduction. It was music we were interested in? Then we should hear the children singing in the chapel, it was beautiful. We suggested that perhaps they still played some of their own music? No, he replied, they seldom heard it. Only once during the weeks we stayed in the southern Sierra did we hear a Bintukua playing an instrument.

We stayed in San Sebastian for nearly a week. We had each been given a small, bare, whitewashed room and a steel-frame bed with a Madonna or crucifix at the head. The children spent most of the day playing in the big cobbled courtyard, while the elder girls worked with the nuns. The young men went to work in the fields in the valley below the Mission with the padres, digging or driving a tractor, their brown cassocks tucked up to the waist. One of the small Bintukua children wandered into Nestor's room one day and looked tentatively at the Kogi cotton *mochila* he had left lying on the table. He eyed it critically. Then his gaze wandered to the *poporo* lime gourd beside it.

'That is bad,' he said, pointing to it and looking accusingly at Nestor. 'It is very bad for the teeth.'

At night the big doors were barred shut. The children would go to their dormitories, and the padres would shuffle to and fro along the flagstones in their sandals. Then all would be quiet. Great mastiff-like hounds bayed as they prowled about the courtyard. We had heard that, centuries before, the Spanish used such dogs to hunt down Tairona priests because of their refusal to be baptized.

We travelled southwards from the Mission to a valley called La Caja. There we had been told by the padres we would see Bintukua Indians living in their own *fincas*. It seemed that here on the southern slopes of the mountain the Indians still presented a pattern of movement similar to that of the Kogi, spending much of their time in their lowland farms, then at certain times of the year migrating with their cattle to the higher grounds below the bare tundra and snow peaks. There, like the Kogi, they cultivated small garden plots of potatoes and onions round small stone houses. Up there, too, they still had their temples – so we were told, for we never saw them.

La Caja was shaped like a box – two thousand feet below us, tucked in the folds of the savannah, like a lush green oasis in a plain of pink. Its green hills and wooded valleys extended as far as the eye could see, surrounded on all sides by the high savannah.

As we descended the winding path, we met Bintukua moving to the higher Sierra, or to the Mission to sell plantains, sugar cane, manioc and maize. The oxen were loaded with *fiqué*-net bags strapped to the wooden frames on their backs. The women trailed behind, clutching *mochilas* and busily sewing as they climbed the steep path. Like the Kogi women they wore a long cotton mantle with great coils of cotton thread about their waists. Sometimes a child would be strapped to its mother's back by a noose across the forehead. Behind, trailing in the dusty path, were chattering children and lean black hunting dogs. Men passed us, leading a horse with a muzzle-loader slung across its back. All usually greeted us with a nod of recognition. Perhaps with our beards they thought we were visiting padres.

The Bintukua houses were like those of the Kogi. They used savannah esparto grass for thatching and made the walls from wattle. But they were square instead of round. They had learnt that a square house is much simpler to construct than a round one.

Inside the houses we never saw pottery, though there were baskets and small wooden stools. Hanging from a wall would be a sixteen-bore shot-gun and machete. A wooden rack extended across the roof. The maize was stored in the attic this formed. All around the walls were cotton and *fiqué* woven bags; some were similar to the coca bags used by the Kogi, though we seldom saw a Bintukua take coca.

Seated on the baked-earth floor of one house we came to, was a woman: beside her on a sheepskin lay a small child. Looking rather anxiously at us a tall Bintukua introduced himself as Carlos Torrés. We told him our names and soon he was beaming delightedly as we explained that we had come all the way from Britain to record the music of the Indians of the Sierra Nevada, and to collect some of their bags and many other things. At this he seemed a little puzzled.

'We want to take these things back to our country far across the sea,' we explained waving our hands expansively to indicate the great distance. 'There we want to put them in a big house, much bigger than the Mission, inside boxes made of glass, for everyone to see.'

Carlos whistled gently through his teeth, as if to show his appreciation of such an idea. Soon we had exchanged our pesos for a *fiqué* hat and some beautifully woven *mochilas*. What we would like most, we explained, was a suit of his fine clothes. At this he seemed very amused, but informed us disappointedly that this he could not do. He was, however, making a new cape and would we like to see that?

Close to the house was a small thatched and cane-walled hut standing on its own. Inside a large fixed loom went from wall to wall. Carlos sat in front of this and, raising the long stick heddle, he shot the weft with the shuttle bound with cotton from one side to the other. Then, beating down the cotton thread and reversing the order of the threads with a shed stick, he shot the shuttle back again. We noticed that some of the vertical warp strands were arranged in bands of colour. Alcibiades had told us that among the Kogi these bar patterns signified certain families or lineages. We also later noticed this use of patterns on the togas of the Motilon. Scattered about the small house were several half-made *mochilas*, and spindles surrounded with cotton and black, blue and red thread.

'The women spin the cotton,' Carlos explained. 'But we always make the cloth. Long ago we used to make our own dyes, but now we buy them from the *pueblo*. That is where we buy the cotton as well and in exchange we give them the coffee you have seen growing around the house.'

As we reached the head of the valley, the misty rain swirled down around us and we soon lost sight of La Caja. Suddenly we caught a glimpse of the snow peaks as the cloud lifted momentarily. Below lay the valley of San Sebastian. Then we realized that this must have been one of the major routes of the early Indians travelling from the plains to the higher Sierra. The Mission had been well placed.

Near the Mission there was a white-walled village which like San Miguel seemed almost deserted. There was only the office of Don Samuel and the shop belonging to his nephew who sold everything from tinned meat and porridge oats to medicines, shoes and wool, presumably to the Bintukua.

Don Samuel was the local Comisario, he had retired many years before but the Indians had requested that he should come back. He spoke their language fluently and seemed to understand them. He was the only official contact between them and the Government.

'My successor was unable to do anything with the Indians. They refused to co-operate and I had to return,' Don Samuel told us. 'They are extremely independent and very proud, and unless you try to understand them, they will do nothing for you. Of course it helps to speak their language.'

We asked him if he ever heard the Indians playing their own music. He told us that he did but very seldom. He would try to find us some who would play.

That afternoon there was a Christian burial for an Indian. It was a large gathering. Many were dressed in their traditional mantles, others wore European trousers and shirts and nearly all seemed to be drunk on *panela* rum.

That evening an old Indian brought an *embra* flute and proceeded to play it, using the thumb and first two fingers of his left hand and two fingers of the right hand to cover the five holes. The flute was very ancient and bound in many places with cotton to cover the splits. The musician managed only a few very wheezy notes. Then, stopping abruptly, he said, 'I would like five pesos for playing, and twenty pesos for the flute.' When we suggested something less, he swept out of the house without answering. That was the first and last music that we heard from the Bintukua.

We had arrived in Atanquez from San Sebastian early in the morning. The village had soon sprung to life, as people arrived for the festival of San Isidro from the surrounding *fincas* and villages, some walking, others coming in old lorries along the trackway from the plain. Now the celebrations were starting and standing on the edge of the crowd we had an opportunity not only to record music, but to see all the people who lived in this Indian-creole village.

The procession slowly moved up the dusty pathway between the rows of white-walled, thatch-roofed houses. In the centre several bearers held high a newly painted effigy of the saint. Every so often the procession stopped and a surpliced, black-bearded priest raised his arm and called out a blessing. It was a hot day and an umbrella was held to shade the padre's bald head; near by the shawled women shielded the dripping candles from the wind.

The blessing over, the padre moved forward, climbing the steep path. The effigy and procession followed. Behind, a brass band of trumpet, trombone, tuba and drums started to play a march. In front of the priest two *mestizos* walking backwards played flutes identical to those we had seen played by the Kogi only a few weeks previously. Everyone started to chatter, the flutes shrilled out, children shouted and the brass band played. Again the padre halted to call a blessing, and everyone fell silent.

The procession continued on its way through the village. Starting from the bare dusty square outside the corrugated-iron-roofed church, it had moved slowly up the stepped pathway between the straggling houses to the very fringe of the village. As the procession returned, a young choirboy in red cassock and white surplice carried a bronze cross at the head.

If San Sebastian had remained an isolated area of missionary activity among the Indians of the southern Sierra, Atanquez, once an Indian village, seemed to represent a more logical advance, the integration of the Indians with the creole peoples of the plains. For decades the Indian had been retreating further into the mountain, but it was inevitable that the advancing virile and prolific creole culture would reach them. If this is an advance which has as yet left most of the Kogi untouched, it is because in the south the terrain is easier and there is more agricultural land. This movement

Our Kogi escort.

has reached far into the Sierra, leaving the Bintukua with a few isolated refuges.

It is strange that the Indian should feel a sense of inferiority and inadequacy towards the creole, who stands perhaps as representative of the white culture. For the Indian in his approach to life, his reticence, his mystical sense and intense introversion, stands far closer in personality to the European than does the creole, who though partly of Spanish stock is to a great extent the descendant of the early immigrants from Africa. The tragedy of integration is this Indian sense of inferiority and his endeavour to become like the creole whose nature is entirely alien to his own.

In Atanquez, even though creole and Indian had intermarried for many decades, there still remained a social distinction between those who were considered descendants of the creole and those of the Indian. Perhaps here the Church acted as a levelling factor; certainly as we watched the festival there seemed to be no sign of social distinction.

There were similar festivals all round the Sierra Nevada at this time of year, at the beginning of the rainy season. The Kogi had prayed to their mother deity. In Atanquez, though the Indian descendants of the Tairona may have forgotten their goddess who lived in the eternal snow, they, like the creoles themselves, probably saw less significance in San Isidro than in the ritual itself. The beliefs might be obscure but the ritual was understandable. It was to bless the crops, to bring rain, in other words to bring prosperity to the villagers, and in this respect all were united. For a few short hours everything else was forgotten, everything centred around the newly painted effigy, shining blue in the sunlight, as it was carried high above their heads.

The procession over, the effigy was once more returned to the church beside the dusty square, and the padre went to rest after hours on his feet. Now the dancing and drinking began. For though it was the beginning of the new season, the year's coffee harvest had only just been collected and taken to be sold in the markets of Valledupar and further afield, and there was still a lot of money about. Much of this was spent on drink and new clothes for the festival, for this was an opportunity to show one's wealth with a new hat or shirt.

The music was in itself a reflection of the people. Early on the morning of our arrival we had been fortunate to record the music called *chicote*, played with instruments identical to those of the Kogi, flutes similar in construction to those once played by the Aztecs of Central America, and holed *maracas* like those used by the Maya: instruments which suggested past influences from these people on the Indians of the Sierra Nevada.

The Kogi temples of Macotama: the racks on the roof hold sacred potsherds.

Of the several rival groups of musicians, one we recorded was playing a type of music known in the coastal regions as *gaita*, only here there was a blend of Indian music with negro. The five-holed *embra* flute was played together with a pair of holed *maracas* and a drum. The emphasis on the rhythm in this music came from the *maracas* and the typical single-membrane negro drum, played between the knees with the fingers and palm of each hand. The tune was carried by the flute and the singers, several of whom took it in turns to sing in couplets, which to judge by the attention and amusement, must have concerned village affairs and personalities.

Here we found no difficulty in recording. Everyone seemed happy to sing and play and even more delighted to hear the playback. They still had their own type of music, evolved from the two cultures. That necessity of life to the village creole of the plain, the popular loud-speaker system, had not appeared. Later we saw groups of villagers dancing *chicote*: the players in the centre were encircled by men and women holding hands who moved three steps forward and one back, then turned to face their partners. This too was essentially Indian music, but we recalled how we were told that Kogi men and women never danced together.

The night came on and with it the rain. As if in answer to San Isidro, it roared down on the tin-roofed houses. But this did not stop the dancing. Once or twice we came upon more sophisticated groups playing the guitar, accordion, drums and the *guacharaca* – a grooved bamboo whose strange scrapings imitate the warning call of a tropical bird and help give the rhythm to the music.

We had been warned that we would hear a lot of music at Atanquez, but we had hardly been prepared for so much. Nor after our experiences with the Kogi and Bintukua did we expect to be allowed to record so freely. Perhaps this was due to the nature of the creole, but there were times, we had found, when he could be equally truculent. Perhaps it was the spirit of the festival. If we had come at another time, it might have been different.

Before we finally left the Sierra Nevada we returned to a village near San Sebastian which we had passed through on two previous occasions. Almost the first person we met was Otto Naeder, tall, gaunt and silver-bearded like a patriarch.

'I am too old now,' he told us as he showed us his house. 'I shall never leave. What more do I want? The savannahs, the snow peaks, the Indians who have hardly changed for a thousand years. It is a different world.

'I lived in Tanganyika once when it was German territory, I had a big plantation on the slopes of Kilimanjaro, but it was confiscated during the First World War and I lost everything when it later became a British mandate. Then I came to Colombia to settle, I built up a business; then the war came, I was interned and all my property was confiscated for the second

time. Now I have little left, so I live here with the Indians as my neighbours.

'Do you see this?' he said, indicating a delicately shaped oval pot. 'This is
very old. It belonged to the people who used to live here before the Spaniards
came. I found it at the bottom of my garden. The burial sites of these people
are everywhere in this valley, you should see one of them. Many of the
sites have been robbed of their contents as some contain gold ornaments. A
Swedish archaeologist came here once and excavated many of the urns. They
were so large he broke them into small pieces, numbering each piece in order
to ship them across to Europe where he reassembled them for several mu-
seums. Are you archaeologists?'

No, we were not, but we would be interested to see a site.

'I would take you myself, but it's too far for me now. I know a villager,
Arturo, who will take you.'

We set out the following morning with Arturo before the sun had reached
the valley. We travelled fast along the winding paths, but the sun was high
before we started to climb the fringing slopes. There on some terraces Arturo
showed us a number of small rock circles set on the level ground on the hillside, facing westwards into the setting sun.

One of them, we found, had been opened at the top by treasure hunters and
near by were the shattered remains of a large urn. We measured the urn
inside the open grave. It was nearly two and a half feet high, with a narrow
lip. Inside it we found broken pottery. This, Arturo explained, was a pot
fitted over the top of the urn to seal it and prevent the earth from getting
inside. We found several small quartz and jasper beads inside the urn but
nothing more. The grave robbers obviously knew their work. Inside these
urns the Tairona placed their dead. Perhaps these graves high above the
valley had belonged to a certain lineage or priestly family, or it may have
only been a communal graveyard. Certainly there was no distinction between
the rings of stones. The urns themselves must have been used for secondary
burial; it would have been difficult to place anything inside one but the bones
of the dead man, together with his precious possessions, his ornaments and
bead necklaces.

'There are many of these old burial sites in the Sierra,' said Arturo as we
started on our way back. 'You can see the old Indian roads as well, and near
them are drawings carved in the rock.'

When we reached the village he asked us to accept a pot he owned and
necklaces of shell. He had heard we were collecting for the British Museum
and would like to present them. This we would have been delighted to
do, but we explained that it was not possible – for the government were
understandably reluctant to allow anything of archaeological value out of the
country, so they would reside in the Museum in Bogotá instead.

'That is very beautiful,' said Naeder as he looked at the neck ornaments we had been given by Arturo. 'But I am not sure whether they are real or moulded lime imitations.' Strung together and rattled they sounded like bells, and their shape was almost identical to that of the conical metal bells found in Peru. Perhaps we had found another musical instrument?

Then we showed him the red jasper necklaces and the individual white quartz beads we had found in the urns. 'They grind the stone down to this fine texture using sand and water, and the holes are bored with hard *macana*-wood spikes. It must take weeks of work and they probably had some magical significance.' We recalled the day Brian had found inscribed tablets near the *mamas'* temple below San Miguel. These too had probably been amulets which gave the owner the right or blessing to do something, to build a house or sow a plantation.

'This pot is interesting. Compare it with my own one here, it is totally different. There were two peoples living here before the Spanish came. The Tairona lived around the Sierra Nevada and a different people lived on the plains. Of course, there were roadways and probably interchange of trade. This pot of mine I consider to be Tairona, but it is a different shape, colour and construction from yours. The valley people made rougher pottery. For instance, they did not know how to wash clay.

'There are two types of burial here as well: urn-burial you have seen, but higher in the Sierra they have found people buried in the foetal position in graves facing east – west, with pots on either side.' In the high Sierra we ourselves had found small stone cairns near the outlet of one of the Sierra lakes. Our Kogi guides had never gone near the lake; they had seemed afraid. It was then that they had disappeared, leaving us to make our own way across the rocky *paramo* to climb into the snow.

Perhaps this had been one of the lakes where the *mamas* could prolong their life by bathing in its water and where they may later have been brought for burial – to travel to the land of the Mother like all Kogi – on a path from east to west, through the nine villages, to the eternal snow and the land of Nabulwé where it was warm, where there was plenty of food and they could live close to the Mother.

As we left by mule the following morning Naeder asked us to take his Tairona pot. 'I have looked at it long enough,' he said. 'You should have it now.'

When we reached the edge of the savannah, before turning north again to the coast, we caught one last glimpse of the snow peaks. Somehow, we thought, the missionary Bintukua and the *mestizo* villagers didn't really belong to the mountain any more; they could be anywhere – but the Kogi did.

Part 4

Guajiro and Motilon

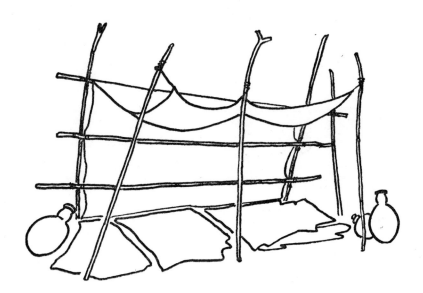

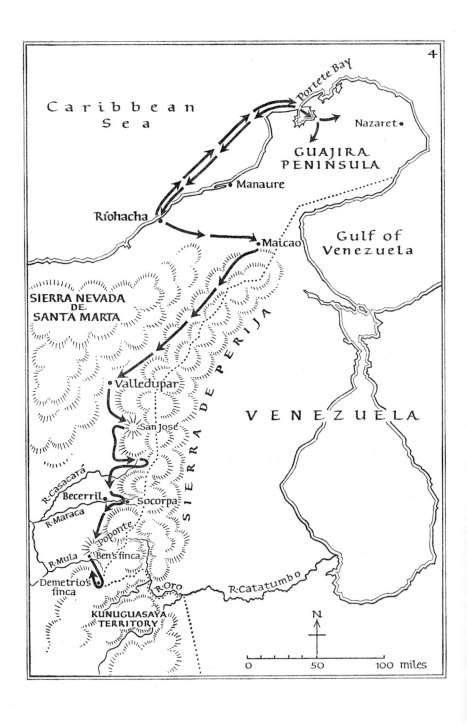

I

Peninsular and Oriental

Several times the night bus stopped by the wayside and in the half-light a saronged figure stepped on board, a string of gutted rabbits in his hand. Greeted by the jovial driver, the Guajiro would sit down, and the three of us, Nestor slumped over the seat in front, continued to bump along semi-consciously, away from the Sierra across the scrubland towards Ríohacha.

With the exception of a herd of goats it seemed that the rabbit was the only animal which prospered on this desert land. Dawn broke and the sun streamed low across the sand over the rooftops to shine on whitewashed walls at the far side of the market square. Shutters rattled upwards, traders arranged their lengths of cloth and gaudy shirts along the roadside and another day had begun in this outpost of Colombia.

At the beginning of the sixteenth century Ríohacha was one of the first settlements to be established by the Spaniards along the edge of the Caribbean. But later, perhaps owing to its isolated position and arid condition, the town declined and gave way to the strongholds of Santa Marta and Cartagena, farther west along the more lushly vegetated tropical coast. Today the town gives little inkling of its early Spanish ancestry. Sandy streets of yellow- and white-walled houses, the modern customs buildings on the waterfront, and small launches bobbing up and down on the sea give the capital of the Guajira the air of a frontier town.

The Guajira Peninsula stretches north-eastwards to form the northern arm of the Gulf of Venezuela. For three-quarters of the year, much of it, especially the north, is barren and desolate – a no-man's land – but from late September till the end of November the scene changes: the rains arrive and the desert turns green. Yet these rains can be so sudden and so severe that roads become impassable and people locked within their settlements. This remote peninsula is distinct from all other parts of Colombia.

Here were the long-robed figures of Guajiran women with bright cotton headscarves and woollen pom-poms on their sandals. The men, also with scarves, and shirts tucked inside their sarongs, looked quite different from their Colombian counterparts. It seemed as though we had left South America and floated to a point somewhere between Arabia and the Far East. Together with this atmosphere of exoticism went an air of opulence, for the inhabitants of Ríohacha were people concerned for the most part with contraband. Young men with an eye to profit had come to the town, opened stores and reaped their reward. Many were Syrians or Lebanese.

The Guajira, adjacent to Venezuela and only a short distance from the island of Aruba, a free port, had been a centre of contraband for many years. The merchants owned high-powered motor launches which either made a trip to Aruba or took their cargo of whisky, canned foods and cigarettes from coasters which anchored off-shore. Then the goods were brought to a secret rendezvous along the deserted coast and disappeared inland. Yet such transactions were small in comparison with the giant trans-shipments which occurred in the depths of the desert peninsula. Convoys of trucks, secretly loaded with coffee or cotton, had been known to pass through Ríohacha on their way northwards. Later, with the help of Guajiro tribesmen, they transferred their loads to other lorries which slipped over the frontier and vanished.

When we arrived times had begun to change. Customs authorities and secret police had been increased. Leading articles appeared in the press, the Government instructed patrol boats to keep watch on the coast and sent fighter planes to reconnoitre the frontiers and report any unusual developments. There was in fact an all-out effort to put an end to the illegal shipment of goods into and out of the country.

'Only last week Mahmud had his launch confiscated by the Aduana,' El Turco, one of the wealthiest traders, was telling us. 'He lost all his whisky and now he's in prison, so you can understand why my prices have gone up. I had hoped to go to Aruba next week but now I don't dare. The Aduana men have all been changed and I can no longer do business with them!'

El Turco's face dropped as he said this. He had originally come from Beirut, just after the war; he had first worked with a friend in Bogotá and then branched out on his own. There were no unnecessary embellishments to the interior of his whitewashed store, just a counter and shelves piled high with goods worth a fortune in any other part of the country. Everything from canned Chicken Maryland to Super-Colossal Greek Olives appeared in front of us and one end of the counter was especially devoted to a display of Scotch. We counted at least eight brands. Here they never cost more than one pound, in Bogotá they would reach five.

A stiff salt breeze blew off the water and white waves constantly beat the shore. Running into the bay was a long timber jetty; at one end a boat was moored. It appeared to be an old coaster, but the black hull and white superstructure looked new against the blue of the sky and sea. Out of curiosity we walked along the pier to where the boat – *Rigtender* – lay. The English name seemed strange, we presumed she must once have been American. From on board came the sounds of music and gaiety. A crowd of the belles of Ríohacha leant over the rails and beckoned us up; we needed no persuasion and in a moment were surrounded by bottles of gin and whisky and the lively young talent the town had produced. We were introduced to the Captain as *Fidelistas* and were in no time the best of friends.

With a smiling dark face and smart new white uniform, the good-looking Captain was everlastingly filling people's glasses, and Colombian rhythms rang out as he wended his way through the dancers.

'Why,' we asked, 'are you celebrating?'

The answer was simple: 'Whenever I come to Ríohacha we have a party. Drink costs nothing, there are plenty of pretty girls, everyone comes on board and we have lots of fun. When we recover, we sail north to pick up a load of gypsum.'

'From where?'

'We collect it from the mines at Portete, a large bay in the north-west corner of the peninsula. The whole trip takes about a week and then we carry the gypsum to cement works in Barranquilla.'

'Are there any Indians at Portete?'

'Yes, scores, they do all the loading and live in an encampment at the edge of the bay.'

Our minds wandered. Portete, a bay in the far north of the Guajira Peninsula; Indians working in gypsum mines; the whole thing seemed strange and fascinating. We asked the Captain whether he would take the three of us.

'Yes, of course, my friends, but you must get on board before ten tonight or else we'll leave without you.'

By midnight *Rigtender* was buffeting her way northwards along the coast. She was flat-bottomed and tended to roll in the swell. The Captain told us, 'She's really an old American landing craft and in the war carried five hundred soldiers at a time to the beaches of the Pacific Islands. Ten years ago I found her lying in New Orleans. We sailed her over to Barranquilla, had her converted and now she carries four hundred tons of gypsum instead.'

We wondered whether *Rigtender* ever went further afield than Colombia, and Cappy, as the good-humoured Captain soon came to be known, replied, 'Once we took a cargo of cement to Puerto Rico, we also carried timber from Buenaventura through the Panama Canal to Barranquilla, and at that time flew the Panamanian flag to avoid difficulties with the Aduana. Now we sail only to the Guajira. The owners were talking of sending *Rigtender* to Egypt to help in the scheme at the Aswan Dam, but I don't think she would survive the Atlantic.'

By dawn we had left the open sea, rounded a point of low sand cliffs and entered a huge, still, deep-blue bay. The air shimmered, and in the distance, above the yellow haze of sand, rose an isolated peak of grey and purple. Otherwise everything was flat. A flock of pelican, fishing off the point, poised in the air, then dived bolt-like into the sea with a neat splash to retrieve the fish in their fleshy beaks. They seemed so powerful and cumbersome,

compared with the terns which skimmed like swallows. We progressed towards the far shore. At first only a black rim – a narrow ribbon of mangrove
– broke the yellow white sheen of the coast. *Rigtender* dropped anchor some
hundred yards off-shore. A small encampment of poles and old sacks rose
out of the sand at the water's edge. Groups of donkeys stood nonchalantly
near the shelters, others laden with urns and driven by cloaked women
joined them, and clouds of dust blanketed the view as trucks arrived, dumped
sacks of gypsum and then returned to the shimmering desert. Our overnight
journey might well have taken us across the Atlantic to the coast of Morocco
or Algiers. The sun streamed down from a pale blue sky and as the crew
struggled to attach a line to the shore, we lazed and read in the warmth, deep
in *Lolita* and *The Devils*, while Nestor, surrounded by newspapers, enthusiastically caught up on the news. The continuous rumble of the engines
ceased, now there was a new and more persistent noise. The crew had begun
their never-ending task of scraping paint. Above the din came the ring of a
bell, and it was time for lunch with Cappy and Francisco, a beaming negro
from Buenaventura and an excellent chef – with blue beret at a Breton angle,
bulging jeans and a twitching moustache.

Soon Cappy started on his stories: 'This bay and the next one up the coast
have quite a history. You may have noticed the water is very deep and we
can come close inshore. During the war the Germans got to know about this
and they are reputed to have refuelled many submarines here. The fuel was
brought across the Guajira, from Venezuela, and then left at points along this
deserted coast. Nobody quite knows how it was done but certainly it was a
very clever idea.'

We too had heard, in Ríohacha, how one crew had been stranded when
their submarine had broken down, and how German secret agents had been
caught infiltrating into the country from the north coast.

'Now there is little excitement like that,' the Captain continued, 'but the
Guajira still retains its contraband fame. The Indians are astute people and
some of the chieftains are among the richest men in the country. The amount
of whisky that passes through their hands is anybody's guess.'

From Indians the conversation turned to politics, and here we left Nestor
to become embroiled, often for hours on end, while we returned to read and
sunbathe on deck.

There were few signs of wealth among the Guajiros who started to come
on board. A line had been fixed to the shore and two craft, one a pontoon,
the other a native canoe, were shuttling back and forth, loaded high with
gypsum. The men were of medium height, on the whole taller and certainly
tougher than other Indians we had met; dark-skinned with short-cropped
hair, broad foreheads and wide-set eyes. They wore loin-cloths and woven
belts with woollen tassels. Nearly all had shirts and many a pirate-like strip
of cotton wound about the head. Some wore rings of silver on their index

and second fingers, others a single string of black beads coiled round the neck. But on the whole their appearance was not colourful. With the dust rising from the sacks of gypsum, their bodies became caked in clay and sand. Yet the faultless white teeth and gleaming pink gums which every Guajiro possessed always came shining from behind a dirty face. They seemed happy, good-humoured workers but they were rough and it took little to excite them. The mate let a sack of gypsum fall near one of the men in the hold. Shouts came up from the bowels of the ship and lumps of gypsum were hurled to the deck. Proud and individualistic, they did not like to speak Spanish and were ashamed of the slightest physical disability. Often if we tried to take photos they threw stones at the camera and it was only possible to evade this by appealing to their sharp sense of humour.

In contrast to the roughness of the men, the women were shy and quiet, talking in soft, cooing tones. They too came out to *Rigtender.* On these occasions the canoes were filled with their red clay urns which were normally carried from the head in rough string bags. They delicately climbed on board in flowing cotton gowns, their faces covered from eyes to chin in black or burnt ochre paint like Muslim veils. The paint, made from a mixture of goat's fat, charcoal and ground fungus, protected them from the strong rays of the sun. Their black hair was straight, their wide-set oval eyes a deep brown, and their skin fairer than that of the men. Bright print headscarves, gold ear-rings, a string of black beads around the neck and orange ones on each wrist gave them a gypsy-like quality akin to nomadic people. Their faces possessed an air of dignity and authority, an air of sophistication which we had not seen in other tribes. Their sole object of coming aboard was to collect water, the most precious of all commodities in this arid land, and they used their charm to the utmost of their feminine ability. Francisco was the person most in demand, for he had a store of old tins in the galley and so received the girls' most amorous advances; though acquainted with Western civilization, they had lost little of their own primitive charm.

To these people the arrival of *Rigtender* was like manna from heaven, and during each of the five days that she stayed a continuous stream of donkeys came down to the shore, laden on either side with the globular water pots which the women then filled. Fashioned smooth and fired from red clay, they often bore a dye design of blackish purple; some had dancing figures, others a star-like pattern based on the five-pronged breathing pores of sea urchins washed up on the shore. The desert and the sea had an overriding influence on these wandering people, and it was this very aridity which gave the area its source of wealth. Gypsum, like rock salt, is an evaporation product formed when a land-locked sea is subjected to intense and constant heat. Gradually the water evaporates and first aragonite, then gypsum, and finally salt crystals take its place. These deposits of gypsum packed between thin layers of white clay beneath the sand formed the mines. They were in fact no more than areas of desert where small gangs of Guajiros under their own Indian foreman dug the rock, put it in sacks and then on to trucks to be taken to the coast. The lorries belonged to *mestizos,* and in charge of all the people working at Portete was a man called Baria. Part of the year he spent in Ríohacha; for the rest he lived in Portete with his Guajiran wife. Each day he came to the boat to supervise the work and it was through talking to Baria that we were able to learn a little about the life which these people led.

'Three boats come regularly to Portete to collect the gypsum and take it to Barranquilla,' he told us. 'The mining concessions are owned entirely by a Syrian, Señor Naser de Daez. He is a very rich man but he treats the Indians well and often comes by jeep to see them.' Baria was sitting with us at the galley table, and the answers to Nestor's questions flowed back. He was young, thin and wiry, with alert eyes and an intelligent face.

'Who discovered the gypsum?'

'The Banco de la Republica originally sent geologists to the Guajira to look for salt, but one man who came to Portete discovered the gypsum. He wanted to exploit it, but no one was interested, and later the entire concession was sold to Naser who by now must be one of the wealthiest men in Barranquilla.'

'And what about the salt?'

'That is mined further south at a place called Manaure. The Banco owns the land and from March to April the Guajiros collect the salt. Thousands of sacks are stored in vast warehouses, and later trucks distribute the salt all over the country. But the Indians can only work there for two months in the year and since the Guajiro covets wealth he goes off to look for other employment. A few are satisfied to hunt and fish, to look after their flocks of sheep and goats, but others come to Portete to dig gypsum and many cross the frontier to Venezuela. There they can work on the roads or further afield on the oil derricks in Maracaibo, and they earn *bolivares* which are worth twice as much as our pesos. They become rich, but they still continue to lead their nomadic lives.'

For four days canoe-loads of gypsum pulled out continuously to the boat. We went ashore to the encampment where the workmen lived. Here, with their own dug-out canoes dragged on to the sand in front of the shelters, they lazed in string hammocks strung between poles and beneath old sacks which protected them from offshore winds and the overhead sun. Suspended from the poles were their personal possessions, cotton gowns, bags and earthenware pots. On the ground were more sacks, a jerrycan or two, and in front of each shelter a fireplace dug into the sand. It was a makeshift gypsy-like encampment where the women, with their donkeys and children, spent more time than the men.

Once we travelled further on the back of a truck. The Guajiros were dropped at the mine where they busily set to pick-axing the shiny gypsum from the ground, but we continued across the desert over the ruts of a pot-holed track. On all sides were the yellows and browns of sand and pebbles; a thorny bush grew over this desolate waste, with a distinctive flat top to its leafless branches and a strange yellow fungus coating the twigs. At times the bushes were replaced by tall tubular cardon cactus like skyscrapers in the sand. Each branch of the cardon was a deep olive-green but its surface was covered in rows of ominous spikes. As the truck lurched forward, we often had to dodge low to avoid the thorns from overhanging globes of prickly pear. The *tuna*, as it is known, with its extraordinary mass of fleshy pro-jections, was the third of the drought-resistant plants which grew in this wilderness.

We rounded a bend and a settlement came into view. It was small: eight houses grouped in a semicircle and a clear space in front of them. All round was the tall cardon cactus, and the huts, little more than shelters, were made from its branches. The great tubes had been felled and the spikes stripped away to leave the inner wood. Cut into equal lengths these strips formed the roof, supported by one ridge pole, and a wall of cardon protected the family from the prevailing wind. Slightly apart from the huts and on the road was a square house, built from the same strips of cactus, but with four walls filled by wattle and a roof of corrugated iron. This was the local store, and here the truck driver dropped us to walk to the Indian settlement.

Few people were about, most had left with their donkeys for the coast. Outside each hut forked posts were stuck in the ground. From one of these an old man was skinning a goat. An agile figure in no more than a loincloth, he carefully nicked the skin from the legs and pulled the dappled hide from the flesh—a macabre sight as the lean corpse hung upside down above the blood-spattered sand while two dogs waited hopefully by the old man's side. He spoke no Spanish, but a boy of about fifteen ran over to us. It was his son, Kechenko, who enquired who we were and why we had come. We explained and started to talk about the goat. Did his father have many?

'Yes, he has nearly two hundred.' Kechenko replied pointing to a pen also made from odd trunks and strips of cardon. Some pigs rummaged near the roots of a cactus and there were chickens close to the house. As we neared the pen we noticed another smaller, circular enclosure, standing on its own.

'That's a *jaguey*. From September till November rain-water collects in these wells which we dig, sometimes three metres deep, and encircle with cardon. The water rarely lasts until the next rains, but recently the Govern-ment were here and dug huge holes with giant machines. There's one over there, behind that mound, and it still has water though our *jaguey* is dry.' Drought was the problem which haunted the Guajiros' lives; Kechenko's father thought it had become even drier since he was a boy. In the last few years many of his long-haired sheep and some of his goats had died; certainly the ones in the enclosure were almost like skeletons.

'But when the rain does come it really pours,' Kechenko added. 'Great stretches of desert are flooded, all the tracks become rivers and the trucks can't reach us. Then, in early December the rain stops, the sun shines and everything is green. Flowers cover the sand and we can sow corn.'

As we walked back towards the settlement we imagined an area transformed, and people no longer desperate for water. Inland, hazy blue cones of mountains rose out of the sand. Kechenko and his family had once lived in a village called Nazaret, on the far side of the range. Some Italian missionaries had settled there, built a school and taught the children Spanish. Both he and his sister Ortelia had learnt the new language but his parents had not. Then one day, when he was still a small boy, his father had a quarrel with another man whom he killed. The man's family united and threatened to take vengeance on Kechenko's father, and because their enemies were much stronger, he, his wife and children had had to flee. They left Nazaret, never to return, and Kechenko could only just remember the cool air, the rain and the smell of the lemons which grew on the hills.

'My father sometimes tells me how he hunted deer in the mountains,' he continued, as he brought down a sheath of arrows from the roof, 'small red animals standing close to the ground, which could run extremely fast. The stags had short horns and my father would lie behind a boulder overlooking their drinking pool, his two dogs beside him. We still keep two hunting dogs but it's rare that I see deer. When I do, I use this steel-pointed arrow.' He fingered the razor-edge of a six-inch blade. 'But more often I shoot rabbits with hard *macana* heads which I notch to make sure the arrow does not fall out when the rabbit tries to run off.'

Kechenko then showed us a leather guard which he strapped to the inside of his left wrist. It was for protection against the sting of the bow string; there was great power in their tightly strung bows. They shot dove and partridge with smaller arrows, while in the marshes were duck and even sea-snakes which they skinned and ate. Among the arrows was one unusual implement with three sharp wooden prongs bound to the end of a short stave.

'We use this to collect the fruit from the cardon,' Kechenko said and walked to a tall clump of cactus behind the house. He stopped in front of a murderous array of spines and reached up to a bright red fruit growing at the point of one of the tubular branches. He deftly slipped the prongs over the fruit, plucking it away from the stem; he plucked another and yet another until the prongs could hold no more. Once the red skin had been removed, the flesh tasted just like a strawberry. After the rains, water melons, marrows and beans grew outside the house, not to mention maize. There were some luxuries after all.

Kechenko's mother and his sister Ortelia now returned from the coast. Tethering their two donkeys to the posts, they unloaded the water urns, like giant Chianti bottles, and hung them from the poles by their string bags. Ortelia was shy and hid her pretty face in her hands. Her mother though old had a strong, fine aquiline nose; her face was entirely covered in black fungal paint. This was applied so thickly that she might have been masked, with thin black lines from the bridge of the nose to the forehead and thick rims over her eyebrows. She carried a baby; placing him in the string hammock with her, she started to embroider a *faja*, a new belt for her husband. She carefully separated the green and red wool, holding her hands high above her head and disentangling the strands with her long bony fingers. Then with a needle which had probably come from Ríohacha, she embroidered a bold linear design which coiled its serpentine way along the belt. Perhaps this had a symbolic significance; it would soon be wound round the old man's waist with tassels and pom-poms of wool, and a woven money bag dangling at his side.

A loud horn blast shattered the silence. It was late afternoon, the men had stopped work and the truck had arrived to carry us back to the coast. *Rig-tender* lay peacefully anchored offshore. There was excitement in the air as one of the dug-out canoes, its square sail hoisted, glided round the point to the beach. The fishermen from a nearby settlement had caught a sea turtle. As the craft beached, three men bent over the vast, almost prehistoric form, and with the help of others lifted the five-foot beast to the shore. They placed it with its shell to the sand and belly plates upwards. With a vicious swipe a fisherman decapitated the helpless turtle and the dismemberment began. The plates were ripped away and the flesh was attacked with the nerves still twitching. Portion by portion great hunks of the bloody meat were handed round and the Guajiros retired to smoke these over their fires. Even the intestines were carried away. The price was high, as this was one of the rarest animals they killed.

The dawn was grey, almost threatening, with the sun's beams piercing the clouds in shafts of yellow light. A mist hung low over the mangroves as we left the boat and walked barefoot across the open desert. We were going to record the marsh birds and try to reach the fishermen's encampment. Inland all was shrouded in haze, but already small groups of robed figures led their donkeys coastwards through the dunes. A flat expanse of sand lay ahead and coating it was a soft velvet carpet of strange brown algae, cracked and wrinkled, tortured by the heat of the sun, remnants of floods during the torrential rains, which covered the low-lying basin. Two fish hawks, with square-cut wings and forked tails, skimmed and dived over the open sea. Near the *manglé*, as the laurel-like mangrove with spidery roots is called, a pair of fan-tailed blackbirds swooped low overhead, perched on a bush and chattered furiously, then a pink-breasted dove cooed to its mate across the muddy water where we stood. Gradually the smaller birds returned, and a pair of warblers with slate-blue backs and cream-yellow bellies flitted between the bushes. The *manglé* had thick shiny leaves and the birds twittered to one another as they collected minute insects from the bark and plucked the small white flowers from the foliage.

It seemed we stood in the water for hours. A green snake zigzagged across our front. The offshore breeze arrived, the wind increased, the sun shone and the birdsong died. Skirting the green ribbon of *manglé* we continued along the coast. A single shelter rose from the sand ahead. It was deserted, only terns called from a nearby spit and a canoe lay high on the shingle. The single massive trunk had come from a river mouth, west of Dibulla. Only there did the trees grow large enough for the Guajiros to make their seaworthy craft. Thirty feet long and over three feet wide, the sides of the trunk still curved inwards, for it had not been fired. Inside lay four seven-foot paddles with long flat blades, and two poles for punting in the reeds. There were also slatted wooden traps, like pots, for lobsters and crayfish whose remains lay scattered over the sand. Tough line was wound round a wooden spool but the hooks must have been taken by the fishermen. They had left, we later discovered, long before dawn to reach a favoured haunt of the *robalo*, one of the commonest fish in the Caribbean.

Back in *Rigtender*, over a lunch of turtle stew, Baria told us about the fishermen: if a fisherman dreams that someone is going to die, he will lie in his hammock all day long, but if he dreams that he is with a woman and she accepts his embraces, then he knows he will have a good catch and will find pearls in his oysters:

'South of here, at a small village called Carrizal, there are underwater banks where the oysters breed, and in April many of them grow pearls in their shells. At this time of year the men go out to sea and dive to the banks all day long; then they return and their women string beautiful necklaces.'

The conversation changed from pearls back to dreams and Baria explained what great importance the Guajiros attached to their interpretations.

'The *piache*, the Guajiro shaman, can be a man or a woman. He interprets dreams, but his main task is to cure illnesses and this he does at a ceremony called the *chichamaya*.'

Baria paused, looked at Nestor and after a moment went on: 'An old man is very ill in a settlement which lies about an hour's journey by truck from here. They say the *piache* is going to cure him tonight, and a *chichamaya* will be celebrated. Do you want to go?'

Such luck was quite unexpected and for much of the afternoon we talked about the feasts and social customs of the Guajiros. They live in a matriarchal society where the mother is head of the family, and even the maternal uncle has more importance than the father. He makes all the marriage arrangements and no one can marry outside his or her own 'class'. Indeed there almost seems to be a caste system and a boy has to pay for his young wife in animals, according to her status. Some girls may be worth as much as one hundred cattle, fifty horses, twenty-five mules and large quantities of donkeys, goats and sheep.

'A rich man may have as many as twenty wives, for the more he has, the more he is respected,' Baria related. 'The children always belong to the mother, but if she quarrels with her husband, he can reclaim all his animals, leave her and search for another wife. Often fighting breaks out between the men over their womenfolk. There are family vendettas, clans are formed and the blood feuds may last for years, causing bitter warfare throughout parts of the peninsula. Nowadays murder can often be settled by payment, for the Indians have their own courts of law, but before there was continuous war and any Government official who tried to enter their territory was killed on sight.'

It was late afternoon and the last sacks of gypsum were brought to the shore. One of the trucks was to take us back, into the desert to the settlement where the *chichamaya* was going to be held. The sun was low as we jolted from side to side across great stretches of wind-blown quartz with a rusty shine. Occasionally a group of two or three donkeys moved off to one side of the track as we went by. Soon these family groups increased, for they too were going to the *chichamaya*; the women dressed in bright new cloaks, many with woollen pom-poms hiding their toes, the young girls in shawls. Even the donkeys were decorated with tassels and leather thongs on their harnesses.

At sunset we came to a small white house, a trading point on the road northwards. The owner was the truck driver's father. He said the celebration might be called off since that afternoon the *piache* had been displeased with the bull which was to be sacrificed. Darkness came and the wind, which had been calm all day, began to increase. Sand blew through the doorway as we talked over bottles of beer. Then, as if from many miles away, a faint drumming reached our ears.

'The *chichamaya* is beginning,' the old tradesman said. 'We must go.' Outside, dust swirled, perhaps the wind was gaining strength in readiness for one of the storms which sometimes occurred at this time of year. The intermittent drum rolls grew louder, and the path left the cactus to open out on to a wide area of sand. In the distance pin-points of fire flickered in the darkness. As we drew near, three ridge-pole shelters were silhouetted by the glow against the black horizon. Groups of figures crouched near the fires or stood in clusters next to the huts, trying to shelter themselves from the wind. Standing apart from the people and taking the full fury of the gale was a young bull tethered to a pole. It looked thin and this was the reason for the *piache*'s objections.

At first only muffled voices could be heard, then once more the drumming began, this time loud and distinct. A young man stood close to the largest fire, an oval drum slung by a thong from his right shoulder to his left side. It was similar to the tenor drum in a military band, with a skin at each end kept taut by strips of hide. He struck both the skin and the side of the drum with single emphatic strokes, but soon changed the rhythm to a rapid roll. Faster and faster his sticks vibrated against the skin, the high-pitched sound ringing out like the reports from an automatic gun. Sometimes they increased in volume, at others they died away, almost to silence. After some minutes, the single beats were played again and the man rested his hands on the side of the drum.

This was repeated several times. The clusters of people remained motionless, their donkeys tethered to the poles of the houses. The drummers changed and, to our surprise, Kechenko, wearing a broad yellow *faja* with long woollen tassels, took up the constant roll. Suddenly a man darted into the open space, skipping backwards, his feet moving rapidly in time with the music. Ten yards behind him came a girl, her golden cloak held fan-wise out from her sides. She glided over the ground just like a bird, following in his footsteps as he wove a circular course over the sand. With no apparent signal he would suddenly reverse to move anti-clockwise, and she gracefully followed his new direction. Round and round, backwards and forwards, the two figures skimmed into and out of the darkness. Their bodies appeared for an instant when close to the fires; then they were lost again in the night. For that one moment the sight was incredible, first the man with his green *faja*, tassels flying in the air, hands hanging close to his side, legs taut, the muscles like fibres as he sped backwards on his toes. Head aloof, his eyes fixed constantly on the girl whose serious yet beautiful face reflected his gaze. She flitted over the desert towards him, graceful as the flight of a hawk, like a Madonna with her blue shawl draped over her head and held out at arms' length. Her feet could not be seen, only the sound of her footsteps re-echoed on the sand to the beat of the drum. On occasions the man seemed to taunt her with a piercing yell, and the pace would quicken. Sometimes she would reply, yet they always remained apart. All of a sudden she fell crumpled to the sand. But the man did not stop, he continued his backward steps to be joined by another girl who came gliding after him from the crowd.

More and more figures came and watched, many awaiting their turn to take part in this exquisite dance, the Dance of the Fly. The men only stopped when they tired, but it was rare to see a girl complete more than four turns over the 'floor'. Their bodies and movements were unbelievably elegant and swift as they flew through the night, raising low clouds of dust to be dispersed by the wind.

'The Dance of the Fly is a courtship dance,' Kechenko told us. 'The young people always dance this during the *chichamaya*. Tonight my uncle, who is lying ill, is going to be cured by the *piache*. He will come at midnight, but you cannot stay – he will never kill the bull if a white man is near.'

This was a great disappointment, but we could count ourselves lucky to have seen the dancing before the main ceremony. We asked Kechenko what would happen and he went on, 'When he arrives he goes up to the bull, cuts its throat and drinks the blood as it dies. As he does this he summons the ancestral spirits and continues to do so, while the women smoke the meat over the fires. We eat the meat and later start to dance again. As we do this the *piache* will sit by my uncle's side till dawn, waving a *maraca* over his body and calling on the ancestors to draw the evil spirit away.'

We listened to Kechenko as the drum rolls filled the air and fires crackled merrily. The beautiful forms continued to glide by and the bull stood tethered to the post awaiting his fate, but we had to go. As we recrossed the desert the drum rolls died and the wind blew.

Next morning *Rigtender* steamed slowly away from Portete Bay. Our surprise sea interlude had come to an end and we had to return to the planned course of the expedition. A pile of letters was waiting in Ríohacha and good news greeted us. The Trustees of the British Museum had agreed to give us a grant and Niels, our Dutch cameraman, was returning to Colombia. He had left for Holland six months before, in December 1960, and now he was coming back on a Norwegian cargo boat. To our surprise he was bringing a wife. With luck the entire plan could be completed, something we had hardly dared envisage before, and in our enthusiasm we decided to anticipate at least four more months in the field. The expedition would reprovision in Maicao, a contraband town on the Venezuelan frontier, and then travel southwards to Valledupar.

Two days later the scene changed as the sun filtered over the green slopes of the Sierra de Perijá. Once more we were in a bus. Roped to the roof were crates of Argentinian corned beef, Californian prunes, Dutch cheese and Portuguese sardines, all carefully concealed in dirty old sacks. At each customs point the bus halted, the police came to search, but Nestor flourished an official letter of recommendation and we were waved on. Unfortunately he had been asked to return to the Institute in Bogotá, but we remained a few days in the heat of Valledupar, the legendary palace of the 'Queen of Gold'. Here in the plains between the two sierras, the ancient Tairona were reputed to have hoarded their gold, and the Spaniards had established one of their first inland settlements. A sleepy atmosphere pervaded the old colonial town, with its two churches, carved balconies and engraved brass plaques marking the homes of old aristocratic families. By noon the heat and the humidity increased and we became anxious to move to the Perijá and the Motilon.

2

Holes in the Thatch

Leaving Valledupar and the dusty heat of the plains behind us, we started to wend our way through the greener valleys of the foothills of the Sierra de Perijá. Rattling and banging along in the old Ford bus, our driver seemed oblivious of the sentiments of his anxious passengers, as we lurched around corners at break-neck speed. With only a cursory glance at the road ahead, he nonchalantly crashed his gears, then continued his discussion with a passenger, waving his arms over his head to express his argument. Above, the wooden luggage rack creaked and swayed. We wondered how long the ropes would hold the pile of luggage – and what would happen if they didn't. We had visions of baggage strewn along the dusty road behind, and the battered remains of precious tape-recording equipment.

Then, by good fortune, the sky began to darken. In a few minutes the rain started, at first a few drops driven before the wind, then a downpour. The bus lurched to a halt, and we hastily drew an ancient tarpaulin over the baggage and the loudly protesting hens of a fellow-passenger. We resumed our journey, but the rain continued and the road soon became a quagmire. The driver, who had by now forgotten his argument, was driving with great caution. It was all he could manage to keep the bus from sliding into the ditch or down the precipitous slope. Our equipment survived, but it seemed a very long journey to the crest of the last hill.

In the valley below lay the tin roofs of San José, a cluster of white-walled houses, stretching along the valley bottom, and scattered among the steep hillside plantations. It was one of many similar villages springing up along the fringe of the Perijá, built on what until recently had been the territory of the Motilon Indian. It served as a centre for the farmers and planters working in the surrounding hills and valleys, with its store, café-bar, local magistrate's office and church. No one owned a car, but there was a bus service two or three times a day. Loads of cabbages, avocado pears and onions would be brought down from the hills on muleback and loaded on these

---

Looking across the valley to the Kogi hillside village of San Miguel – in the foreground our three guards.

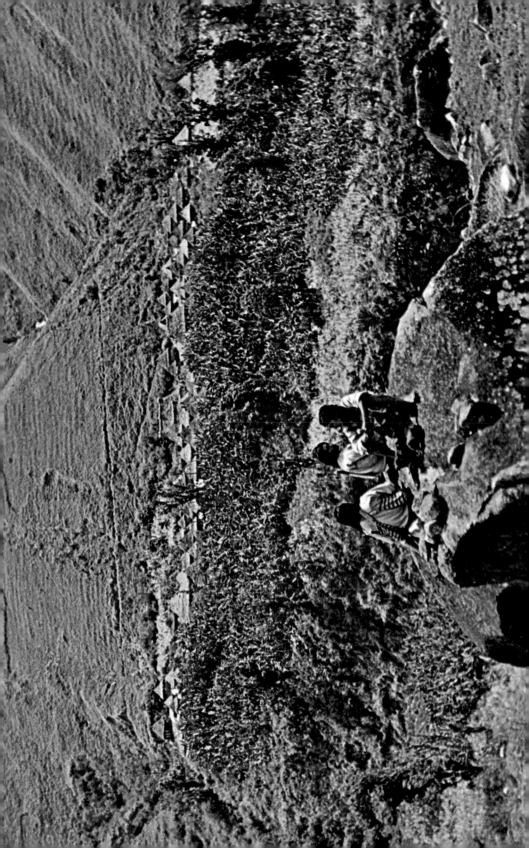

buses. This was the first stage of the long journey to the markets of Val-ledupar and far-away Barranquilla.

Among the generally peaceful and law-abiding people who lived in the community of San José, there were a few who had come here to be out of the reach of the law, men who perhaps in the past were guilty of murder, robbery, or no more than their political convictions – for this is a country where politics are taken very seriously. Many of the settlers had mixed Indian blood, and this seemed to exaggerate the more violent side of their nature. Crime in these circumstances was not infrequent. Sometimes an argument would start, or a vendetta would be remembered, and a fight would ensue. More often than not someone would end up with a knife in his back.

Life in San José was never dull and for Alec Clark – a Canadian missionary whom we had first met some months before in Bogotá when we had arranged to make the journey to the Yuco Motilon – it was a mixed blessing. Politics were something he never worried about, but his own small mission church on the hill was a thorn in the side of the Catholic pride. His feud was a religious one. Only a few days before our arrival, a visiting padre from a nearby village had accused him of withholding the rain the villagers needed so badly for their crops. For the rains were so late that year that many feared their crops were already lost. It was because they allowed this man to live amongst them, ranted the padre, that they were being punished in this way. Naturally this sort of accusation did not make life any easier for Alec; never-theless, his work continued, and certainly the following Sunday there was no noticeable decrease in his congregation.

Bespectacled, slight and intensely active, he had lived with his family for the greater part of thirty years around the Perijá both in Venezuela and Colombia. He knew perhaps more of the Motilon of the northern Perijá – the Yuco – than any other man. Though himself an intensely religious man he seemed to us less concerned with the conversion of the Indians to a parti-cular creed, than with giving them a better understanding of the change in their own lives. Towards this end he had spent years of work studying the Yuco language.

Only two days after arriving in San José we again loaded ourselves and our equipment on to a bus, and returned with Alec to the sweltering plains of the Magdalena. Continuing south along the side of the Perijá, we travelled through some of the richest cattle and cotton country of Colombia. After some fifty miles we left the main road and travelled eastwards over a rough track in a jeep. That night we slung our hammocks in the two-roomed, mud-floored hut of Ramiro, a *colono* hill farmer.

Next day, riding Ramiro's horses, we set out at dawn so as to cross the last

---

A mama, *priest of the Kogi.*

stretch of open ground and reach the shade of the forest before the sun rose overhead. The track was narrow and often precipitous. It was one which Alec had only just completed with the help of his Indians. At times the horses, less nimble than the mules following behind, stumbled and gave us anxious moments. The forest was hot and humid and we sweated profusely. All morning we climbed. We passed a gap in the forest and there ahead of us, perched on a shelf in the valley, lay a village of thatched, open-sided houses. A few moments later we were surrounded by a group of toga-clad Indians; they were the Casacará, a clan of the Yuco Motilon.

That night, for the first time since we had lived with the Tukano, we slept under the same roof as the Indians. Firelight flickered on the grass thatch, silhouetting the hanging baskets. Indians stretched on their mats, muttering in their sleep. A dog suddenly barked and several of the Indians started talking, then fell silent. Probably it had scented a puma as it passed on the far side of the valley, on a nightly foray. In the early hours of the morning a wind swept through the open-sided houses – a cold mountain wind rushing valleywards. Leaving their mats, some of the Indians huddled about the glowing embers of the fire, puffing on their pipes till dawn.

The houses, thick-thatched with mountain grass, were grouped on a small, bare, mud-caked river terrace. On one side the plantations extended sharply to the tree-line above. On the other side of the narrow strip of level ground, on the valley bottom, was the river, reached by a precipitous path. The houses, wall-less, eight of them in all, were small compared to those we had seen in the Amazon; barely twenty feet from end to end, the largest being less than fifteen feet from mud floor to ridged roof.

From the roof of each house hung clusters of baskets: large ones for carrying maize from the plantation, slung from the forehead on a *fiqué*-weave headband; smaller ones for holding raw cotton. The palm-weave sleeping mats which were spread on the floor at night were rolled during the day and placed in the roof-beams, next to the bows and arrows slung in loops from the roof.

Many of the village women had abandoned their diminutive front-cloths and their barkcloth and cotton-weave capes for print dresses. Squat, heavy-limbed, thick-lipped, fair-skinned and blackish-eyed, they were awkward when walking, yet graceful in repose. Smoking small clay-bowled pipes of exquisite fineness, the stems bound with different coloured threads, they spent much of the day threading cotton. They pulled out the raw cotton by hand and turned it on the toe or through a ring hanging from the roof. Then it was wound on a spindle-stick resting on the leg and spun between the palms of the hands. The women wove the cotton on a fixed loom and made a new toga or cape for husband or child. Some togas were plain, others decorated with red or brown bars and zigzag insignia. Made from one piece of cloth with a hole for the head and open slits for the arms, these capes extended from neck to ankle and provided excellent protection against the rain and cold mountain winds. Their length never seemed to impede the men while hunting or fishing in the forest.

These oval-faced, agile forest-dwellers, expert hunters and fighters, well adapted to their mountain forest existence, were at one time not confined to their present fastness. Descended from Carib stock, they apparently once extended far across the plains to the Lake of Maracaibo in the east, and almost to the Magdalena River in the west. With the arrival of the *conquistadores*, and with the later expansion of settlers, this once-powerful tribe numbering thousands was forced gradually back, into the foothills, then into the mountains of the Perijá. Year after year, as they were increasingly hemmed in by the *colonos*, the new-era farmers, their life had become a struggle to survive.

The word Motilon is the Spanish for short hair; these Indians keep their hair extremely short, using the sharp edge of a hunting arrow to cut it. Whether this habit resulted from an outbreak of measles at the beginning of the last century which almost decimated the tribe, when they cut their hair to lessen the risk of contagion, or whether it stems from a custom long since forgotten, is debatable.

Though all the Indians who live in the Perijá are named Motilon, there are two, possibly more, distinct groups. In the northern part of the mountain range live the Yuco and Chaké Motilon. These people are descended from Carib stock and speak that language. To the south live the Kunuguasaya. From what little is known of these people – for they are a killer tribe – they may be of Chibcha origin. Though there is some trade, intermarriage and fighting between these two main groups, they form distinct cultures. Moreover, to a great extent, the Yuco-Chaké are now considered a 'peaceful' tribe, though on occasions they still fight extremely fiercely among themselves. The Kunuguasaya, on the other hand, though once passive, are now extremely fierce and will not tolerate any incursion on their territory.[1]

Early one morning, we descended to the river and climbed through the plantations on to the ridge above the village. Although it was cold at night, the day soon became hot and we were glad to reach the shelter of the high forest and rest our packs. We climbed higher along a half-used track, sometimes cutting our way with machetes, and sliding down the banks to cross the small mountain streams.

Just as we were climbing the steep bank of one of these streams, our Indian guide, who was leading, leapt back almost knocking us all over. Only the fabric of his tattered trousers had saved him from the fangs of a fer-de-lance. There it lay coiled and waiting for the next one of us to pass, its back a line of yellow- and black-fringed diamonds, and its viper head raised aggressively.

[1] Since this was written, mission contact has been made; also two French anthropologists have been working there since 1963.

'That's a snake that will attack without provocation,' said Alec, as he hastily stepped back. 'The man is afraid to kill it, because his wife is with child. If he does, she would never be able to bear children again.'

As we would have to return this way later in the day, and as we had no wish to meet the snake again, Brian advanced cautiously and managed to kill it instantly with a blow behind the head. To a Motilon this act may have seemed strange, for Carib legend relates that the tribe is descended from the snake. Perhaps for this reason they both fear and respect them.

Further up the slope we suddenly came upon a small cluster of huts. Compared to the village we had left that morning, this collection of small, lean-to, grass-thatched shelters was very primitive. Often such small plantation hutments were used by the Motilon as a retreat when their own villages were attacked. Sometimes they used them during long spells of work in the plantations.

We had no sooner arrived than the headman came to greet us. He seemed friendly enough, though Alec warned us he was a murderer and the son of a great chieftain of the Yuco. What his real name was we never learnt. To us he gave the name of Severeeno. A powerfully built man with beetling brows and piercing black eyes, he wore a toga and a broad-brimmed hat. He invited us to sit on a mat in the shade of his shelter. He offered us a maize drink and began to speak in hesitant Spanish, waving an arm expansively, stabbing the air with his finger and rattling his hunting arrows together with his other hand. He would suddenly change into Yuco, then back to Spanish. Around him stood the men of the village, silently watching, each one clutching this bow and bundle of arrows.

We admired the magnificent sheaves of arrows strung from the roof of each shelter. Some in patterned sheaths of red dye looked as if they were of lighter construction and had colourful bindings. We learnt later that these were made on occasions by the Indians to trade in Codazzi as exchange for cloth or beads. Many of them were bought by the Mission and sent back to Spain as curios.

'But these ones,' said Severeeno, handling a magnificent set of long arrows, some with metal blades, others with long barbed points of a hard blackish palm wood, 'these are the arrows we use to hunt puma, deer and the wild pig – and sometimes to kill men.'

Near us, seated on the earth floor of his shelter, an old Indian was pounding a piece of metal from a machete between two stones, beating it flat so that he could shape it into an arrow head. As we watched he began to cut the metal into a heart-shape with a metal wedge. He notched the arrow head at

---

ABOVE: *A Kogi settles himself comfortably to make a hat.* BELOW: *A Bintukua at his loom weaving a cape.*

one end and carefully drilled a hole below the notch. As we waited he sharpened the blades to a razor's edge, filing till the surface shone like stainless steel. With infinite care he inserted the finished metal head in the white slit foreshaft, a shaft of cane already straightened with his hands and teeth, and in the heat of the fire. He tested it for balance, weight and straightness, for on these the accuracy of the arrow in flight depends. If the arrow missed the target, he might only lose a meal, but at the worst he might lose his life.

The old man deftly ran a blackened cotton thread through the hole in the metal head, looping it back on to the foreshaft, crossing it, recrossing it, and looping it again. Completely absorbed, he inserted the foreshaft into the heavier hollowed-cane shaft. In his hand he held a ball of *bréo*, a compound of beeswax and the bitter ash of the calabash, an insecticide and preservative all in one. Rubbing this on the cotton, he revolved the arrow in one hand and wound the taut cotton with the other, carefully working a cross-diamond pattern along a section of the shaft.

'This pattern symbolizes the poisonous viper,' commented Alec. 'The circular design, seen more often on the arrows of the Kunuguasaya, depicts the deadly coral snake. Perhaps in this way they hope to increase the power of the weapon.'

The patterns were varied in design and colour. Black, red and plain white cotton is used to make the crosses, chevrons, zigzags and diamonds. It has been suggested that these represent clan or family insignia, like the marks on the feathered arrows of certain Amazonian tribes.

The arrow is the most treasured object a Motilon possesses. Even the children make miniature bird arrows and hunt for days in the forest with a diminutive bow of slit palm. The special fighting arrows never leave the Indian's side. Walking, eating or sleeping, he always has them within reach, for he never knows when he may see an animal or expect a sudden attack.

In the forests of the Perijá game is diverse, but not plentiful. Bands of monkeys roam through the high trees. The long-drawn moan of the brown howler could be heard from a great distance. Sometimes we saw smaller monkeys kept as pets, especially by elderly women, who treated them as if they were their own children.

Squirrels are seldom seen. Of birds the wild turkey is the most sought after. They weigh up to fifteen pounds and provide excellent food. Wild pigs roam the forest and the high grassland, as does the puma, with which the Motilon is constantly at war. Given the opportunity, it will take the village dogs, the tame turkey and the chickens.

ABOVE: *The great south gate of San Miguel.* BELOW: *Nestor Uscátegui preparing narcotic specimens.*

In the foothills of the Sierra the small plains deer are fairly abundant, while higher lives a red deer, the size of a mule, with a shaggy coat.

'The Casacará Yuco eat a type of fern grass, which has a V-shaped stem like the antlers of a stag,' Alec told us. 'They eat it before they go hunting, believing that it will bring them luck. Sometimes they roast the legs of a pink-footed wood pigeon. They then rub the claw on either side of the nose and under the eyes, believing that by doing this they will have a surer eye to shoot the next one.'

The Motilon hunts for birds alone. Often as we walked through the forest we saw small leaf-shelters built high in the branches. Usually they would be near some tree with fruit or berries which attracted the birds. Sometimes an Indian remained for hours on end crouched in one of these, waiting for a bird to approach close enough for him to shoot.

Many of the birds Indians want for their feathers; the yellow parrot, black turkey and the toucan for its belly feathers. These he fashions into a colourful hat which he may wear at the 'Feast of the Dead'. He uses one of his light bird arrows to catch them, with a blunt head of beeswax or a piece of maize cob. This only stuns the bird and does not damage the feathers.

To hunt the heavy turkey the Indian uses a metal-pointed arrow, whereas for a pigeon he uses a hard-barbed, *macana*-wood point with eight fan-shaped subsidiary points. This is designed so that if the main point misses the target, the others are certain to pierce the bird.

When the Indians hunt bigger game they travel in groups of two or more. They may be away as long as a week at a time, especially when the First Fruit or the Corn Festival is due. They never seem to take dogs with them when hunting. Yet there are always several in each village, probably kept more as watch-dogs than pets. Certainly some we met could be vicious – as we found to our cost.

On the eastern slopes of the Perijá the rains continue more or less throughout the year, and the streams and rivers running into the Lake of Maracaibo are seldom dry. On the steeper western slopes, the high streams often dry up during the rainless months. When the rain does come the water cascades down the steep stream beds, through the valley bottoms and into the meandering Magdalena, as if it cannot get there fast enough. For the Motilon who live in this region, this means that the fishing season is a short one. Even then it adds little to their diet. To catch the fish the Motilon uses the seeds of a type of plant similar to the lupin, which he pulps and places in the water upstream of a small dam. The fish are poisoned almost instantly and float towards the dam where they are scooped out of the water with baskets. When the water is low, the fisherman sometimes drains a pool to catch stranded fish.

But more often he fishes with his bow and a light two- or three-pronged arrow. He positions himself on a rock in the river, or on a fallen tree trunk spanning it. If he can stand directly over the fish in the water, there is less refraction and he can be surer of his mark.

The Indian has evolved a different design of arrow for almost every type of animal, even for certain birds. Some are long and thin: the metal-bladed head of one was fourteen inches long, and would have been made for puma. They kill monkeys with smaller heart-shaped arrows. Others with a harpoon-type, detachable head, they may use on squirrels and pigs. These are designed in such a way that, as the wounded animal rushes through the undergrowth, the head of the arrow remains buried in the flesh. But the shaft, attached by a string, catches on the branches, and impedes it, so that it cannot easily evade its pursuers.

Of all the hundreds of arrows we saw, virtually no two were identical. If the design was similar, then the binding was different. Perhaps the most perfectly made and the sleekest of all, are the notched *macana*-headed arrows. The barbed point alone is upwards of two feet long – or the breadth of a man from shoulder to shoulder. These arrows released from their powerful black *macana* bows are those which have always been found in the bodies of planters, oil engineers and adventurers, who have had the misfortune to fall into a Kunuguasaya ambush.

We bade farewell to Severeeno later that day. He seemed almost sorry to see us go. One wondered what might have been the outcome of such a meeting under different and less friendly circumstances.

When we moved off up the hill we seemed to have half the village as an escort, trailing along behind us in their long togas, each man clutching his sheaf of arrows. We climbed higher and, leaving the forested valley, followed a path across a wide ridge of grassland. Below us lay the valley which we had left that morning. In front lay the wide sweep of the Sierra, the high tableland stretching to the border of Venezuela.

It had been our original intention to travel to the Irapa, a group of the Chaké Motilon, in the headwaters of the Venezuelan eastern slopes. We had heard that they were an intensely musical people, singing war songs and walking songs in chorus. The distance was great and, especially at this time of year with the arrival of the rains, the journey might be difficult. Moreover, there was the question of carrying our recording equipment, and the risk of damage was considerable. But the Casacará themselves made the final decision, for they would not even entertain the thought of going. Only recently they had been fighting with the Pshikakao who were friendly with the Irapa. They knew that if they passed through their territory, they would exact revenge for the twenty or more men who had been killed in the last ambush.

The sun was directly overhead and we were glad of the opportunity to rest as we topped the ridge. We listened to the villagers, who had followed us, talking amongst themselves. One of them wished to show us something. Following him to a spot of high ground, we found some old charred house posts. In the centre of the ring of stumps was a small trench, no more than five feet long and perhaps three feet deep.

'This is a temporary grave,' Alec began. 'The Motilon believes in the existence of a soul or spirit. When a man dies, his spirit remains near the body until the burial rites are completed; only then can it depart . . .'

Just at that moment there was a cough in the grass near by. The Motilon with us instantly rushed forward, drawing their bows as they moved. Fast as the Indians were, the puma was faster. With a bound he was out of range, and soon lost in the tall grass above the valley.

The Indians had moved with extraordinary speed, positioning themselves, their arrows ready to shoot, before we even realized what was happening. No wonder even a well-armed man stood little chance against these people in an ambush.

Many of our days with the Casacará we spent moving from one village to the next. Wherever we went, on arrival we would be given a maize drink from a gourd or bananas and a weave mat to sit on. It was difficult to say how well the Indians would have received us had Alec not been there. For many years now they had become accustomed to his visits, and if puzzled by his interest in their lives, they seemed happy to welcome him.

Crossing some high ground one day we had a magnificent view of the mountains along the border, with a sweep of wide valley lying almost at our feet.

'That is where I used to have my house.' Alec indicated a place high on the far side of the valley, remote and almost treeless. 'We lived there for several years with the children, seldom going away. There was no need to, for we could live off the land, and what provisions we needed we would bring in by mule.'

Some of the villages were surrounded by fortifications. One village we came to had a palisade eight to ten feet high running around the whole settlement, even enclosing part of a plantation. The palisade served a dual purpose. In the first place it protected the dogs and the livestock from the ravages of the puma. In the second place it was a defence against Indian marauders. In the case of an emergency, the villagers would quickly close the two or three entrance gates, and, firing their arrows between the wattles of the barricade, they were prepared to withstand a siege. Often the marauders would be a local group of Indians, but sometimes the Kunuguasaya would come into Yuco territory. Ostensibly they would come to exchange maize, cotton and metal for arrowheads, but they would also be looking for wives. The outcome would usually be a fight.

It was while we were staying in this village that Marty, an old chieftain, told us some of the customs of his tribe. A young man goes to live with the family of his prospective bride, working in the plantation under the surveillance of her father until she reaches the age of puberty. Then the two are married during a feast which may last for four days. The young man continues to work on his father-in-law's plantation until he builds his own house.

On one occasion we unearthed potsherds from a nearby cultivation plot. We spent a day searching in vain for a great rock carving of a frog. We also heard of a cave high in the mountains where there were many potsherds and the bones of many dead. Marty attributed all these things to the Manapsa, the people who lived in these hills before the Casacará.

One evening the old chief began to talk of the early days and the origins of his people. He told us some of the legends which had been passed down from generation to generation.

'In the beginning, long, long ago, Papsh, the father of all, married a toad and from her twins were born. These became the twin stars seen for six months of the year. No sooner were they born than their grandmother, also a toad, tried to eat the twins. The twins in retaliation tied her up, and passing a rope about her neck forced her to exhale fire, for she possessed the first fire. But no sooner did they release her than she swallowed it again. So once more the twins made her vomit the fire and this time they threw it on to the trees. Since that time there has always been fire.

'One day the jaguar – the wife of the stag and mother of the puma – killed the twin's mother and ate her. When the twins heard this they were very angry and resolved to take their revenge. They broke the supporting fork of a tree bridge (this according to the legend was the Milky Way, a bridge of stars which was originally formed by spray when the crab threw a red-hot stone into the water). As the jaguar walked over the bridge, it gave way and she fell into the water. The twins who had been waiting in ambush wounded her with their arrows. An opossum and a skunk then took up the chase with the twins, following her until she was overcome by the smell and her wounds. So long ago the jaguar died and the twins had their revenge.'

Alec had heard the legends before, and he had little difficulty in translating them as old Marty talked on. He told us no less than twelve legends that night. Many were repetitive and he would say a phrase over two or three times, perhaps to put a more subtle meaning to it, or to imply the great time since these events were enacted. A few of the stories were difficult to understand, they were disjointed and seemed to have no reason. Others like the story of the vulture had a touch of humour.

'Once there was a vulture who found the first manioc. He kept his discovery a secret between himself and his daughter. But the day came when his daughter married and she, knowing the secret, told her husband where the manioc was hidden. In this way man first came to know about manioc.

When the vulture heard this he was greatly distressed. So vexed was he that he almost scalped himself while preening his feathers with a lice comb, and he has remained bald to the present day.'

In another legend Marty told how the Ataposh, his forebears, had defeated a people who used iron arrow heads. From these people they learnt how to beat the iron, shape it and bind it on to their own arrows.

As the last of the daylight faded, there was a brilliant flash of lightning. A long rumble of thunder echoed down the valley. Hens and turkeys, dogs and children standing outside, all rushed for shelter as the rain came pouring down on to the thatch roof above us.

Old Marty went on. This time it was the story of a great flood, a legend which, though told in many different ways, seems to be common to many Indian tribes.

'There was a dual god who lived long ago called the "water drinker". This god took the form of two rivers who swallowed all water. Once the dual god was drinking and a tree lodged in his throat, and the water could not pass. Gradually the water began to rise . . . . Many were drowned, but some survived. The survivors were the ancestors of the tribe.' Perhaps this legend dated from the time when the Caribs inhabited the plains of the Magdalena or Maracaibo, where flooding was not unusual.

Marty continued all that evening and well into the night. As an old chief his authority had lessened with the years. For the Casacará were no longer a powerful tribe as they were in his younger days. He had been nominated a chief by the tribal council, for his father had also been a chieftain; this was the usual Casacará custom. But in some of the tribes contending claimants for office would fight with the sharp sides of their bows, striking each other on the head, parrying blow for blow until one, his head gashed with bloody cuts, would be forced to give in – or die.

Many days had now passed since we had first come to the Casacará. Alec felt that he had to return to his work in San José, whilst we planned to journey southwards again to visit a clan of the Yuco Motilon who lived on the borders of Kunuguasaya territory.

We set off down through forest-clad valleys to the plain below. The sky suddenly darkened overhead, and as the rain started we hurriedly took shelter in an abandoned village site close to the path. One of the houses was still standing, though there were gaping holes in the grass thatch, holes which the rain now poured through, forming puddles on the dusty floor.

Along one wall was the rack on which the sleeping mats and the baskets would have been placed. Hanging from a beam was an old basket and inside it a few black turkey feathers – perhaps the remains of a once proud head-dress. We wondered who had lived in this house and who had owned the black feathers. When he had died, what had been the burial rites – before his spirit had been free to go to the wind and the ancestors?

3

Kippered Corpses

Ever since we had seen the Casacará grave above Severeeno's village and Marty had spoken about the Manapsa and their tribal burial grounds high in the hills, we had been intrigued by the question of death amongst the Motilon. Alec had told us how they mummify the bodies of their dead and how they hold, not only burial, but exhumation ceremonies. However, little more had come to light. We had decided to visit the Maraca, another clan of the Yuco Motilon, living in the headwaters of a river by the same name. Recently a Catholic missionary had moved eastwards to live among this still relatively warlike group in the village of Socorpa. It was here we planned to record more of the music of the Motilon, and now hoped we might learn how they buried their dead.

Pedro, our new muleteer, took us across the savannah and into the foot-hills, to a ranch where his family lived. His mules were sturdy beasts, much stronger but also more excitable than any we had seen, and as he loaded them he threw his thin cotton *ruana* over their heads. The sun was high when we reached the open thatched house. As we sat biting great chunks of juicy red water-melon, we heard how they had left Bogotá some two years before, after a family feud, and for the time being could not return. We could not stay talking if we were to reach the Maraca on the same day, so we hurriedly exchanged the loads on to smaller mules and continued with Pedro's younger brother, José. Always climbing, through forest or beside tall, green maize plantations, we clung to the backs of the mules as they picked their way along the stony track. The air became cooler higher up, tall trees gave way to dense scrub and occasionally through this scrub a view stretched back to the haze and flatness of the savannah. Darkness came and we passed through a maze of overhanging boughs and creepers. Quite abruptly, we left this trackless tunnel and emerged on to a wide plateau. Overhead the clouds raced by, lit by a fleeting moon. The wind blew, tall grass shone white in the moonlight and huge boulders loomed like sentinels. Far beneath us little pinpoints of fire glowed in the blackness. 'That is Socorpa,' said José.

Descending the steep slope, the mules cautiously put one foot in front of the other, often sliding forwards on the loose stones. The fires drew closer, a dog began to bark, he was followed by others and in a moment the whole valley was alive with echoes. We crossed a small river, one of the headwaters of the Río Maraca. Ahead were houses, some no more than lean-to shelters. A band of toga-clad, gnome-like figures ran out to look at the mules as we passed by. José called to them in words we did not understand. From our brief glance they seemed like an army of Lilliputians, so small were they by comparison with ourselves. In front an unfinished timber hut rose out of the darkness. As we dismounted a fair-haired good-looking man in a silk dressing-gown and a goatee beard came to the doorway, shielding a candle from the wind.

As far away as the Sierra Nevada we had heard of Padre Atanasio. He had first worked with the Bintukua and only recently moved to the Motilon. He had the reputation of being the most zealous of the Catholic missionaries, and, although they were rivals, even Alec had good words to say for his work of conversion amongst the Indians.

Outwardly he had an air of *bonhomie* and, unusually for a priest, he spent most of the day in ordinary clothes. Perhaps because of this we felt more at ease with him than might otherwise have been possible. On one occasion he joined us for a long walk, all the while talking vivaciously a Valencian Spanish which flowed so fast that at times it was unintelligible. He frequently suggested that we should join him on an expedition into the territory of the Kunuguasaya. Our presence may have been a form of release for him and the endless talk a break from the discipline of his own life. No matter how we felt about the ultimate object of his work, we could not help liking him, and he in turn was pleased that we should visit the Indians.

On the occasions we saw him with the Maraca his manner was always gentle and they in turn were willing to do what he asked of them, which seemed little enough. During the days we stayed at Socorpa we never witnessed any form of service or religious teaching, although some of the villagers had learnt a few rudimentary words of Spanish. If any fighting broke out he acted both as an arbitrator and doctor to the wounded. We noticed that several of the villagers had small bags of imported maize flour in their houses, distributed by an American welfare organization, and given to them by the Mission. Why it should have been necessary to subsidize their food remained a mystery. It is possible that a gathering of so many Indians around the Mission created a land problem, forcing them to rely increasingly on the Mission. A course which, though meant in good faith, could lead to the economic disruption of their lives.

The Maraca people are striking because they are so small. Unlike any other tribe we had seen, they could be called pygmies. Their dwarfed bodies

---

ABOVE: *Takina, sacred village of the* mamas *with its temples.* BELOW: *Brian talks with the Kogi.*

barely rose to our chests. They have large heads, short-cropped hair, oval brown eyes and round faces. Their tiny arms and legs end in stubby hands and feet, their knees often seem to splay outwards and their stomachs, especially those of the women, are large and distended. Their gait is clumsy. Even their chickens were malformed, with shrunken legs, and we began to wonder whether we were living in a world of imagination. What is the reason for such extraordinary stature? Perhaps it is the result of chance mutation and inbreeding in this one group, or a lack of protein. Yet these cloaked excitable gnomes are friendly and jovial. They talk in slow linked monosyllables, each word emphasized by a sharp consonant. It is a musical language.

Like the Casacará the Maraca live in small huts and shelters near the edge of their plantations. For some days we walked among them, noting our observations. They did not seem to mind, they even showed great interest, peering over Donald as he drew their houses and looking in amazement through the camera viewer when we took photographs. One day a taller man came up to us and asked, in Spanish, whether we could give him some red cotton to bind a new arrow. It was a surprise to hear Spanish. Karkamo, for this was his name, said that he used to live in another village closer to the savannah and had learnt the language when he went to trade his arrows in Becerril. Later he had worked for a frontier farmer but did not like it and so had returned to Socorpa.

He seemed very different from his fellow-villagers. He was about our own height and had a fine physique. Unlike the rather shy and uncertain villagers, he was proud and treated us as equals. In a way he reminded us of a younger Severeeno. It is possible that he was not a Yuco at all but a Kunuguasaya. This might explain why he lived separately from the villagers. He had often been involved in bow fights, in which he was known to have killed several men, including his own father. To us he was always polite, answering whatever questions we cared to put to him, and offering us the shade of his lean-to shelter and his mat, rather than letting us stand outside in the heat of the sun. He soon became invaluable as an interpreter.

We climbed up the steep valley past bananas growing along the river bed, past maize rising high above our heads, and reached the tableland of grass and cactus. The forest in the valley beneath was broken by the green patches of the cultivation plots. During the dry season, from December to March, the trees are cut down and, just before the rains, are burnt by the men. Pointing across the plateau, Karkamo outlined an area which he and his brother had cleared the year before, where their two families had planted maize and bananas.

The festival procession of San Isidro, Atanquez.

We walked through the grass towards Karkamo's plantation on the far side of a smaller valley. On the near side the ground was also cleared and planted with a patchwork of different plants. Bushes of small Indian beans were near the crest; the slope descended in ridges covered with the creeping leaves of a root similar to the sweet potato; these changed to manioc which grew in profusion. Large elephantine leaves spread across the track, the leaves of *malanga*, another root which the Indians eat. Karkamo stopped, cut some roots and put them together with the leaves into the basket, and we continued to a small hut among banana palms and tall *papaya* trees.

The Motilon do not store maize or root crops in their houses, through fear of fire, but erect special huts in or near the plantation. Inside, raised off the ground and walled in with a mesh of banana leaves or bark, is a crib where the maize is stored.

'This,' said Karkamo, picking out a white cob, 'is *wortrepa*, the strongest maize we grow. Only men can plant this white seed, women would bring a bad harvest. We prod holes in the hillside with long wooden staves and drop the seeds inside.' He showed us cobs ranging in colour from yellow to black through slate-blue and a lovely chestnut. Each was different, and each had a special area on the hillside where it could be planted according to its strength. In this way, with the wind and the wild bees carrying the pollen downhill, they preserved their different types of Indian corn.

When the maize is ripening in July, wild deer, monkeys, squirrels and birds raid the plantations; the Indians erect hides in the trees where they wait patiently with their bows and arrows. In addition, a small insect bores into the cob, leaving a white powder behind instead of the corn, so that much of the crop is ruined whilst it lies in store. The only method of insecticide is to smoke the cobs over the fire. As he filled his basket, Karkamo told us that they always took maize with them when they went on long journeys to visit other peoples: 'Thus we show we have come as friends and not to fight.' He put the basket on his back and we returned to the village.

Once home he gave the maize to Ishishik, his plump young wife, who, with her baby still tied to her back, started to grind the grains between two stones. He put two *papayas*, long marrow-like fruit, in the ashes of the fire and arranged the *malanga* leaves on sticks to smoke over the embers. Ishishik scraped the *malanga* as we would potatoes. Such a mixture of maize, roots, baked fruit and smoked leaves constituted their midday meal. The Maraca eat three times a day, but while we stayed with them we rarely saw meat being eaten; it seemed animals were scarce. Maize is their staple food and they believe that it originated from Mishk, the god of Indian corn. He visited the tribe only once, during a thunderstorm, and when he came he appeared as a giant whose hair was a tangled mass of coloured cobs and whose nails were beans. He taught the people how to sow the seeds, and told them that they must never bake the cobs, or their mouths would be twisted permanently to the right. He then left in another burst of thunder. Many Indians believe that they can prevent a storm from reaching their houses by waving fire-brands in the air, thereby keeping Mishk within his own kingdom.

Underneath the eave of the house, behind a long string of tobacco leaves, were two intriguing objects. Karkamo brought one down: 'We play this during the feast of *wortrepa* after we have brought the first maize into the village.' It was a very curious musical instrument, a kind of flute. The head, fashioned entirely from beeswax, was in the shape of an axe, and projecting from the blade was a tiny bird's quill reed. This was moulded on to a hollow stave of light wood, the same wood as the Tukano had used to make their dancing-staves. He took the flute to the fire and poured water down the reed. Then, warming the wax, he moulded the head more securely to the wooden shaft.

Sitting cross-legged near the fire, Karkamo put the quill to his mouth. With the flute running diagonally across his body, he positioned the thumb and first finger of his left hand over the first two stops, covering the second two with the index and second finger of his right hand. It was an awkward position and, to begin with, nothing more than air escaped. Slowly a deep note came, then he obtained five different tones. It was a strong penetrating noise, rather like the deep notes of a bassoon. Indeed, with his air of concentration, Karkamo looked much like a member of a tribal orchestra.

He explained how they went into the forest to collect wild bees' nests, climbing up trees with smoking firebrands; the honey they kept in gourds, the wax they melted to make flutes and coat their arrow thread. Ishishik came and sat next to him. In her hands she held what appeared to be a small children's bow. To our surprise she put one end of the bow in her mouth and, keeping her left arm outstretched to hold the other end, she drew a slither of wood backwards and forwards across the *fiqué* string. The faint whining sound altered as she moved her lips. It was a musical bow and the sounds were in imitation of the frogs they heard when they went down to the savannah near Becerril.

To record their music was no problem, for the Motilon have a keen sense of humour. Once they had heard their own voices and laughed at themselves, they soon became enthralled with the tape recorder. The most striking of their dances was also connected with the First Fruits Festival, the feast of *wortrepa*. The men brought the cobs into the village in baskets on their backs, their heads bent low to the ground. At first they moved slowly round in a circle, suddenly the headman emitted a short high scream and was followed by all the other men uttering the same cry in answer. Soon the whole valley resounded with the cries and the women joined the circle, each one placing her hands on a man's shoulders, and always looking to the ground. They did not scream, but in unison uttered low shivering ululations. One of the loveliest tunes was that of the toucan bird, played on two panpipes; on one the Indian calls, on the other the toucan replies. The descending notes were similar to a tune we had heard in the Amazon, but the panpipes were different: the five pipes diminished in size towards the centre rather than to one end, and they were smaller. Some panpipes were even made from birds' quills, minute in size, with a sound as piercing as a whistle. Most beautiful of all are the songs they sing when they go to their plantations, out hunting or to war. First the men whistle the tune, then they break into a hum which grows louder until it becomes a part-song, often in harmony. They tell how they are going a long way to a place they have never seen before, how they may encounter wild pig on the track or monkeys high in the trees. The women sing as well, in soft melodious voices, sometimes accompanying the men, more often to lull their children to sleep.

One night, after hours of recording, we were suddenly awoken by shouts outside in the darkness. All around the hut were excited figures brandishing their arrows and twanging their bow strings; it seemed that at any moment the razor-sharp points might fly through the air. An old man, Ikoshmo, was brought to Padre Atanasio, with a gaping wound in his head. Blood poured to the ground, but little sympathy was shown towards him and he himself hardly seemed perturbed as he smoked his pipe amidst the pool of blood. He had been struck with the edge of a *macana*-wood bow. This is how they settle their arguments, often fighting till one is killed. The padre bathed the wound with alcohol, Ikoshmo's young grand-daughter cried at his side and the villagers continued to twang their bows and mutter.

Next morning all the Indians assembled, fully armed. Karkamo was not there; he and Ishishik were in their house, painting their faces red with *bija* mixed with wild bees' honey which makes the paint stick to the skin. Karkamo put triangles on either cheek, outlining them with black lines from a burnt calabash which he had ground. Ishishik only put a large red blob on her cheeks and then dotted the side of each nostril and the bridge of her nose with immense care. We noticed that Karkamo's bow was stained with blood. He explained, 'Ikoshmo came here last night and took two baskets. I went down to his house and fought him but could not kill him.' Now they were painting their faces in readiness for battle.

For two days it seemed that fighting might break out between the rival families. Ikoshmo, his head still clotted with blood, demonstrated to every passer-by how Karkamo had beaten his skull. His hair matted, his toga stained, he grunted as he struck the air with vicious strokes. Karkamo himself, though

---

LEFT: *A Kogi with his* poporo *containing lime, its stick and his bag for coca leaves.*
RIGHT: *A Kogi weaves a hammock.*

young, already had a killer's reputation. In spite of this the battle never took place. Padre Atanasio managed to calm them and peace returned.

During this time the Indians were too excited for us to work with them, and besides Karkamo could not come with us. So we went to a nearby village which had been deserted, farther down the valley close to the river. The houses did not appear to have been empty for long, the roofs were intact and the posts firm, though grass was beginning to grow on the floor. Under the eaves of one house we discovered two bundles, wrapped in Indian togas and carefully sewn up. They were old and the cloth had turned brown. We felt them and suddenly realized they were mummified bodies. Our thoughts again turned to the Casacará grave we had seen and to what Alec had told us. When a person is dying the nearest relatives come to the house and mourn. At death the body is wrapped with mats and cloth in the foetal position, the knees bound to the chest and the hands to the cheeks. Then for three days and nights the corpse is smoked over a special framework which is erected outside the house. In other words the dead are kippered! Afterwards the corpse is either buried beneath the floor or hung under the eaves, and the house is deserted. The whole village moves away, for they believe that while flesh is still attached to the body an evil spirit will hover over their houses.

Some days later we went and saw Karkamo to ask him about the deserted village and the corpses. At first he was surprised and silent, then, looking towards the ground, he said that his mother had died last year and they had left the village. In three months' time they would perform the outburial rites.

Three days after full moon, he told us, they clear a wide path from the village to the house where the body lies, for they believe that all the obstructing bushes possess evil spirits. The women prepare maize *chicha* and as the moon rises they fill a hollowed tree-trunk lying outside the headman's house. No fires are lit while the drink ferments, and the men, later joined by the women, dance slowly round the *chicha*, their faces painted red with *bija*. In the morning the whole village makes its way to the house where the corpse is hung, the men with their bows and arrows, the women with wooden staves, beating the undergrowth as they pass. Here Karkamo would unwrap the body and, together with his brother, clean the corpse before rewrapping it in two new mats and a piece of cloth. They would enclose a small gourd and a packet of maize so that their mother could eat and drink on the journey to the next world. He would carry the corpse on his back and play a flute of

---

ABOVE LEFT: *A Kogi grandmother.* ABOVE RIGHT: *Two Bintukua sisters.*
BELOW LEFT: *A very rich woman, her wealth indicated by her beads.* BELOW RIGHT: *Kogi maraca player.*

human bone handed down from their ancestors. His brother would follow playing another human-bone flute.

The men and women of the village come after the chief mourners, vehemently beating evil spirits away from the path. On entering the village the *chicha* is uncovered and they start to drink. Then they dance *Tuwéwa*, the Dance of the Dead. The corpse is carried through the village; the men play panpipes, followed by groups of women, their arms linked and brandishing engraved staves. The corpse and the two brothers with bone flutes would remain in front. The rest work themselves into a frenzy; paint runs from their faces, their bodies become covered in dirt and sweat. All day the dance of *Tuwéwa* continues, but occasionally they change to the Toucan Dance with the lovely tune which we had already heard. In this the men wear simple crowns of toucan and wild turkey feathers, the same feathers we had seen when we left the Casacará deserted house. By night the *chicha* is finished and bodies lie prostrate on the ground. The corpse would hang in Karkamo's house, but in the morning he would lead the procession to the secret burial cave.

We asked him where the cave was, but he would not tell us. We asked whether we could see the human-bone flutes, again he was unwilling. Two days later we went to the headman's house and eventually Apatchmo, a dwarfed old man, agreed to show them to us. He undid a small cane box and carefully took two flutes out. They were nearly nine inches long, bound in cotton, with only one hole and a specially cut mouth-piece. They had a worn, polished look and we later heard they were the tibia bones of a white man, a missionary, killed some fifty years before. Apatchmo took one flute in his left hand, his thumb and little finger beneath the bone, his index finger covering the single hole. A pure clear note rang out, and he altered the pitch by moving his finger, slightly waving the flute in front of his mouth. Karkamo joined the old headman, playing a simple accompaniment of two lower notes, and we listened to these eerie sounds as we walked away from the village and down the valley.

On one side of the valley was a very steep limestone cliff. One day Juan, Padre Atanasio's muleteer, told us he had heard that the burial cave was hidden high in the cliff-face. We went down towards the river bed, cutting our way through creepers and thorny scrub which turned to dark, overhanging forest. We drank in the cool stream and then started the climb up the far bank; here the undergrowth lessened, but the boulders were loose and came away as we scrambled up the slope. At last a giant crag with lianas hanging down a gully formed what appeared to be the base of the cliff. We hauled ourselves to the top, and there it was in front of us, not, as we had expected, an abrupt precipice, but a series of ledges.

Crawling along the ledges we gradually gained height; suddenly Juan looked back at us, with a bone in his hand. Quite near was a single skull, large and elongated; among the crumbled rock fragments were more bones. All appeared charred as though the bodies had been cremated. On a higher ledge were still more bones and three skulls, two of which had been cracked and the bone had thickened over the fracture. Many years ago two men must have fought with their bows like Karkamo and Ikoshmo. Close to the skulls, partly buried in the debris, were several wooden staves, those the women carry during the outburial ceremony. Each was inscribed with small triangles burnt into the wood; one, lying apart, had circles only. This, we learnt later, would have been carried by a dead man's widow during the procession.

The ledge widened and in front of us, lying next to one another in a dark recess underneath an overhanging roof of limestone, were eight mummified corpses. We had reached the secret burial ground, the sacred place where Serepto the Wind had power over all evil spirits and swept them away from the land of the Motilon. Deep in the recess were the remains of ten more corpses, now no more than charred skeletons. The cloth had been burnt away but lying close to the skull of one was a bundle of stone and horn spindles, intricately engraved with zigzag lines and pierced by thin wooden shafts; this must have been a woman's corpse, mummified with her most valued possessions. It was a macabre sensation to be surrounded on all sides by the dead. Only one living creature was present, the guardian of the burial ground. A nightjar perched vigilantly on one of the bound white bodies – a tiny corpse, wrapped in leaves and entwined with creeper, that of a baby, perhaps a chieftain's son. The nightjar stood his ground, eyeing us with defiance as we approached, then at the last moment silently swooped away.

The mummies were unbelievably light, and one had already begun to disintegrate. The cloth had torn and projecting from the inner layer was a string of minute black beads, a necklace worn by the women which the widow always places next to her dead husband's body – for two years after his death she can not remarry. We left the cave and made our way back along the ledges. The view was magnificent, but it was a relief to leave this cavern of death, to breathe fresh air and clamber downwards through the living forest to the valley bottom.

The Maraca people could not be allowed to know of our discovery, and that night as we packed our rucksacks a sense of guilt crept over us. All too soon the outburial rites would come to an end, the Missions would eradicate their ancient customs, and because of this we felt justified in visiting this secret place. Karkamo and Ishishik came to bid us farewell. Perhaps when he carried his mother's corpse to the burial cave, he would see the footprints on the ledges and would know we had been there.

Loading the mules in the darkness we left the Río Maraca long before dawn and climbed steeply to the high plateau. Beneath, the dogs' barks died away; above, the moon shone and the night was clear. Far away on the horizon were lights, moving like beetles through the night. They were trucks passing through Becerril, far below us in the plains. By mule this was a ten-hour journey, a long ride, but in fact so very close; in no time the Sierra de Perijá would be colonized and the Indian would disappear.

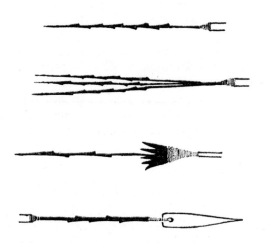

A Guajiro desert shelter.

4

An Arrow in the Rafters

The joyful sounds of a Mozart symphony filtered through the trees, down to the river where we swam. All around the frogs' night-chorus mingled with the constant *put-put-put* of the single-stroke power plant. Two days earlier, when we had loaded our kitbags into the bus and were about to return to Valledupar, a passenger had stroked his chin and pointed to a figure standing in the village street, exclaiming, 'Don Benjamín!' – and now we were at his *finca*.

We had always intended to come and see Ben, for we had known one another in Cambridge, and his farm not only lay close to the two groups of Motilon we had just visited, but even closer to the dangerous territory of the Kunuguasaya – the Bravo Motilon as they are known all over Colombia. After our chance meeting, he asked us to come and stay a few days – perhaps we could discover a little more about these fierce people, possibly make plans for an expedition into their territory at a later date. No one had managed to make friendly contact with them from Colombia and their raids on the frontier farmers along the Perijá had increased steadily over the past few years.

It was a thatched, wattle-walled house, surrounded by fly netting, where Ben sat, silhouetted against the bright light of a naked bulb, with Heraclitus, his faithful Alsatian, at his side. Red-bearded and bare-backed, his figure hunched over a pile of papers. It seemed to us that the years spent in these harsh surroundings had changed him little, although he was merrier than he used to be and more vitriolic; he still had a strange humping laugh, the only vestige of a total paralysis which he had suffered as a child. Always a slight recluse with an intelligent, rather academic outlook, it is possible that university life might have suited him better. But seeing him working on his *finca* or regaling the *colonos* with the dry wit of his fast colloquial Spanish, one knew that he was happier here.

'How do you like Mozart in the wilds of Curucucú?' he asked. 'When I arrived four years ago there was nothing, just those two little mud huts behind us, the river and the forest. Now it's a bit different, but the gramophone

---

A Guajiro family rides out to collect water.

is still my only luxury. More often than not it breaks down, and I have to wait months until I go to Bogotá and buy spares.' Like ourselves he had first come to Colombia on an expedition, but he had stayed. To farm had always been his ambition and he now owned some five thousand acres of land. 'There was dense jungle over the fertile soil,' he continued, as we sat round the table drinking cool *panela* flavoured with lemon. 'And what wasn't forested was no more than rocky scrubland. However, a river, the Mula, runs through the *finca*, and it was this more than anything else which made me buy the land. During those early days it was a struggle and an exciting one at that, for the Motilon were, indeed still are, right on my doorstep. Often they'd come down from the hills, raid the outlying plantations, sometimes kill a *colono* and disappear, generally unseen.'

His was a lonely life of competing in a battle to open new land. As a foreigner, the local people first looked on him with suspicion; then the more unscrupulous tried to cheat him, but he was not to be fooled. In a very short time the bearded figure of Don Benjamín, driving down to the main road in his old jeep, riding across country on one of his horses or into the village of Poponte on a rickety bicycle, became something of a living legend.

A small sandy track left the farm to wind through cleared forest out to the bare savannah which surrounded Poponte. A single wide dusty street ran the length of the village, bounded on either side by low whitewashed mud houses with open doorways. The scene was little different from other villages at the foot of the Perijá. The men, with their broad-brimmed straw sombreros finely woven with black designs, wore their machetes in long leather tasselled scabbards dangling at their sides. Sometimes quarrels broke out and it was not unusual for them to end in violent death. As we rode along the street, the horses' hooves kicked dust into the hot morning air and nothing could have seemed more friendly. A group of *colonos*, their mules laden with maize brought down from their hillside plantations, stood talking in the middle of the road and greeted Ben with the customary '*Buenos días, Don Benjamín.*' They may have been surprised to see not just one but three bearded figures riding through Poponte.

On the far side of the village the desolate scrubland changed to a uniform green. A vast area of cotton stretched towards the hills. 'That's Don Howard's *finca*,' Ben explained, 'The two sources of wealth here are cattle and cotton. The cotton has to be fumigated at least three times a year, and David, one of Don Howard's sons, sprays the fields from his plane. He's there in the *finca*.'

The low white ranch stood apart from the array of workshops, barns and machine stores. Inside as we talked, looking out over the verandah towards the Perijá, David brought down an arrow which was hanging on the wall. 'Some time ago, one of our men was working on the edge of the forest. He never returned and we later found him dead with this through his ribs.' With a long, savagely barbed *macana*-wood head, it was the first Kunuguasaya arrow we had seen. As we sat comfortably in the ranch with a view on to the very hills where the Kunuguasaya roamed, the whole situation of the frontier farmer and the Indian became a reality. Modern man and machinery convert the plains into vast cotton lands and cattle pastures. The *colono* strikes further and further into the foothills, cutting back the forest to make his plantations, while the Indian desperately tries to retain the territory which he believes to be his own.

Crossing the Río Mula the sturdy mule-like horses climbed up the steep bank, the brass stirrup guards jingling against the rocks. An extensive plateau of high grass and low twisted trees lay in front of us. The land rose to bare rock ridges, parched and dry, the deep red sandstone flaking away in the heat of the sun to leave contorted forms jutting out of this barren wilderness. 'There in the north are the foothills of the Sierra Nevada,' Ben said as he pulled in his horse, resting the reins on the pommel of his rancher's saddle. 'About Christmas time when the atmosphere is clear I look out across the plains on to the peaks of snow and can probably see the mountain you climbed.

'Each year the *colonos* move further into the hills, slowly opening the land towards the Venezuelan frontier. The forest they can fell is their own, but the valley beneath us belongs to me. One side is being fenced, the other is bounded by the river. Now that I have secured the titles I hope to stock it with cattle.'

We rode off the ridge and up the valley, on our way to visit Lolo, the man who looked after this part of Ben's farm. The sun rose higher and the horses, which kept up a continuous running jog, snorted when we reached the river, dipping their nostrils deep in the water. 'It was here,' Ben called from ahead, 'that a *colono* saw three Indians crouching on the rocks, waiting with their bows and arrows for fish. They were stark naked. Luckily they didn't notice him, and he returned to Poponte, one of the few people ever to have seen the Bravo Motilon.'

A chicken strolled unconcernedly across the bare earth floor as we sat eating *sancocho*, a *colono* stew. On the table was a bottle of liquid which looked like water, a broken maize cob projecting from the neck instead of a cork. Lolo poured some into a mug and with a laugh Ben exclaimed, 'Beware. – It's got a kick like a mule!' Rough and fiery, the alcoholic content of this local brew was such that, when some spilt and Ben set a match to it, the flames leapt high in the air.

Some days later we had the opportunity to see a private still. As a precaution against possible discovery, the small thatched hut was set well back in the forest. Two fifteen-gallon petrol drums, one on top of the other and joined with clay, had been placed over a fire of steadily burning logs. Projecting from one side of the drums was a narrow cane tube through which condensed liquid slowly dripped into a bottle.

Ben was roaring with laughter at our incredulity at the sight of the distillery and the stacks of bottles. 'The recipe is quite simple,' he said. 'Just four or five blocks of *panela* melted down and allowed to ferment for three days with plantains or maize. Add aniseed and pour the mixture into the still. Light the fire and the steam rises to condense on the sealed lid. The drips run down to a dent in its centre, on to a wooden spoon and out along this cane tube into the bottles, and it's ready for market. It's good business. I wouldn't mind one myself, but it's illegal, and if you're caught the fines are very heavy.'

As we rode back across the plain to Curucucú that evening, we could not help thinking how easy it was to produce this powerful spirit. It cost little and its effect could be disastrous. Only the month before we had seen a similar drink made by the *colonos* of the Sierra Nevada and sold to the unfortunate Kogi. Here in the Perijá it was the *colonos* themselves who enjoyed the effects or suffered the consequences.

One night we found ourselves round a small table in a Poponte bar. Oil lamps blazed down on crowded figures, many in broad-brimmed sombreros shielding their often scarred faces from the light. It was Saturday and the village had filled with people, for this was the one night in the week when everyone came, the *colonos* leaving their *fincas*, some riding miles on the backs of their mules to come and drink, spin yarns and do a little business. A crowd gathered round the table where we were sitting, and Ben became deeply engrossed in a conversation over the price of some cattle. Then the subject changed. A man called Demetrio asked what we were doing. Ben jokingly replied that we had come to look for the Bravo Motilon. The man's wizened face hardened as he looked at us over the empty beer bottles.

'Only five weeks ago, this very night, my wife was murdered by the Motilon.' The crowded figures bent their heads closer towards the quiet voice. 'I had come to Poponte late that afternoon, my mules loaded with maize, and left my wife Maria alone in the *finca*. I would often stay away for the night and return the next morning. In this way the animals could rest between journeys. The Indians must have attacked early, for Maria would sit in the entrance with a lantern at her side, before she went to her hammock. There, framed in the doorway, she was killed; an arrow pierced her side.' Demetrio paused, but the bystanders only murmured and then fell silent. Indian forages on their *fincas* were a danger which always preyed on their minds.

'They fired many arrows at the house, some were broken or the shafts split as they pierced the blank walls. When I returned that day I found one buried inches deep in the wood through Maria's body. It was a terrible sight. I just can't bear the thought of going back to live there again.'

We then asked Demetrio what else the Indians had done and he told us: 'They raided my maize store and tore up the manioc in my plantation. They also stole plantains, bananas and six of my chickens including the cockerel. There were no feathers on the ground, so they couldn't have killed them, they must have taken them away to breed. The whole *finca* was ransacked, machetes, salt and *panela* vanished, but Maria's body was left untouched where they had killed her.'

A tall, gaunt man pushed forward through the crowd and greeted Demetrio. His name was Felíz and he owned the *finca* beneath Demetrio's on the Río Mula. He had been there the night the attack occurred:

'It was about one o'clock in the morning and my dogs suddenly started to bark. I could hear a noise at the top of my plantation but in the darkness could see nothing. When it was light I went up there and found the manioc had been uprooted, but the dogs must have frightened them.'

After the raid the Indians were said to have roamed the neighbourhood, but they made no further attacks and the *colonos* decided to take revenge. 'Six of us, armed with our guns,' Demetrio said, 'banded together to go and kill them. We rode up the Mula, past my ranch and then went high into the hills until we reached the headwaters. Here, to our surprise, we discovered a wide track which the Indians had made, and that night we camped on the same spot where they must have been some hours earlier. The embers of a fire were still smouldering and near by were the skins of stolen bananas. We also found some hollow branches with burnt beeswax inside, which they used as torches to travel by night.'

Perhaps through fear, perhaps, as Demetrio said, because their provisions ran out, the *colonos* returned after only three days. There were no reprisals and the journey had been fruitless. Now the two men wanted to accompany us into Bravo Motilon territory, they knew the way and would be only too willing to take us. But when they learnt that we would take no arms, they looked aghast. 'Perhaps,' said Felíz, the more vehement of the two, 'we can hide pistols in the baggage.' Still we insisted that were we to go we would have to be unarmed. Our purpose was a peaceful one, theirs was to seek revenge.

Beer bottles piled higher on the table, and with the end of Demetrio's story other *colonos* started to talk with hatred and fear of the Bravo Motilon. At one point Ben asked Demetrio what had happened to the arrow which had killed his wife. Demetrio replied, 'It is in Rinconhondo, in Anastasita's house. If you want to see it, go and ask her, but I think there are arrows still in the *finca*. One, I remember, I put in the rafters.'

It was very late when we left Poponte and rode back to Curucucú in the darkness. To have tried to go far in Bravo Motilon territory was at this stage out of the question; none the less, the very existence of marauding bands in itself intrigued us.

We started from the *finca* at first light, and only the dogs seemed to notice as we jogged up the empty road between the silent white-walled houses. One of them, braver than the rest, rushed out to snap at the hocks of our horses. The end of a leather thong flicked on to his back and he disappeared yelping in the trail of dust behind.

Cantering across the flat grassland we soon reached the bend in the Río Mula at the point where it debouched from the valley. There only two days before, armed with small garden trowels, we had spent an evening rummaging over the site of an old Motilon village. We had been lucky to find several broken sherds of fine reddish clay with incised lines and scrolls. We presumed they belonged to the Motilon villagers, though they were very different from the coarse grey ware we had found in a Casacará plantation. About twenty-five years previously, when the village had been abandoned, a *colono* had occupied the vacated land, only to have his son shot through the neck with an arrow by a Kunuguasaya raiding party. He had left the place and the *colono* expansion along the Mula valley had been renewed only recently at the risk of further clashes with the Indians, who for generations had been accustomed to roam over these foothills and plains, hunting, fishing and collecting turtle and crocodile eggs from the bigger streams. Their activities now included raiding the new plantations, taking maize, plantains, manioc and the occasional chicken. It was usually during the first half of the year that these raids were most frequent, for the Indians then suffer most from a shortage of food in their own territory around the Catatumbo and Oro rivers on the south-eastern slopes of the Perijá.

For some time Ben had been thinking of going to Demetrio's outpost *finca* to see how far the valley had been opened up since he was last there. It was interesting for him to see what sort of land it was, for the valley, divided by a line of ridge-backed hills, ran almost parallel to his own boundary line, and although for the present he had enough land, one day he might want to expand.

He waved his hands about him: 'This was all forest the last time I was up here. Look at it now, there are a lot of rocks and boulders, but there is good soil between. The only trouble is you're likely to get an arrow through your stomach if you stay around too long.'

Demetrio had said we were welcome to go to his *finca*. He himself did not like to stay up there for any length of time, at least while there was a possibility the Indians might return, for this was still the time of year for raids. It was mainly at Ben's suggestion that we were now all three going to Demetrio's. There was a chance that we might find some evidence of the raid, something they had left behind. We knew there was an arrow in the roof of one of the houses, and Demetrio had told us we could take it.

In spite of their notoriety, the Kunuguasaya have managed to keep their lives a complete mystery. Their possessions likewise are little known, except perhaps for the arrows found in their victims. Strangely enough, the first contact with the people had been a peaceful one. It was at the end of the last century, when a cattle trail was made from the Magdalena valley over the Perijá to the Venezuelan plains, that the herders met some Indians. Tall and well-built, long-haired and wearing only a loincloth, they were totally different from the Yuco Motilon of the north. From the descriptions these people could only have been the Kunuguasaya, living in large communal houses and speaking a strange language quite unlike that of the Yuco. At first they were friendly towards the herdsmen. Then the trail workers started to raid their plantations for food and the Indians defended them. At the turn of the century there was a brief contact with the first oil explorers. Then, as in the case of the herders, the situation deteriorated and fighting broke out. These were probably the first and last friendly contacts with the Kunuguasaya. For the last sixty years it has been a war to the death.

We came to a divide where one branch of the Mula came in from the east through a narrow defile in the sierra. In front of us the valley continued. Just across the stream was a small planked house. Splashing through the stream we passed by without seeing anyone, not even a dog.

'That is Feliz's *finca*, where the Indians came after killing Demetrio's wife. It is strange that they left him alone. Perhaps he was well armed and inside the house. I don't think the dogs would have frightened them.' Ben pointed further up the side of the valley: 'That is where Alec Clark tried to make contact with the Indians, putting beads, thread and needles, and even food for them beside one of their trails, but they never touched it.' Alec had told us about this, he had left trade articles on various occasions, and only once, he thought, had anything been touched. He had hoped that should they take anything they would leave something in exchange. By repeating this many times, he felt that he might one day be able to approach the Indians. This reminded us of a Venezuelan missionary who had flown over an Indian settlement on several occasions, dropping gifts and photographs of himself. Then one day he parachuted down, hoping the Indians would recognize him, and was never heard of again.

The *colonos* and the petroleum workers suffered most at the hands of the Indian. Frequently single oil workers and surveyors or small groups would be surrounded and attacked. They always had to carry arms and travel along the forest tracks in vehicles with steel mesh against the arrows. On one occasion two Kunuguasaya women were taken, but both committed suicide within hours of their capture. Some years later two Indian boys suffering from a serious lung disease were found by the roadside and taken to hospital where they were cured. They were then sent to a mission in the Amazon, where one died and the second was never heard of again. A unique opportunity for a direct contact with the tribe was lost.

Usually after a killing there would be reprisal raids. Quite often the

Yuco-Chaké Motilon would suffer these reprisals, for even now some of the people on the fringes of the Perijá do not differentiate between these Indians and the so-called Bravo Motilon or Kunuguasaya. From 1935 onwards the petroleum companies intensified their work in the Catatumbo–Oro regions, and the Indians likewise intensified their attacks on isolated camps and groups of workmen; woundings and deaths resulted on both sides. In the same year the Colombian and Venezuelan governments organized a commission to demarcate the frontier between the two countries. Though a large force and heavily armed, they were nevertheless subjected to frequent attacks and only with difficulty managed to complete their work.

Alec Clarke and Padre Atanasio had spoken frequently of the Bravo Motilon, how they would like to contact these people, even at the risk of their lives. They presented a challenge. Like many missionaries about the sierra they hoped one day to be able to pacify and christianize these fierce people. In fact we had heard of a Venezuelan mission who with the assistance of the Government had only recently made an approach to one of the Catatumbo groups, and according to their account had established relations with them. They apparently used helicopters, landing near the houses and exchanging gifts with the Indians. At this very time the Colombian Government was parachuting supplies to some settlements; it was hoped that the starving Indians would lessen their attacks on the fringes of the sierra.

We were now passing through forest land bordering the river. We knew we must be very close to Demetrio's plantation. 'If we don't get there soon we shall have to turn back, or we'll be travelling in the dark. It's rather farther than I thought.' Ben looked up at the sun through the branches of the trees. 'The Motilon usually prepare an ambush with great care. Sometimes they make leaf-covered hides beside the track, or a platform in a tree, and lie in wait.' We had seen a tree-top hide with the Casacará, but that was for birds. 'Did Alec tell you what they do when they kill someone? They don't always just leave the arrows in the body. Often the head will be hacked off at the neck, and the hands at the wrists. Sometimes the sexual organs will be removed, and, as an afterthought, they will defecate around the corpse.'

When we had been with the Maraca, we had noticed young children firing arrows at one another in a sort of game. The tips of the arrows were of beeswax or maize cobs, so that they could not wound each other. In the past when the Maraca went to war, they would enact a type of war dance in which the men, standing in two lines about thirty paces apart, would take it in turn to fire their arrows at one another. Standing sideways on, they

---

Kechenko's mother makes a belt; her black mask of paint protects her skin from the sun.

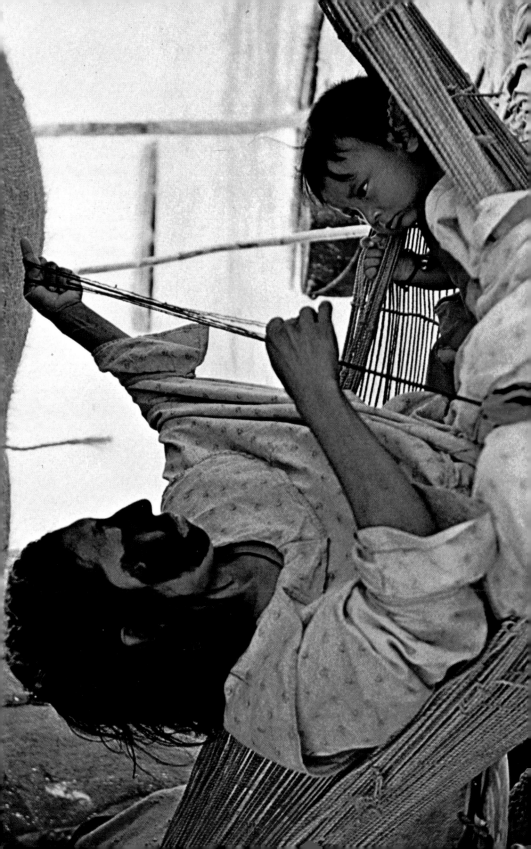

would dodge the arrow as it sped towards them, slapping their sides to keep a form of rhythm. There would often be injuries before the real fight even started. Between the Indians themselves a declaration of war was usually made by crossed arrows or crossed palm leaves left in a trackway. But the white man seldom gets such warning. The Indians usually attack at daybreak. Moving through the forest, they give the appearance of being in greater numbers than they actually are.

Suddenly we broke into the open on the edge of a small plantation. On the far side of the river were three newly-built wooden houses. The plantation was fringed by the forest, which rose sharply on each side to the open savannah, two thousand feet above us. Crossing the stream, we dismounted and tied the horses. An old brown bitch with a litter of puppies growled at us as we approached the huts. We wondered how she had escaped. Usually the Indians kill a dog – for they have none of their own – and hacking the head off impale it on an arrow placed in the ground.

'It seems strange that they should have attacked at night. Perhaps they knew Demetrio was away. This must be where she was killed. She would have been silhouetted in this doorway with the lamp behind her.' Ben stooped as he entered the doorway. The room was bare except for two chairs, a wooden table and a hammock slung in one corner.

We found the arrow in the rafters overhead. Its two-and-a-half-foot *macana*-wood head was notched in four places on each side. The point seemed blunt and the cane shaft, bound with black thread, was split along half its length. Presumably it had hit the wall of the house and the shock had forced the head back into the cane.

There were no more arrows in the house and we walked round the perimeter of the huts to see if the attackers had left anything, but there was nothing. Except for an occasional snarl from the bitch everything was silent and deserted. The sun was beginning to fall to the west and we knew we had to go, or we would still be in the valley at nightfall.

As we turned the horses' heads down the valley, we took a last look at the deserted wooden huts, the surrounding plantation with the freshly cut timber spread-eagled among the maize shoots. We tried to picture the scene as Demetrio would have seen it that morning when he returned to find his wife dead. Perhaps it was his rage which had carried him and the posse far into the Perijá along the Indian tracks, till fear or hunger forced them back, frustrated, unable to find a trace of the assassins.

Why had the Indians done this? Perhaps by killing they felt they could put fear into the heart of the *colono*, and keep him out of their territory. For

---

ABOVE: *A Guajiro encampment on the shores of the Caribbean.* BELOW LEFT: *Skinning a goat.* BELOW RIGHT: *Kechenko picks fruit from a cardon cactus.*

sixty years since their initial friendliness was abused, they have never relaxed. Yet slowly and inevitably they are pushed back. The forces against them are too great. Without land they cannot grow food, and without food they cannot live.

Epilogue

1. COLOMBIAN KALEIDOSCOPE

It was July before we left the Motilon. Nearly ten months had passed since we first set out. We had visited four Indian tribes, each for a few weeks, and had had a glimpse at a fifth. Now it seemed time to take stock, not only of what was left to do, but of what had already been done. What in fact had been done? All our experiences seemed fragmentary, superficial. We had a veritable kaleidoscope of memories of Indians – impressions, no more.

Perhaps it would have been better to have lived with one tribe during those ten months and learnt more about them. But then we would have defeated our purpose which was to record the music of several tribes. Had we lingered with one group we should never have completed the whole. This was always our dilemma. But what could we have gained by staying longer? None of us, with the exception of Nestor, was academically qualified to study an Indian tribe, and to our misfortune he could come on only two of our journeys. What were we then? Perhaps we could have called ourselves adventurers or explorers, but these names are anachronisms in the twentieth century. Perhaps we were just travellers, human beings trying to catch a glimpse of another kind of man, the South American Indian, that strange perceptive being who is fast disappearing off the face of the earth.

What surprised us most was the diversity of these Indians. One tends to think all Indians alike, living in primeval forest, wearing barkcloth and covered in paint. But every Indian we met was very much an individual personality. Some were gay, others sad, some shy, others aggressive, tall, short and fat, fine-looking and ugly; taken as a whole one might describe them as introspective, reserved and very independent.

Like the individual, the tribes also were diverse, each one to a greater or lesser extent influenced by its environment – Noanamá, Tukano, Kogi and Motilon, and also Guajiro, though of these last our impressions were as fleeting as our days among them were few.

The four tribes could be more simply classified by grouping the Noanamá and Tukano together. They were living under fairly similar conditions, those of the tropical forest. Their fishing and hunting existence was in many respects alike, as was much of their material culture. Moreover, in the social sense, both tribes showed an absence of any central authority or chieftain;

the only authority lay with the heads of the houses, and the considerable but not excessive influence of the shaman. In addition, the family groupings within the scattered forest *malocas* and waterside stilted houses, in the ceremonies and, to a lesser extent, their art and music, all seemed to show a certain relationship.

They recognized a supreme being. He had little effect on their everyday lives, he was something remote but nevertheless present. What the Tukano called him we never knew – he may have been Jurupari; to the Noanamá he was Evandama. There were also the spirits of the forest and the ancestors. To them Severiano sang his Canta Haí, to them the Tukano shaman chanted during the festival on the Piraparaná. There was the custom among Noanamá boys and girls of putting flowers in their hair and in the holes bored in their ears, which prompted Nestor to remark that they were almost Polynesian, and we found later that the Tukano had the same habit.

There were differences too: the partly sedentary cultivation of the Noanamá and their dependence on maize, compared with the shifting agriculture of the Tukano and their staple of manioc. There were differences in craftsmanship and design: pottery, basket weaving and the methods of making canoes, to mention but a few.

But what does all this tell us? Here were two peoples living six hundred miles apart, divided by the high Andes. It only tells us that at some time in the past there was a contact, perhaps a migration, or even that they formed one major group which was divided by the Chibcha advance.

The Motilon and Kogi – and this includes the Bintukua – were essentially highland dwellers, the one living in the lower 'cloud forest', the other in the high savannah tundra. The most noticeable thing about them was that they wore clothes; the Motilon a long cloak reaching to his ankles, the Kogi a jerkin, trousers and a sash. They had developed the use of the loom and wove cotton, *fiqué* sisal and even wool, unlike the forest dwellers who would still have gone naked or worn barkcloth but for the influx of trade cotton. Moreover, they rarely used body paint. We only once saw a Motilon painting his face – which they do when they go to war.

Perhaps their most distinctive feature is that, unlike the tropical forest dwellers, they live in small settlements and villages: the wattle-walled houses of the Sierra de Perijá with the surrounding barricade as a defence against the depredations of wild animals and warlike neighbours, and the small, round, wattle-and-daub temples and houses of the high Sierra Nevada.

It has been said of the Amazonian Indian: 'One word from the chief and everyone does exactly as he pleases.' This is a dictum which could apply equally to the Tukano or the Noanamá. In a way this lack of authority, this

---

Guajiro women take in water from Rigtender.

nonchalance seems to add to their charm, it makes life a little happy-go-lucky. But not so with the highlanders. Here one senses authority and a martial spirit, particularly among the Motilon who were always itching for a fight; frustrated perhaps at being unable to fight other groups, they resorted to fighting amongst themselves, always clutching their sheaves of arrows and twanging their bowstrings in anger. Here – and among the Kogi too – we found aggressiveness; underneath they were still the same humorous, perceptive people, but outwardly they wore an air of purposefulness, as if life had become a serious matter. To the Kogi life had become more than that; they had a duty to live by the rules of their priests. This was the wish of their mother goddess Nabulwé, the supreme power in their lives. It seemed to us at the time that a Kogi set down beside a Tukano would have found him as alien to his conception of a human being as we ourselves were; yet both are Indians.

The most primitive of all South American Indians is the wandering nomadic Maku, still to be found in the isolated depths of the Amazon forests, living solely on what he can gather with a stone axe as his only implement. He still represents Stone Age man. At the other end of the scale is the monotheistic Kogi, the nearest present-day equivalent we saw to the highest state of culture the Indian has reached. Between these extremes are such tribes as the Tukano, Noanamá and Motilon, each in a sense representing a different stage in development.

On the one hand are cultural traits which denote common origin or the influence of early migrations. On the other hand is the diversity representing stages of social development which were still evolving at the time of the Spanish conquest and which since then have each, in varying degrees and at different times, been subjected to a completely new force – European culture in all its complexity.

And how did the different tribes react to this influence? Generally speaking, the forest lowlanders like the Tukano have survived longer because of their remoteness. Yet when a contact is made the shock is great and their lack of cohesion may lead to rapid extinction.

The highlander, who in most instances has been in contact with the European for centuries, has – perhaps because of the greater cohesion imposed by the Kogi priests and the Motilon chiefs – either wholly resisted or adapted himself to the new influence in such a way that much of his own culture is incorporated in the new, as has happened in Atanquez, and indeed in the case of countless thousands who in the past four and a half centuries have become fully integrated into a European society.

There are very few places left in the world where the notion of Western

---

Ortelia, Kechenko's sister.

culture is unknown. There may still be one or two isolated hill tribes in New Guinea; and wandering-nomadic groups of foresters like the Amazonian Maku. The Tukano certainly were not isolated in this sense. Some of them had had direct contact with the rubber collectors of the early part of the century, and many of them today still tap rubber. It is possible that the obvious signs of depopulation among the people of the Piraparaná are due to this yearly migration of the younger men. Essentially, however, they remain simple uncomplicated people believing in an amazing world of spirits and demons and quite happy in that belief; taking part in their festivals with great gusto, extremely creative with their beautiful head-dresses, woven baskets and pottery, to mention but a few of their artefacts, and delighting in their music. Perhaps we influenced them unduly in this last respect. Perhaps when we left, the panpipes were put back on their neglected wall. But this is unlikely.

Nor were the Noanamá completely isolated. Among them one felt a growing conflict between the negro settlers and the Indian. We recalled an argument between Severiano and an old negro: in a rage Severiano had shouted, 'Respect me!' Perhaps the negro's cheerful arrogance infuriated the Indian more than the taking of his land. Then there was the Mission. We had seen Severiano calling to the ancestors with his Canta Haí sticks in front of him, facing a lighted candle under an image of the Virgin Mary. The Indians were gradually disappearing from the San Juan and moving northwards to Panama, in a pathetic attempt to continue the only way of life they knew.

But the Motilon were different, and the Kunuguasaya had adopted an openly hostile attitude towards all intruders. To this day they remain, like the Maku, almost unknown – but not because of inaccessibility or remoteness. The Yuco-Chaké, however, whom we visited, though still extremely war-like among themselves, are not so much under the influences of *colono* expansion from the plains as of the work of the missionaries.

If only in the past the missionaries could have concentrated less on the outlawing of those aspects of tribal life which constituted the very basis, the very roots of Indian existence – their spiritual and ceremonial life, which ran completely contrary to the teaching of Christianity. If only they could have restrained their overwhelming zealousness to eradicate these and tried to understand them and show tolerance instead. Then the inevitable shock to the Indians would have been less – of losing their own beliefs in the face of a religion apparently far more terrible, one that involved only one alternative to eternal damnation and hell, which was so totally at variance with their own charming optimism for a better life to come. This was followed by a second more lasting shock, the realization that few but missionaries really practised this faith – and to the Indian religion was part of his being. Then their despair and disillusion could have been softened.

The real tragedy of it is this. Why should it be necessary to change the lives of these people at all? Why cannot they all be left like the Kogi who, it seems, have survived four and a half centuries of independence? But one has to consider the strength of Kogi society, something which the Amazonian has never acquired. Moreover, the Kogi have isolated themselves in such a way that the land they occupy can be of little use to the *colono*. If change does come, as it surely must, then it will take place in the same way as has happened to the Bintukua, the Atanquez creole and countless thousands of Colombian Indians.

Nevertheless, whether integration with another culture is involved, or simply extinction of the tribe, in the long run it means the loss of a way of life, be it the disciplined life of the Kogi or the insouciance of the Amazonian – a way of life from which we ourselves have become extraordinarily removed, a life which in its own way is very down to earth, realistic and natural, and which we regard as primitive. ...

So our discussions went on, after that journey to the border of the territory of the Kunuguasaya. Sometimes in Ben's *finca* we talked far into the night. From Ben, we began to appreciate the point of view of the *colonos* among whom he lived: the need for more land as these smallholders were pushed off their own by the magnates; the move into apparently empty land; their natural desire for revenge after the Indians' sudden attacks; the armed posses riding into the hills. It was like the early expansion in North America and the Indian wars.

We argued too, endlessly, with Padre Atanasio and Alec Clark, pointing out the terrible things they were doing. They would tell us equally convincingly their own point of view. In a sense their work was utterly selfless. It was done for no gain on their part, and were they not giving the Indians the rudiments of Christian education? Who else would do it? Was it not better to do something than nothing, than to stand aside like ourselves and criticize? It was an anachronism to say missionaries were ignorant of the lives of the people they worked among. Many knew their languages and had studied their customs.

When we look back now, from a distance of many months and many thousands of miles, there are certain recollections which stand out more clearly: the first Indian we saw from the boat on the Río San Juan, suddenly appearing out of the dusk and balancing his canoe over our wake as if he were part of it; the Tukano dancing in the glow of burning beeswax, bodies glistening with sweat and head-dresses flashing in the darkness; a Kogi with his long hair blowing in the wind, the stone cairns beside the mountain lake and the glacier in the moonlight; the Motilon with the blood from his gaping wound forming a puddle about his feet, and the outburial cave with the mummified bodies and the lone nightjar.

Then there were the rock carvings in the Amazon, archaic yet extraordinarily alive. If art is an expression of a culture, these drawings could not have been the work of tropical foresters like the Tukano. From a hunting-fishing people you might expect to see fish or animals drawn naturalistically or in the abstract; yet we only once found this side of their existence expressed, and that was not in the Piraparaná. Many of the figures portrayed suns and moons, yet as far as we were aware neither had special significance in Tukano life. Moreover, Ni, standing as he did, isolated on a pinnacle of rock high above the river, made an almost emotional impact, as if the artist had wished to identify himself with the figure. It was drawn with an intensity of feeling completely foreign to the personality of the Amazonian. Yet José was able to tell us of a legend about it and the Indians had identified their own mystical spirit or water god with it.

Most of the figures were cut in sandstone and might have been sculptured by chipping with a harder rock, perhaps flint. But a fair number, including Ni, were cut as much as half an inch deep into granite rock which blunted our own knives. It is puzzling to know what implement could have been used, and staggering to consider the work involved.

Then there were the strange squared figures on the Apaporis, like the cardmen in Alice. We had noticed half-moon shapes like necklaces with pendants. These, like the squares, reminded us of Inca and Chibcha ornaments and loom-worked cotton cloaks, unshaped by the hand of a tailor.

In the Caquetá there seemed to be a third style of art, abstract, rather intellectual. Here the human form mattered little. Heads were squared, bodies were contorted into extraordinary shapes. There were large carvings covering ten square feet, a mass of intricate squares, frets, coils and spirals. It was as if the rocks had for ages been used as a vast sketchbook on which passing travellers had engraved their own conception of artistic design.

An Indian came to us during those endless days of waiting at the frontier post and told us of a cliff-face which was covered in drawings, many of them coloured. He offered to take us there if we wished. But it was several days' journey through the forest and we dared not go, for while we were away the gunboat might have come and gone, and that would have meant waiting for months.

What is the significance of all these drawings? One immediately begins to think of past civilizations in the forest. They may be some form of writing or communication. Perhaps they are the work of migratory peoples, moving north – south or east – west, from Panama to the Pampas, from the Andes to the mouth of the Amazon. In time it may be possible to make a compre-

ABOVE: *Maraca woman playing a musical bow.* BELOW LEFT: *A boy with bird arrows and a pet toucan.* BELOW RIGHT: *The Motilon discover the wheel.*

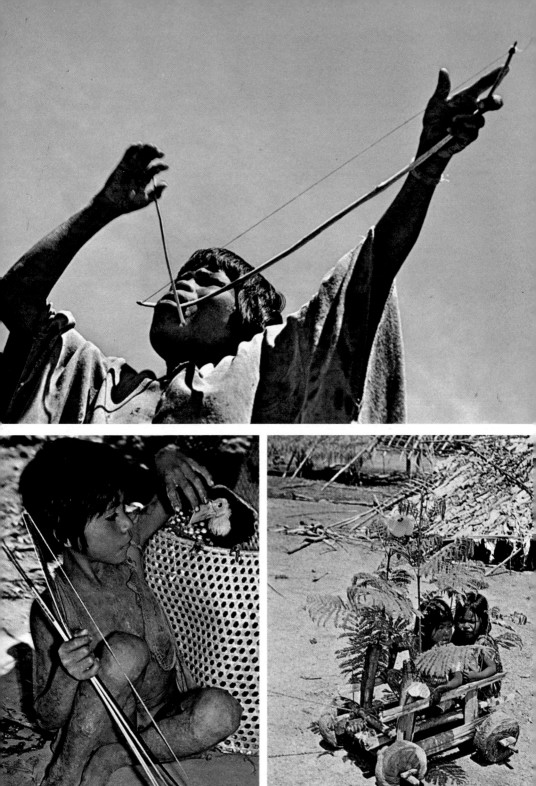

hensive study of these designs all over South America. Certain trends might be found, early migrations might be illustrated by particular styles. The study might also tell us something of the character of these people. It could show the course of their migrations and possibly even date them, though, unlike the cave art of Europe, it is impossible to date individual drawings. But if the diversity of the trends of art in the small area we visited is any indication, a survey of the whole would seem an almost superhuman task.

Among the highlanders artistic expression had less of the foresters' spontaneity. Their art had a particular purpose. The coloured stripes and markings on their cotton mantles showed the lineage or family of the wearer. The Kogi, we were told, had gold ornaments, face-masks and even feather head-dresses in their temples. But they were kept hidden as objects of religious ceremonial. The Motilon found expression in the bindings of their arrow-heads, but these, again, were probably once tribal marks used for identification.

The foresters seemed to decorate everything: the patterned basket-weaves of the Noanamá, their bead caps and gourd designs; the musical instruments, the clay or charcoal designs on the front of a Tukano *maloca*, and their gay festival paraphernalia. Here there was a more natural outflow of creativeness, which had become inhibited among the highlanders. There were a few signs of outside influence, yet it was essentially traditional art. The head-dress we brought back to the British Museum was compared with one obtained on the Caquetá by the botanist Richard Spruce over a hundred years ago. It is impossible to tell the difference. Here as in all Indian art is evidence of the supernatural, the power of an unfathomed spirit world. There is none of the triumph of mind over matter, none of the intellectualism we find in European art with the evolution of classicism and the baroque. In this sense even the work of the Maya or the Aztec was still primitive.

The forest dweller's art has the spontaneity of a child, yet his approach is both sophisticated and intelligent. He will weave a pattern for a basket because the idea appeals to him and shape a paddle with the finish of a craftsman and the design of an artist.

The Indian is something of a connoisseur. This is the result of a natural critical sense. The Tukano would never accept cloth, fish-hooks or beads from us without a thorough previous inspection. The colour of the cloth is of prime importance, its strength would be tested, as would be that of the fish-hooks and nylon line, and the test for a good bead was to place it between the teeth – to see if it cracked! Pottery or baskets we had obtained by barter

---

LEFT: *A Motilon playing an axe-head flute.* RIGHT: *A child at his mother's breast; in front of them is ground maize.*

would be carefully inspected by Indians we met later, who would disregard them if they considered them inferior work.

Sometimes we would play music we had recorded in the Amazon to see what the highlanders' reaction was. Then we would play classical music or jazz. Usually a simple tune or one with a distinct rhythm conveyed something to them. There was some interest in Bach or Mozart, but none in Brahms. As for their own music, once we had shown our interest or they had heard the play-back on the recording machine, they all – with the exception of the Kogi – would play to us for hours, and the range of sounds and instruments was astonishing.

Astonishing, too, was the realization that an Indian besides being a cultivator, a hunter, a fisherman, a boat-maker and house-builder, besides knowing the tribal legends and myths and the arts of basket weaving, wood carving and design, was also a musician, not only playing but himself making, with considerable skill, a wide range of musical instruments.

Among the Tukano alone we counted fifteen such instruments. A jingle-rattle is admittedly not very difficult to play, but it requires skill to make one and to design it so that each shell produces a certain note. A panpipe or a deer-bone flute may not be difficult to make, but it takes practice and determination to play one.

The Indian is deeply involved in the natural world about him, and just as he incises on a calabash the representation of a beetle or a frog, he will try to imitate the calls of birds or the sounds of the forest. All his instruments reflect this forest environment: snail and tortoise shells, deer-bones, nut-shells and gourds. But his music is also deeply involved with myth and ritual. We found the giant *jurupari* flutes were never placed where women could see them. They were used during the ceremony to call their god. When the women heard the flutes, booming like alpine horns in the distance, they fled into the forest, not daring to return till the flutes had been returned to the stream bed. The sacred significance of many of the instruments may account for their elaborate designs.

Very little is known of the origin of Indian, as of all music. Perhaps it first evolved during religious ceremonies, through the waving of a stick in the air or its being beaten on the floor; or perhaps through the rustle of marsh reeds held in the hand and shaken as Severiano did during the ceremony of Canta Haí. This may have been the first sound to suggest the use of nutshells and seed-rattles.

When we were living with the Casacará-Motilon Alec Clark told us that the Indians put the mark of a stag's antlers on their foreheads to bring them luck. He also gave us his interpretations of the legend of the puma and the deer, from whom the clan was descended. In the Amazon the shaman is said to be able to disappear at will and travel through the forest in the guise of a puma, because this animal was the most dreaded of all. Both these animals occur constantly in the myth and legend of the tribes, as does the Motilon legend of the twins. It is a legend known from Mexico to the tribes living in Tierra del Fuego, which suggests a considerable antiquity.

Just as the puma is usually the symbol of fear, so the deer is credited by the Indian with fairy-like, almost feminine, qualities, perhaps because of its shyness and speed. It has been suggested that the deer is the symbol of new life, having been regarded as such by early migrations of hunting folk moving south along the chain of the Andes from North America. It was thus associated with first menstruation and all the accompanying rites when a girl reaches puberty and is able to create new life, and its hooves were used by women as ornaments or rattles. The deer-bone flute may have been the first musical instrument used by the Indians.

Several tribes have no musical instruments at all. Possibly these were the first people to reach South America. Later migrations may have brought instruments with them, possibly others evolved on the spot. The similarity of some Kogi and Motilon instruments to those used in Central America suggests a more recent influence.

At first we found it difficult to distinguish the sounds of the different instruments if we could not see them. But after a while we learnt to recognize not only the instrument but also the many different tunes of each tribe. A Noanamá girl would sing to herself for hours on end. The Motilon had a vast repertoire of walking, war and harvest songs. Instrumental tunes were fewer and some, as in the case of the haunting call of the snail shell, tended to be very repetitive. The Tukano, however, had innumerable panpipe tunes.

Indian music we at first found strange because we were accustomed to the European tone system. They have no conception of note vibrations to obtain an octave. Yet they can tell whether one instrument is in tune or not with another. A panpipe can be cut to a certain length to produce a particular sound, but it is difficult to produce the exact note, so they may raise the pitch by adding sand, or putting water or even *chicha* inside.

The panpipe tunes in the Tukano festival were the nearest thing we heard to orchestral music; each group played antiphonally, with sometimes two or three groups playing different tunes. We could not however make out whether combination or competition was the motive behind this weird performance.

The Tukano had no conception of counterpoint, though their playing was often harmonious. We did find it in the singing of the Noanamá – perhaps the result of mission teaching. One Tukano chant is almost identical to a western Irish folk lament.

In contrast to African negro music in which stringed instruments and drums predominate, Indian music is mainly that of the rattle and the flute. Every type of construction is found, from humming top and conch shell to panpipes and the whistling jars of the Andes. Since the time of the Conquest European music and more particularly African music has had an increasing influence on the conservative Indian. The Noanamá and the highlanders showed signs of this influence, though the Tukano were still free of it. In some cases the instrument had been adopted and was played in the Indian idiom. The Noanamá had a type of drum probably copied from their negro neighbours, but they still played their own halting rhythms. The Motilon had a musical bow, but its use was entirely Indian in conception.

In the Sierra Nevada we found a direct clash of musical idioms, in the *chicote* and *gaita* played by the Indian-creole inhabitants. Perhaps in this are the seeds of a new music combining the atonal, remote and sad Indian music with the gay, sophisticated, ebullient harmonies of the negro-creole. Perhaps the folk music of Colombia as a whole, from the Spanish mountain songs to the negro rhythms of the coast, is a manifestation of a Euro-Afro-Indian music evolving like the arts and the people themselves into a new wholly South American dimension.

Such are the idle thoughts of travellers written in retrospect. But of all our memories – Kogi temples, Noanamá children paddling to their stilted houses in a Pacific sunset, a Tukano *maloca* at dawn with the steam rising off the night-wetted thatch – the one that will remain longest will be that of the Indian himself, whether a Kogi regarding us with the scorn of a man who knows himself to be a superior being, or a Tukano who never looks *at* you, rather into you with a strange trustful-untrusting eye, as if to try and penetrate your innermost thoughts.

Walk with him long enough in the forest and you too will learn to see the track of a tapir; to tell if it was running by the depth of the spoor; to tell if it was wounded by the clot of blood beside the path; even to tell the time when it passed, by the dryness of an upturned leaf, the only one on a shower-soaked forest floor. Perhaps if you could speak his language he would teach you how to walk through the forest for days and never lose your way, to use a bow and arrow, to kill a parrot with one dart from your blowpipe. You might even come to accept the forest for what it is. You would become part of it and it would be the only world you knew....

If you ever reached that stage, then you would be like an Indian. Then you would understand the shock of civilization. It would be like going for a very long holiday in a remote countryside, perhaps the Outer Hebrides, never seeing another soul, and then returning to the heart of a city. Only it would be a hundred times worse.

You would take cocaine because to you it would be perfectly natural. Your father took it and his father before him. You were told as a child that you could not live without it when in the late summer, at the end of the dry season, you had to travel great distances to find deer at the water holes.

Without that small bag you would never reach your destination. The sun would travel many times across the sky before you could return.

It is fairly obvious now that in those few weeks in the Piraparaná when we became unduly agitated at the break-down of an engine or the disappearance of our guides, at the delays and frustrations, we had not begun to acquire the philosophical detachment of the Indian.

'When I feel like that,' Horacio would say, 'I just sling my hammock and let the world pass by,' and so saying would proceed to do precisely that. An Indian might have given us the same advice could he have understood the cause of our agitation or the complex mentality of the *civilizado*.

Perhaps if we could recall our childhood impressions before familiarity blunted our senses, before our minds or the pictures or images they formed were channelled along a specific course by what we were taught, before in fact we became specialists, we might understand the way an Indian looks at life – and perhaps even learn something from it.

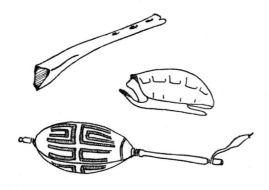

Epilogue

2. ONE LAST BAD MOMENT

The Catalina rumbled slowly southwards through the rain and darkening cloud. That morning we had left Villavicencio in bright sunlight. At first we flew over the parched green mosaic of the Llanos. But once over the Río Guaviare, the dividing line between plains and forest, the weather had suddenly changed. Now, as we pierced our way through the storm in this old relic of the war, our chances of finding the rendezvous seemed remote. Of all the gambles, this was the greatest we had taken. We were attempting a return to the Tukano, this time taking only a few hours to get to a point which previously had taken us over two months to reach.

Four days before, we had met Mike, an American tropical-fish expert from Leticia. He told us that a Catalina was going to leave Bogotá on the inaugural flight of a new Amazonian freight and passenger service which would link all the rubber and trade posts otherwise accessible only by river. Probably they would take us at very reduced rates if we promised to film the amphibian in action and make a two-minute commercial advertisement for Colombian television. We decided to go ahead. Radio messages were transmitted to two mission stations and to a *cauchero* living at the frontier post of La Pedrera. Somehow the news had to reach Don Carlos at his home on the Miritiparaná, and the only way to do this was to have Indian messengers sent by canoe. He must be told to meet the expedition at the mouth of the Piraparaná. We were returning to make a film and would land the Catalina on the Río Apaporis at this point.

Would he be there, would we be able to find this pinprick in the heart of north-west Amazonia? In this cloud, almost certainly no, but at least we were in the hands of an excellent pilot and there was still an hour to go.

As the plane bumped and shuddered and the rainwater trickled down from the joints in the fuselage, an aria from *Rigoletto* pealed forth from our pilot in the cockpit. Niels and his young wife Hanna sat on our kitbags, wondering what was to happen next. They had returned newly married to Colombia in June, and after the Motilon journey they had joined us to come and make films. Niels only agreed to come on condition he could bring his wife. At the time we were dubious. Little did we know how Hanna was to thrive on fresh air and rough conditions – perhaps we should have taken our two applicants after all!

Suddenly, as though fate was on our side, there came a break in the cloud. Below, a river twisted its way through the forest carpet.

'That's the Apaporis,' shouted the pilot. Our faces were glued to the portholes as the flying boat followed its course. Excitement was high. Only a few moments before, word had come back that fuel was running low; there would be no time to search for the mouth of the Piraparaná and we would have to fly on to the final destination, Leticia on the Amazon. Everything depended on the pilot's judgement and our own knowledge, for maps were of no use and we had elected to try and land where the two rivers joined.

'There's a river coming in on the left bank.'

'Yes ... it's the Pira. ...' The Catalina circled to come in closer.

'Look at the boat,' shouted Niels. We could see a speck in midstream, a canoe with some figures, who seemed to be holding some kind of a sheet.

'All right, I'm coming in to land – hold on ' The Catalina plunged abruptly down. We ploughed through columns of spray, the engines roared and we came to a halt. On each side was the tall forest wall, ahead the river and coming towards us Don Carlos, in his long canoe. He had travelled day and night from his home on the Miritiparaná. Our meeting seemed unbelievable. Soon the kit was transferred, farewells exchanged and the Catalina was revving its engines to take off. They promised to return in three weeks' time.

Two days later our small party was moving up the lower course of the Piraparaná. We arrived at the first rapids by night. With the higher water the treacherous currents were cause for concern. Our objective was the *maloca* where we had already seen the manioc festival and where we knew we would be welcome, doubly so because Don Carlos and Alirio, now our interpreter, were both known and accepted by the Makuna clan. Don Carlos in fact had married one of Bréo's sisters, and he returned to the *maloca* at least twice a year to try and find Indians to come and work for him, and to get *farinha*.

It was approaching midday when we left the main river and started to move up a smaller sidestream. We passed one series of rapids and soon came to a second: *Cachivera Nakaheydoo*, the Falls of the Sacred Box of Plumages. Here the canoe had to be completely unloaded. Niels scrambled through the water to film and we carried the kit over the rocks.

What happened once we set off, Brian's diary for 19 September can tell:

'Suddenly the motor cut out and we were swept backwards by the raging torrent, so fast that before we knew where we were we had gone stern first down one fall and were heading straight for the second. Niels, holding his camera in the air, asked whether he should jump. I said "No", and Carlos desperately shouted to Alirio to start the motor. Carlos tried to grab hold of a branch, but it broke and we crashed over the second fall broadside on. In a moment we were upside down in the foaming water, clinging desperately to anything we could lay our hands on.'

The rest either sank or floated away. Donald struggled towards one bank, endeavouring to hold his rucksack high above his head; inside was the Kudelski recorder, the most valuable piece of equipment we had. Niels too tried to keep his cine-camera out of the water, but with little success. Luckily both he and Hanna reached a rock ledge on one side of the torrent where Alirio joined them with the waterlogged boat. Carlos and Brian seeing no one ahead swam downstream to grab the remaining kitbags before they sank. It was fortunate that most of these were plastic-lined and so the air which remained kept them afloat. Of the cameras only the two Rolleis in their hermetically-sealed cases remained intact. Five others had sunk together with the medical chest, a sixteen-bore shotgun, the best tarpaulin and all our shoes. Now they lay somewhere on the river bed.

Niels, his tall bedraggled figure bent over the boat, tinkered with the outboard motor and eventually got it to work. Brian scrambled back along the bank and went downstream with Carlos and Alirio to collect the equipment which lay straddled across tree roots and rocks at the water's edge. Donald was still cut off on the far bank, and as he waited for the boat to return he buried his thoughts in Dylan Thomas's poems. There was nothing else to do and in itself this seemed to epitomize the apparent hopelessness of our situation.

At this stage it was impossible to know whether we could continue and make the film. With a soaked cine-camera and two water-ridden tape recorders, our chances seemed virtually nil. But the reels of colour film had been saved, sealed in a watertight milk churn. To turn back would have been to admit defeat, so we reloaded the boat and continued upstream to the next *cachivera*, the Falls of Thunder. Here we laid everything in the afternoon sun over the granite boulders to dry – soaked cigars, telephoto lenses and fifty-yard lengths of cloth. It looked as if a giant trading store had suddenly appeared in the midst of Amazonia.

While Carlos and Alirio unrolled the cloth, the bright reds, greens, yellows and blues spread like Tibetan banners across the rocks, Niels carefully started to dismantle his Bolex and laid the parts in the sun. Hanna, remarkably controlled, looked after the hammocks and clothes, while we tended the tape recorders, shotguns, pressure lamps and the food. All this had kept afloat and the rice, which was sealed in plastic, had somehow kept dry.

At last we could relax by the fire, while Alirio boiled a great can of rice

---

Donald with the mummies in the burial cave.

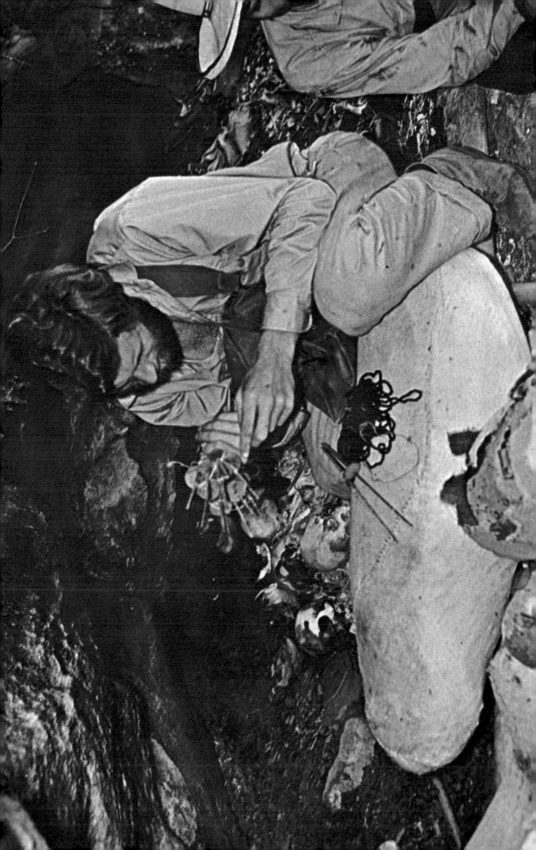

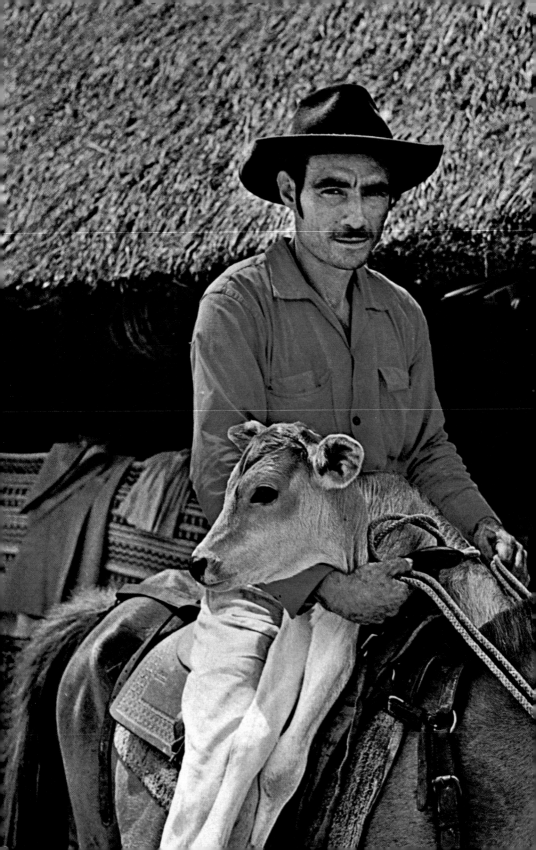

over the flames. As we drank tea, the same tea which had been our saviour time and time again, we hardly uttered a word. The disaster had been too great, our senses were numbed and there was nothing to say. Instead, each one of us occupied himself with a different piece of equipment – a lens, a tape recorder, microphones or a shotgun, trying in the darkness to dry them out. For a time Niels placed his camera on a rack over the embers of the fire, then Brian remembered how Dr Schultes had said that he never used desiccators but found dried rice much more effective. Our own desiccators were at the bottom of the river, so we followed his advice and sealed the remaining cameras in plastic bags filled with toasted rice.

Next morning the sky was clear and once more everything was spread over the rocks. Suddenly Niels' voice rang out gleefully – 'The camera's working,' he shouted as he wound and rewound the Bolex and then loaded a reel of film. Gradually the mainspring worked itself free and though a mixture of oil and water ominously oozed out of the compartment, the motor continued to run. In his enthusiasm Niels jumped from rock to rock, with the viewer still misted, eagerly filming.

We moved upstream once more. Niels and Hanna sat closely together in the bows, Alirio perched watchfully on the prow in front of them, we were on the kit amidships and Carlos managed the motor from behind. On reflection it seemed a miracle that things had not turned out much worse – no one had been injured, the film was safe and the boat intact. Above all we had to admire Niels. In a moment he had lost practically everything, his camera was his life and now a virtual write-off. He had every right to insist that we return, for he had other contracts to fulfil in Bogotá. But the expedition must have meant more to him than just another job. Like ourselves he had always had an overruling wish to visit Indians. It was this which originally made him sail a yacht single-handed from Cartagena to the Islands of San Blas, near Panama, there to make his first film.

It rained unremittingly as we continued up this tributary of the Piraparaná. Not once did we see an Indian. Then, only two bends before Bréo's *maloca*, we came upon two Makuna boys fishing from their slim dug-out canoe. At the port were more canoes, moored to the floating log pier and bumping side to side in the swift current. A sandy track led away from the water to the long rectangular *maloca* which stood alone on higher ground.

We lived here for the next two weeks, the last time we were to stay with an Indian family. To spend our last weeks in a Tukano *maloca* was a fitting climax to our travels, for the Piraparaná had been the essence of the whole expedition. On the first visit we had found it difficult to get to know the different families, for we had always been travelling and José was not a

A colono *rides to market.*

co-operative guide. This time we returned to one specific *maloca* which we already knew. Bréo was happy to see us and we were welcomed by all his family.

We were given a corner of the vast interior, to sling our hammocks and keep our stores. Bréo's father, the old Makuna shaman, was fortunately away, preparing curare poison in the forest. He did not like strangers and he certainly would not have allowed us to film.

In February Carlos had said that the only way we could ensure that a Tukano household would do everything we wanted, was to give the headman a shotgun. To part with our own would have been a very expensive gift, but Carlos had brought a sixteen-bore Winchester which like many others had reached Colombia as contraband from Peru. We gave this to Bréo and from then on he did absolutely anything we asked. The gun became his proudest possession. Still a young man, he was the one Indian whose face and eyes always seemed to radiate happiness. He proved one of the most strong-willed Indians we met and his control over the *maloca* was absolute. His people liked him, and this was the measure of his worth.

Through Alirio we explained to Bréo what we had come to do. That evening as the men squatted round and took coca, he in turn told them why we had arrived; they were to help us and not once were they to look at the strange 'eye' which the tall fair man might point at them. The consultations went on far into the night in the half-light of the *turi* torchwood and smouldering embers. At dawn the doors were hoisted to their hooks, the fires stoked and the Makuna went about their daily tasks.

These were what we had come to film, and we quietly followed them out to the *chagra* to watch the women dig manioc and the men pick coca. Most of the work away from the *maloca* was done in the morning and we often had difficulty in keeping up, for now we had to go barefoot like the Indians, and the soles of our feet took time to harden.

'I don't like the signs of rust appearing round the rewind mechanism,' Niels remarked one day, as he was filming a canoe being hollowed out. 'I suspect the mainspring is getting more and more coated with rust, and I can't get in at it. Eventually it will rot and snap, and that will be that!'

The most striking feature we remembered about the Tukano was the manioc festival and the amazing feather head-dresses which the men had worn. Bréo told us they were due to have a manioc celebration in about two weeks' time, but we persuaded him to celebrate sooner, and he agreed to send messengers into the forest and up-river by canoe, to warn the other *malocas*. Two of these were nearly fifty miles away in Brazil.

Canoe-loads of people soon arrived and the *maloca* filled to bursting with families slinging their hammocks. Well over a hundred Indians came and the preparation of coca and *chicha* went on for four days. On our part, too, there was preparation. We had promised everyone a present. Bréo had received his shotgun which he flourished at all who came. Now we cut the cloth into three-yard lengths to make skirts for the women, skirts which they wore only when white men came. For the men the most sought-after presents were our tiny glass beads. Each man was delighted with two spoonfuls and they carefully strung them on strands of *cumare* which they coiled round their necks.

One of our greatest problems was to film the festival in the dark interior of the *maloca*. At first we had thought of getting a special battery-operated flood lamp from Europe, but there was no time. Then a friend from Cambridge wrote and told us to try using pressure lamps. We brought six of these with us, together with sheets of tin and tinfoil to act as reflectors. The tin had been lost in the rapids, so we cut up all our empty cans and fitted them around one side of each lamp. Our problems were not at an end; the light was too dim, for we had brought pink petrol when we should have had the more refined white.

When Niels did start to film in the dark, he found that even with the lamps held almost next to a subject there was barely a reading on his exposure meter. Also the condensation in the viewer made it impossible to see.

'I don't know how this can come out, especially on colour film, I can't see a thing!' But we took a chance and with hands and arms wrapped in cloth against the heat held the lamps as close to the Indians as we dared. They must have wondered what was happening as four mysterious figures carrying dazzling lights descended on them. Yet amazingly, whether pounding coca or baking cassava, they remained themselves and carried out their tasks quite naturally while Niels filmed. We had to adopt different tactics for the dances. Here the lamps were useless. After a lengthy discussion Bréo agreed that they would dance outside, but only for a short time, since the shaman was annoyed – it was unnatural to dance outside the *maloca*. Then Niels had an idea: he would use the beams of the afternoon sun. For half an hour the light streamed through the women's doorway and he was able to film the dance.

Although the film was the major object of this last journey, recording music was also important. Before, we had not dared to descend the Pira-paraná with the precious Kudelski; now we had it with us. Water had penetrated only the battery compartment and we were able to record a large part of the Tukano music afresh. In both these aspects of our work we could not have had a better person than the talkative Alirio to help us. He would organize the Indians just like a kindly army sergeant-major, and with an old leather forage cap stuck firmly on his head he strutted about the *maloca*, proud to serve all our needs.

The collection had always remained a prime aspect of our travels, all the more so after the British Museum gave us a generous grant – one of the only ones we obtained. Sometimes we had found it easy to collect: when we left the Noanamá we went down the Río San Juan with five wooden crates filled to the brim and three dug-out canoes lashed to the side of the boat. But when we left the Kogi of San Miguel we had nothing to show but the stone tablets we had 'stolen' and a coca bag and *poporo* which had been presented to Nestor by the cacique of San Francisco. On the journey down the Piraparaná we met with varied success, the *malocas* on the upper reaches of the river would part with nothing, but on the lower course we found bartering much easier as the people had met *caucheros*. Then a canoe capsized and we lost over half of what we had obtained. Now we could recoup our loss and were spurred on by Niels' and especially Hanna's enthusiasm. They too wanted to make a collection and friendly rivalry ensued which at times became anything but friendly! The Museum was given first priority but Hanna had an initial advantage over us men. She was on much closer terms with the *maloca* women, and, for instance by sewing their skirts, could obtain almost anything she wanted from them. Until now we would never have admitted that a girl should be allowed to take part in an expedition, but we had to change our minds. She had been through our worst disaster and come out unscathed; we lost all the medical supplies but she remained as fit as ourselves. True, the clouds of minute black sandflies, the sweat bees and the *nigwas* which laid their nests of eggs in our feet were a new discomfort for her, but both she and Niels soon came to accept these and enjoy the other aspects of a life they would probably never see again.

Here a small nucleus of people went about their lives in a way which was entirely their own. We had literally descended from the sky, into their home, and for a very short time were able to experience at least a part of this life with its routine tasks, the drudgery of a hard existence and the joy and happiness of the festival. The Makuna seemed a particularly contented people and had little desire to make contact with the outside world. A spoonful of beads, a machete or a length of cloth were the things they wanted and in exchange they were willing to trade their own objects as well as their services. But even here there was a limit beyond which they would not go. With Alirio we were making a last desperate effort to obtain the *Kurubeti*, the sacred pebble stave festooned with exquisite emerald-green and purple hummingbird feathers at its carved end. It was the one thing with which they would not part and no matter how many spoonfuls of beads we offered, the shaman would not change his mind.

Bréo entered the *maloca*. For a time he watched and then came over to the scene of the bargaining. Never before had we seen such anger in his eyes. In short clipped syllables he spoke to Alirio. No, we could not have the *Kurubeti*, it belonged to his father, the great shaman, and he would never be forgiven. Besides this, we could have nothing more from his *maloca*; we had

With the Maraca: Ikoshmo after his fight with Karkamo.

taken enough. This was a young headman whose power and authority we had to respect. Our action seemed criminal, almost like taking treasured antiques from a friend's house, and that night Brian proposed giving everything back! Many times a sense of guilt crept over us as we went about our almost ruthless collecting. Yet we did give the Indians things which they wanted in return and our collecting encouraged them to continue in what were often dying crafts. Donald numbered each object and covered pages of his diary with drawings and copious notes; we could ease our consciences with the thought that we were trying to do some scientific good.

The festival was over. We started on the return journey to the mouth of the Piraparaná to await the Catalina's return.

By now the food supplies were beginning to run low. A favourite watering-place for tapir, or *danta*, as they were known, lay close to one of our camp sites. Carlos soon equipped himself, manufacturing bullets of lead from the shot in our twelve-bore cartridges.

'I'll be back in half an hour,' he shouted. We hardly believed him but he kept his word. He had killed a female *danta* and for two days limbs, ribs, indeed every conceivable piece of meat, were smoked on a rack which was specially erected over the fire. There was sufficient meat for everyone for at least a week. And by the end of that week, while we were waiting for the Catalina in Alirio's house, we were thankful we had had the extra supply. The air company had broken their word.

For four days we waited in the little hut overlooking the wide Apaporis. Each morning the sky was clear until about 10 a.m. Then the clouds came and it began to rain. On two occasions we heard aeroplane engines approach and then move away. Once the noise was so close that we unstrung our hammocks, packed the final oddments and ran down the steep slope to the river's edge. The food situation deteriorated. Niels became ever more concerned about his film contracts in Bogotá, and Carlos was impatient to return, for the rubber-collecting season had now begun. We had to leave, there was enough petrol to get us to Carlos' home and from there we could go south to La Pedrera, the frontier post on the Caquetá.

With the help of Carlos' men we crossed the five-mile portage between the Apaporis and Miritiparaná. Our bare feet suffered in the process. Once more disaster nearly overtook us. During the night descent of the Miritiparaná, the guide in the bows was supposedly keeping watch with a torch, but he fell asleep and before we knew where we were we were rammed amidships by another powered canoe coming in the opposite direction. Only a bit of water was shipped, but we did not sleep any more.

LEFT: *Ishishik makes herself up.* RIGHT: *Karkamo in warpaint.*

This time the radio in La Pedrera was working. We immediately sent messages to the air company and the British Embassy, to try to ensure that the Catalina would return and pick us up. They had failed to arrive at the appointed rendezvous; moreover we had paid for our return flight. What had happened? We had run out of food and Niels was long overdue in Bogotá. Radio contact with Leticia was of no use, for our friend Mike was still in Miami selling animals and tropical fish. No reply came from Bogotá for two days, then the news arrived: there had been a revolt in the Llanos, the country was in a state of emergency and all Catalinas had been commissioned to fly troops to the area bordering the Orinoco. The plane could not make the journey for at least a week, and even then there was little certainty. Our best route out was from the Brazilian frontier post of Villa Bitencourt, so we went down the gigantic and placid Caquetá to talk to the captain of the station.

'Yes, an Air Force Catalina is coming in tomorrow, but a general will be on board; he is inspecting all our frontier posts. I doubt there'll be room for all of you, and you'll have to ask General Josef for his permission.'

Next morning the four of us, bedraggled and shoeless, watched the smart platoon present arms to a small mustachioed general with a chestful of medals glittering in the sun. He had been told about us and very kindly said we could come. Later we heard that Richard Mason had been killed only five weeks before, on a tributary of the Xingu in Central Brazil. Perhaps this had made the general more sympathetic towards our cause, for he allowed not only ourselves but all our equipment on the plane.

We flew south to Leticia. Niels and Hanna returned direct to Bogotá by passenger flight. Two days later a cargo plane took us and all the equipment, including the sixteen-foot Indian canoe we had brought from the Piraparaná in March and had then been unable to fit inside a plane.

Just as the converted bomber was about to take off, the few passengers and ourselves were told to disembark. A search ensued and two thousand rounds of ammunition were discovered – we were gun-running for the revolutionaries in Bogotá! No one else was allowed to fly, but Mike, who had just returned from Miami, persuaded the police and customs that we were Embassy officials, and we flew.

That was the end of our expedition. By December 1961 we had left Colombia and were on the high seas, bound for Liverpool. With us were the films, hours of recordings, thousands of photographs and five huge crates with the collection for the British Museum. But of all our strange objects the four dug-out canoes caused most concern. The old chief of the liner's holds was worried that one had developed dry rot, and the Liverpool dockers had never seen anything quite like them before.

Almost a year later as we sat searching our brains for words, a letter arrived from Horacio and our journey became a reality once more:

'Now that "the terrors, the agonies and the mistakes", to borrow a well-known expression, have been forgotten, I can sit back and enjoy to the full our experiences on the Ti and the higher reaches of the Piraparaná. Remember that black morning on the Ti when we got bogged down, the scouting party to the first *maloca* on the Piraparaná had not returned and we despaired of their return? Then José and Uriel were found packing their belongings preparatory to abandoning us to perish miserably in that howling wilderness. That was a bad moment, as Peter Fleming would say. Remember the time we had, pushing and pulling *El Diablo* – now the size of an ocean liner – up the last part of that miserable ditch to the portage, and the struggle getting it over? "One, two, three ... ugh, Ugh, UGH!" Yes, we certainly had a hell of a time, but on the whole things turned out quite well.'

Select Bibliography

ALCACER, A. DE, *El Indio Motilon y su historia*. Ediciones Paz y Bien, XIII, Puente Comun, 1962.

CASEMENT, R., 'The Putumayo Indians', *The Contemporary Review*, C, II (1912).

CHAVES, M., 'La Guajira una región y una cultura de Colombia', *Revista Colombiana de Antropología*, I (Bogotá, 1953).

CUNNINGHAM, F., 'A History of Exploration in the Sierra Nevada de Santa Marta of Colombia'; unpublished, Universidad Nacional, Bogotá, 1951.

GOLDMAN, I., 'The Cubeo', Illinois Studies in Anthropology, *Urbana*, II (1963).

HARDENBURG, W. E., *The Putumayo, The Devil's Paradise*. London, T. Fisher Unwin, 1912.

HOLDER, P., 'The Motilones', *Journal of the Washington Academy of Sciences*, XXXVII (Washington, 1947).

IZIKOWITZ, K., 'Musical and other Sound Instruments of the South American Indians', *Göteborgs Vetensk. Samh. Handl.*, Ser. A., V, III (Göteborg, 1935).

KOCH-GRUNBERG, T., *Zwei Jahre unter den Indianern*. 2 vols., Berlin, 1909–10.

— 'Die Volkergruppierung zwischen Río Branco, Orinoco, Río Negro und Japura', in *Festschrift Eduard Seler*, Stuttgart, 1922.

KRAUS, E. and VAN DER HAMMEN, T., *Las Expediciones de Glaciología del Año Geofisico Internacional a las Sierras Nevadas de Santa Marta y del Cocuy*. Bogotá, Instituto Geografico 'Agustin Codazzi', 1960.

MASON, J. A., *Archaeology of Santa Marta, Colombia*. Field Museum Anthropological Series, XX, Chicago, 1931–39.

MOSER, B. and TAYLER, D., 'Tribes of the Piraparaná', *Geographical Journal*, Vol. 129, Pt 4 (1963).

O'LEARY, T. J., *Ethnographic Bibliography of South America*. Human Relations Area Files, New Haven, 1963.

REICHEL DOLMATOFF, G., 'Los Indios Motilones', *Revista del Instituto Etnologico Nacional*, II (Bogotá, 1945).

— *Los Kogi: Una Tribu de la Sierra Nevada de Santa Marta, Colombia*. 2 vols., Bogotá, 1950–51.

— *Datos historico-culturales sobre las tribus de la Antigua Gobernacion de Santa Marta*. Bogotá, 1951.

— 'Notas etnograficas sobre los Indios del Chocó', *Revista Colombiana de Antropología*, IX (Bogotá, 1960).

— *The People of Aritama.* London, Kegan Paul, 1961.

SCHULTES, R. E., 'The Identity of the malphighiaceous narcotics of South America'. Botanical Museum Leaflet 18, 6, Harvard, 1957.

SPRUCE, R., *Notes of a Botanist on the Amazon and Andes.* 2 vols., London, 1912.

STEWARD, J. H. (ed.), *Handbook of South American Indians.* Vols 2, 3 and 4, Washington, 1946–48.

STEWARD, J. H. and FARON, L. C., *The Native Peoples of South America.* New York, 1959.

USCATEGUI MENDOZA, N., 'Contibución al estudio de la masticacion de las hojas de coca', *Revista Colombiana de Antropología,* III (Bogotá, 1954).

— 'The present distribution of narcotics and stimulants amongst the Indian tribes of Colombia', Botanical Museum Leaflet 18, 6. Harvard, 1959.

— 'Algunos colorantes vegetales usados por las tribus indigenas de Colombia', *Revista Colombiana de Antropología,* X (Bogotá, 1961).

WALLACE, A. R. *Travels on the Amazon and Río Negro.* London, 1889.

WASSEN, S. H., *Notes on Southern Groups of Chocó Indians in Colombia.* Etnoloiska Studier, Göteborg, 1935.

WEST, R. C., *The Pacific Lowlands of Colombia.* Louisiana State University Social Science Series, VIII, Baton Rouge, 1957.

WHIFFEN, T., *The North-West Amazon.* London, Constable, 1915.

Index